Consuming Race

From the rise of Nordic noir to a taste for street food, from practices of natural gardening to the aesthetics of children's TV, contemporary culture is saturated with racial meanings. By consuming race we make sense of other groups and cultures, communicate our own identities, express our needs and desires, and discover new ways of thinking and being.

This book explores how the meanings of race are made and remade in acts of creative consumption. Ranging across the terrain of popular culture, and finding race in some unusual and unexpected places, it offers fresh and innovative ways of thinking about the centrality of race to our lives.

Consuming Race provides an accessible and highly readable overview of the latest research and a detailed reading of a diverse range of objects, sites and practices. It gives students of sociology, media and cultural studies the opportunity to make connections between academic debates and their own everyday practices of consumption.

Ben Pitcher is Senior Lecturer in Sociology at the University of Westminster, London. He has written extensively on race and racism, and in the area of cultural studies. He is author of *The Politics of Multiculturalism* (2009).

Consuming Race will be of enormous use and value to students and researchers of race and ethnicity in all areas of culture. It is clear and incisive, yet well theorized and rigorous, and it insists on and lays out a powerful argument: no matter how much we might want to hope, believe or fantasize otherwise, *race will not go away*. Race is always going to be a central topic to any serious consideration of media, culture and society, and Pitcher's book offers a clear and engaging set of readings of race, drawn from many areas of mainstream popular culture and our daily lives.

Paul Bowman, Director of Postgraduate Research,
Journalism Media and Cultural Studies
School, Cardiff University

Consuming Race draws our attention to the ways race finds its way into even the most banal aspects of everyday consumer life. Highly readable, patient, thorough and complex, the book reveals (old) even as it creates (new) articulations. Defining its terms in a most clear and informed manner, the book emphasizes the presence of race wherever capital flows.

Kent A. Ono, Professor and Chair of
Communication, University of Utah

Consuming Race

Ben Pitcher

Routledge
Taylor & Francis Group

LONDON AND NEW YORK

First published 2014
by Routledge
2 Park Square, Milton Park, Abingdon, Oxon OX14 4RN

and by Routledge
711 Third Avenue, New York, NY 10017

Routledge is an imprint of the Taylor & Francis Group, an informa business

British Library Cataloguing in Publication Data
A catalogue record for this book is available from the British Library

Library of Congress Cataloging in Publication Data
Pitcher, Ben.
Consuming race/Ben Pitcher.
  pages cm
  Includes bibliographical references and index.
  1. African American consumers 2. Consumers, Black
  3. Consumers. 4. Race – Social aspects. I. Title.
  HC110.C6P575 2014
  339.4'708996073 – dc23   2013039286

ISBN: 978-0-415-51968-7 (hbk)
ISBN: 978-0-415-51969-4 (pbk)
ISBN: 978-0-203-10204-6 (ebk)

Typeset in Sabon
by Florence Production Ltd, Stoodleigh, Devon, UK

Contents

Preface

This book is an exploration of how the meanings of race are made and remade in acts of creative consumption. It will make the case for expanding and extending the realm of subjects and topics we talk about when we talk about race, for race is important to aspects of our lives that we don't usually think about in racial terms. Rather than regard race as the possession of particular groups or individuals, I suggest that it is more useful to think of race as a practice we are all invested in 'doing' through everyday acts of consumption. This book explores race in terms of bedlinen and bedsocks, in a taste for herring and crime fiction. It considers Kylie and Jason as artefacts of black culture, and the act of buying a sandwich in the street. It looks for race in landscapes, parks and gardens, and examines the racial meanings of novels, microblogs, box sets and children's TV. These all provide us with some useful and interesting ways of thinking about how race works in our contemporary cultures.

Each chapter provides a detailed reading of a particular cultural text or texts, providing examples of some important methodologies for the critical analysis of objects, products, media, images, spaces, places and styles, among other things. I have tried to make this book as clear and accessible as I can, and have not assumed prior knowledge of relevant debates in cultural studies, media studies and sociology. The book's examples provide a way for students to relate some of the latest research to their own everyday practices of consumption. At the same time, I have tried to provide some new ways for academics, researchers and other interested readers to think about some of the complex investments we all have in producing and reproducing race in the twenty-first century.

One of the things that this book is invested in working against is the propensity of work on race to trade on the illusory guarantee of racial embodiment or the rhetoric of experience. While it is customary and good practice to acknowledge one's social and cultural situatedness, this situatedness does not necessarily afford knowledge or understanding that is permanently closed off to others. Certainly, my status as a self-hating left-wing ambivalently ex-working class whitey intellectual will have had some bearing on some of the things I have found it interesting to write about in this book, and it will have brought with it its own insights and oversights, but this is not to suggest that I am any more or less qualified to write about race than anyone else. Race is not a 'minority' subject, and its importance is something I very strongly feel we should all work to understand better: race is everybody's business.

Acknowledgements

I am grateful first of all to everybody who kindly agreed to let me use their images. The cover image is reproduced with kind permission of PLAYMOBIL. PLAYMOBIL is a registered trademark of geobra Brandstätter GmbH & Co. KG, Germany. For the Bob Marley T-shirt photos in Chapter 1, thanks are due to Donald O'Clair, Marie Noëlle Delgado, Renae Simpson, Santi Ochoa, Shyrynn McHugh, Attila Terdik and Wayne Marshall. Thanks to Kevin Sudeith for the Afghan war rug image in Chapter 2, courtesy of WarRug.com. I'm very grateful to Ochuko Ojiri of the Black Nerds Network for the images in Chapter 4. The image in the fifth chapter is provided courtesy of Wahaca restaurant, www.wahaca.co.uk. Thanks to Zodiac for permission to reproduce the *Waybuloo* image in Chapter 6. The killer shrimp in Chapter 7 is reproduced by permission of the GB Non-native Species Secretariat.

The epigraph to this book comes from the film of Stuart Hall's 1997 lecture 'Race: the floating signifier', and is reproduced by kind permission of the Media Education Foundation. The section on *The Wire* in Chapter 8 is largely taken from an article co-written with Rebecca Bramall, and first published in the *International Journal of Cultural Studies*.

For providing some useful references, ideas, comments and suggestions along the way, thanks to Rebecca Bramall, Mica Nava, Sarah Elsie Baker, Mao Bramall, Jakob Stougaard-Nielsen, Leon Gurevitch, Mark Bhatti and Mónica Moreno Figueroa. For help with what were sometimes some rather esoteric enquiries, thanks to Jon Nott of the Woodcraft Folk and BBC Scotland. Thanks to Gerhard Boomgaarden, Emily Briggs and Alyson Claffey at Routledge. Thanks to Sara Marchington and James Sowden at Florence Production. Thanks to Maxim Lucas for the extra pixels and my can of Marley's Mellow Mood™.

I have had the opportunity to present and discuss some of the work in this book in some interesting places with some interesting people. Particular thanks are due to Gavan Titley and the European Communication Research and Education Association for the invitation to Maynooth, and to Suvi Keskinen and the Research Network on Nordic Populism for inviting me to Turku.

Thanks to the students on my Consuming Race module at the University of Westminster, and in particular to Vanessa Brown, Sam-Aaron Butler, Ebadul Haque and Natalie Teltscher for keeping it interesting for me. The reference to Tinie Tempah in Chapter 4 is courtesy of Asif Chowdhury. Apologies for those I've forgotten; as you know, I'm terrible with names. Thanks to colleagues past and present, and particularly to Francis Ray White, Maja Cederberg, Naomi Rudoe and Adam Eldridge for your help, support and general wonderfulness.

Thanks, finally, to Rebecca Bramall for suggesting I do this in the first place and for being such a helpful and constructive reader of my work.

As will become obvious, all this was conceived while hanging around Lewisham with a toddler. For that reason, this book is for Jean, with love.

What might it be in human identification, in human practice, in the building of human alliances, which without the guarantee, without the certainty of religion, or science, or anthropology, or genetics, or biology, or the appearance of your eyes, without any guarantees at all might enable us to conduct an ethically responsible human discourse and practice about race in our society?

Stuart Hall

Chapter 1

Introduction

Race doesn't go away

A longstanding and still very common belief that people hold about race is that it is something that will eventually go away. For some, this belief is based on the anti-racist conviction that assigning people to different races is simply not a valid thing to do, and that through education and understanding we will get to the point where we no longer categorize one another in these terms. For others, it is based on the more commonsense feeling that the significance of race fades away once we have an understanding of someone's personality; that once we get to know what they are 'really like' then their racial identity doesn't matter any more and we stop thinking of them in those terms. Because in both cases it is felt that ideas about race – and particularly the negative and destructive ideas associated with racism – stem from ignorance and unfamiliarity, the suggestion is that race is something we can overcome, get around or see beyond. We can, it is thought, get to the point where it is not something we care about, or even notice. 'I don't see race, I just see another person', someone might say; or, 'It makes no difference if you're black or white, or red or blue or green', or 'It's not the colour of someone's skin, but what's inside that matters'. While these sentiments are in many respects admirable as attempts to avoid or speak out against prejudice or discrimination, they are also patently untrue. They are attempts to *pretend* something that deep down we all know is not the case. Race doesn't disappear. We can fool ourselves that it's not there, but we all know that it is.

If race doesn't go away, then perhaps it's not quite right to think of race as necessarily the product of ignorance and unfamiliarity. What if greater knowledge and understanding of others actually increases, rather than diminishes, the significance of race? This seems to be borne out by our experience of life in the twenty-first century: wherever we live in the world, planes and trains and new media technologies make our social and cultural formations more diverse than ever before. We seem to know more and more about each other than we ever did. Living with difference is normal, and is becoming ever more so, and yet as we all know race hasn't evaporated into thin air. Our multicultural realities don't mean the end of race. On the contrary, race is everywhere. We can't get away from it, even if we try to, because trying to get rid of race is like trying to dig a hole out of existence. For the time being at least, race seems to be very much here to stay.

It is my argument in this book that the recognition that race doesn't go away is not, or need not be, a pessimistic one. As this chapter will go on to suggest, once we are able to acknowledge that race is about more than just racism – which will necessitate some critical thinking about the position of racism in a lot of existing race theory – then we are better placed to think in a less judgmental sense about the profound ways in which we're all mixed up with race. This involvement we all have with race does not necessarily result in racism and inequality, and indeed may provide ways of challenging and undermining it.

Consuming race

So why doesn't race just go away? The answer is fairly simple: because we're all deeply invested in it. This is the case whether or not we're black or white, racist or anti-racist, Chilean or Chinese. It doesn't matter. Our lives are saturated with racial meanings, and often – as this book hopes to reveal – in ways that we do not always fully recognize or understand. Race doesn't just form a backdrop to our lives, it is a medium through which we live our lives. We are all of us actively involved in producing and reproducing ideas about race. The generation of racial meanings cannot simply be reduced to the things we explicitly say about race and how we behave towards those marked out as racially similar or different. Race is made and unmade in countless other ways as we go about the practice of being a human being: the books we read, the food we eat, the TV we watch, the toys we play with, the clothes we wear: all these things (and many others) can and frequently do have racial meanings, even if race is not explicitly marked out in them as a theme. We might use these objects and activities to say something about ourselves and our own racial identity; we might use them to say something about other people and our relationship to them; they might be used to express ideas about racial superiority, aptitude and intelligence, or to challenge and undermine those ideas; they might express our hatreds, our fears, our pleasures, our desires; they might provide ways of communicating with or connecting to others, or of refusing those connections; they might serve as a mechanism to find out about other people beyond our immediate social locations; we might engage with them as a way of pursuing particular interests, or as a way of exploring new realms of human experience.

This is where consumption comes in, as a way of thinking about some of the many different aspects of human life in which race is implicated.

While clearly the circulation of racial meanings does not always need to involve acts of consumption, I want to suggest in this book that consumer culture is an immensely important and rather underexamined site for the making and remaking of those meanings. I use the idea of consumption in this book to refer – in a rather general way that will annoy some theorists of consumption – to a wide variety of practices that involve our engagement with a range of objects, products, services, stories, images, texts, styles, spaces and places. The important thing about the idea of consumption here is its openness as a concept. I don't, for example, want to limit consumption to the activity of commercial exchange; consumption can involve practices where no money ever changes hands, or where money is the least interesting aspect of what is going on. Likewise, consumption is not a passive process, as compared to the activity of production, because consumption produces too. It does not just exhaust or use things up, it creates, reworks and connects. Consumption also describes ways of engaging, understanding and 'reading' the cultures we inhabit. My understanding of consumer culture has quite a lot in common with 'material culture' – a term often used to explore the social value of objects – but in my reading it does not necessarily depend or focus on the materiality of race. What's important about the idea of 'consuming' race is that there is no practice that is off-limits, to be considered too trivial or inconsequential for our critical attention. *Consuming Race* sets out to think about how race is caught up in all the 'small' things, as well as all the 'big' things, that we think and do (and in the process of examining the 'small' things it prompts us to consider that they might actually be quite 'big' things after all).

The idea of consumption helps us to open up our thinking about the generation and circulation of racial meanings. This book is invested in the idea that racial meanings are not the property or possession of certain groups and individuals, but rather that they belong to the realm of culture within which we all operate. This book accordingly sets itself against some approaches (admittedly now rather old-fashioned, but still very dominant) that are committed to thinking about race primarily as an identity that people 'have': that we are either born with it, or that it is given to us (willingly, or otherwise) by others. These kinds of approach do not always rule out thinking about the racial meanings of things like music and clothes, but they tend to think of music and clothes as expressing or commenting upon those pre-existing racial identities. In other words, while in these approaches there is a relationship between race and aspects of consumer culture, racial meanings are necessarily thought to come before consumer culture. In these approaches, consumer culture is understood to represent raced people in particular ways, but it is not itself considered to be a place where race itself 'happens'. While this book is interested in ideas about representation, it is very much committed to challenging the notion that race is something that precedes acts of consumption. Rather, I'm interested here in the ways in which racial meanings are generated *through* practices of consumption. We often define and redefine our own racial identities, our relationship to others and so on, in social and cultural practices that take place within consumer culture. There aren't necessarily any more 'important' sites of racial meaning outside of consuming practices that underpin the generation of racial meaning. What race is or means in any particular instance can be untangled in the ensemble of relations mediated by consumer culture. Sometimes racial meanings are brief, transient and ephemeral, but they are no less significant for that. This does not mean that race is a shallow or surface phenomenon, but rather (and I will return to this in my conclusion), that its 'depth' is to be found in that ensemble of relations, and not guaranteed by blood, history or some other fetishized marker of racial meaning.

This kind of critical perspective therefore represents a move away from the commonsense but actually fallacious idea that race is somehow 'attached' to people and their bodies, which in turn provides them with or represents a racial identity. When I use the term 'race' throughout this book, I am referring to a site of meaning: variously a category, a concept, a symbol, an idea or a resource through which we describe, understand, produce and contest notions of human difference. The meanings of race are diverse, sometimes unstable, and will often contradict one another. They are to be found in the dynamics of human culture, a product of the infinitely complex processes by which we define and understand ourselves and others. Race is not something we 'have', it is always something we 'do'. Because of the strong tendency in our cultures to think of race as expressing innate characteristics or some kind of inner truth, it used to be customary to highlight race's social constructedness by bracketing it in 'scare quotes'. Yet critical attention to how culture works (particularly in the tradition of poststructuralist theory) demonstrates that pretty much all categories of meaning can be thought of in these same contingent and dynamic terms. Just as the meanings of the words in a dictionary change as the culture that uses them changes, it is an illusion to think that the meaning of any concept (from race to gender to class to cupboard to computer to love to kindness) remains static across time and space. Rather than select and single out an especially politicized and controversial concept like race for scare quotes treatment, it should be taken as read that its meaning is thoroughly cultural, and that it does not and cannot exist outside of this. This does not mean, as the facetious and anti-intellectual riposte typically has it, that we can just purposely invent racial meanings willy-nilly, changing the meaning of race simply by deciding to use the concept differently, for this is not how culture works. In the same way that the languages we speak and write are collective and collaborative affairs, the meanings of race involve collective and collaborative processes. While we can work to change those meanings by intentional means, such struggles necessitate a complicated negotiation with existing meanings: this is what we mean by cultural politics.

What I am suggesting, then, is that we think about race as part of a 'language' of cultural meaning, and of particular practices of consumption as instances of language use: we consume race to 'say' something about ourselves and others. Sometimes we are in control of what we are saying through acts of racial consumption, at other times we are not. While we may think we are consuming race in a particular way, there may be other meanings being generated, other things that race is saying that we are not always fully aware of. And so by thinking critically about practices of racial consumption we can interrogate some of these meanings. We can, by reading these practices, try to figure out what race is saying in any particular circumstance, at any particular moment. This book accordingly shares some common ground with the idea of 'everyday multiculturalism' as 'a grounded approach to looking at the everyday practice and lived experience of diversity in specific situations and places of encounter' (Wise and Velayutham, 2009: 3). Though approaches of this kind are a useful attempt to understand and engage with the 'bottom up' experience of cultural difference, there is no reason why we should confine our understanding of how race is 'lived' in 'everyday practice' to an embodied or face-to-face encounter with difference. As Gail Lewis has argued, cultural practices of race, involving transnational circuits of representation, 'stand right at the heart of contemporary everyday life and mediate individual experiences and the social relations of "race", gender, class, sexuality, and age' (Lewis, 2007: 873; see also Gray, 2013). As I will go on to suggest, practices of consuming race can involve forms of meaning-making where racialized others do not have to be physically present, or can be figured by or substituted for objects, images and ideas, even animals, plants and landscapes.

A Bob Marley T-shirt

To introduce some of the ways in which racial meanings get produced and reproduced in acts of consumption, I want to take as an example a particular object in consumer culture, an object with which we are all probably quite familiar, and present some ways of reading it (an object can be 'read' in a way that's analogous to the way we might read a book or a newspaper, that is, as a 'text' that can serve as the focus of acts of interpretation). Over the next few pages there are seven images taken in a number of different places in the world – Jamaica, the East and West coasts of the United States, Spain and Hungary – of people wearing T-shirts featuring the famous musician Bob Marley. The T-shirt is a particularly good object to examine if we're interested in thinking about the intended meanings of its wearer, because T-shirts have of course become a cultural form that we intentionally use to make a statement or convey a message. Because they are relatively cheap and easy to print images, slogans and other text onto, T-shirts have become a conventional means of saying who we are and what we believe in. Frequently

Figure 1.1 © Donald O'Clair

customized by their wearers, T-shirts, like many other objects in consumer culture, are inherently social items. T-shirts quickly and clearly express what we care about and what we're into, regardless of wealth (they can be bought cheaply), sex (they're worn by men and women) and other social categories and distinctions. Nobody intentionally puts on a T-shirt without being very conscious of what it might be saying, because a T-shirt is like a label we have chosen for ourselves. Now of course it's not possible on the evidence of a photographic image to really tell what the people wearing these T-shirts may have wanted to say by wearing them, any more than it's possible to tell what somebody means to say with their T-shirt when they pass us in the street. What I'm going to do here is speculate in a more general sense about some of the meanings that may be activated or produced by this particular object in consumer culture. My reading certainly won't be exhaustive of the possible range of racial meanings, but it will give an indication of some of the complex and sometimes contradictory ideas that are communicated through acts of racial consumption.

Maybe the first and most obvious thing that anybody says by wearing a Bob Marley T-shirt is that they're into his music. Marley remains the most famous reggae musician, and it almost goes without saying that reggae music is in no small part to do with race. Reggae has its geographical origins in

Jamaica, and like other forms of Caribbean popular culture it has played a part in expressing and exploring a complicated social and cultural history that includes the experience of European colonialism, the transatlantic slave trade, and related struggles for freedom and independence. Although it is a musical form that was developed post-independence, reggae makes sense of and comments on this history and its contemporary legacies, and includes among its subject matter themes like racial inequality, black nationalism, rebellion and revolution. As everybody knows, reggae is in some sense 'about' all this, and the wearer of a Bob Marley T-shirt is accordingly in one way or another associating her or himself with it. The wearer does not have to

Figure 1.2 © Marie Noëlle Delgado

be particularly invested in this association – their interest in reggae might ostensibly be focused very specifically on the sound of the music and how it makes them feel – but it is an association that they are making nonetheless. (It is easy to test the validity of this idea: could a white supremacist intentionally wear a Bob Marley T-shirt and not feel as if they were somehow contradicting themselves?)

If reggae music foregrounds a tumultuous history and politics in which race has a particularly significant place, it is important to recognize that what all this means is very much dependent on both who is wearing a Bob Marley T-shirt, and where it's being worn. Take, for example, someone wearing the shirt in Kingston, the capital city of Jamaica, who thinks of themselves as having family connections to Africa. To them, the act of wearing a Bob Marley T-shirt might be a way of drawing on the sense in which Bob Marley and his music have come to stand for a link between Africa and the Caribbean, and a way of communicating a feeling of connectedness with the history and culture of that continent. This particular T-shirt wearer could be intentionally drawing on the association between Bob Marley and pan-African unity, the powerful cultural and political project that developed in the twentieth century to make sense of the relationship between Africa's past and present, and its connections to a wide range of disaporic communities who derive significance and meaning from their entanglements in it. Alternatively, we could imagine another person wearing the T-shirt on the streets of Kingston for whom Bob Marley stands for something very different: imagine someone whose understanding of themselves draws to some extent on a family connection to China. To them, what might be meaningful or significant about Bob Marley is his status as a 'mixed race' Jamaican (Bob Marley's dad was white), and the sense in which he can be understood to stand for notions of culture and identity that do not fix on a single point of 'origin', but which are the combination of many different elements. To this person, the significance of reggae might derive from its status as a creole or syncretic musical form: the way it is constituted from a wide range of influences, and is in a sense a collaborative product that bears the mark of the multiple histories (including, of course, those people of mixed African-Caribbean and Chinese heritage like dancehall musician Sean Paul) that form twentieth- and twenty-first-century Jamaican popular culture.

Move somewhere else geographically and the meaning of the Bob Marley T-shirt is likely to shift again. Consider, for example, someone who doesn't make a claim on Jamaicanness, but for whom Bob Marley is nevertheless a meaningful symbol of personal identity. It's obvious that the significance of wearing a Bob Marley T-shirt is not somehow limited to Jamaicans, but that all kinds of people with historical or cultural or emotional connections to Africa, or to the Caribbean, or to the experience of being 'mixed race', may all draw on Bob Marley and what he symbolizes to say something

Figure 1.3 © Renae Simpson

significant about who they are. Paul Gilroy asks whether 'people connect themselves and their hopes with the mythic figure of Bob Marley as a man, a Jamaican, a Caribbean, an African, or a pan-African artist?' (Gilroy, 2010: 113): processes of identification are open and mobile. Outside of the Caribbean, a Bob Marley T-shirt may in some respects be a more useful communicator of personal identity than within it. Bob Marley's face is recognized the world over, and in social contexts where a T-shirt wearer might find themselves marked out as a racial or 'ethnic' minority, it is an image that works as a kind of shorthand, helping the wearer to situate themselves in a common language and set of meanings. The global communicative power of Bob Marley's image is, it hardly needs saying, largely dependent on its status as a commodity in consumer culture. Were it not for the twentieth-century commodification of popular music and style through the production, distribution and promotion of records and merchandise, it is unlikely that anyone outside of Jamaica would have even heard of Bob Marley, let alone made use of his image to express an idea about who they are (indeed, it is impossible to conceive of reggae music existing at all without the technological and communicative mechanics of commodity culture).

We don't, of course, need to confine our understanding of identity to the narrow terms of family history. By wearing a Bob Marley T-shirt, individuals can identify themselves with a wider range of values or attitudes that have become attached to him. In Figure 1.1 the Bob Marley T-shirt lends itself

Figure 1.4 © Santi Ochoa

to a particular set of interpretations by the way that Marley's image is combined with the words 'soul rebel' and 'freedom fighter'. These terms focus on Bob Marley's meaning as a counter-cultural symbol, and draw on aspects of his music and persona associated with forms of political and creative resistance to the legacies of colonial rule. It is a set of meanings that draw in particular on the associations between Bob Marley and Rastafarianism, the Jamaican Christian movement that expresses forms of black pride, theologizes a diasporic claim on an African cultural identity, and articulates a critique of 'Babylon', the forces of oppression embodied not just by slavery and colonialism but the malign and corrupting influence of Western culture and politics. A number of the original colour images accentuate the connection between Bob Marley and Rastafai, reproducing his image in the characteristic Rastafarian and Pan-African colours of green,

Figure 1.5 © Shyrynn McHugh

yellow and red. Though these connotations might be of particular significance to its wearer if they are a follower of Rastafarianism, this does not
mean that the Rastafarian meanings of a Bob Marley T-shirt disappear or
are rendered invalid if she or he is not. Consider, for example, a Tunisian
wearing a Bob Marley T-shirt in the context of the 'Arab Spring' protests
of 2010–11. Even if this person did not know or care about the Afrocentric
aspects of Rastafari, their sartorial choices will have nonetheless drawn
upon it as a symbol of protest in the context of autocracy and political
repression. When Vijay Prashad first sees an image of Bob Marley in late
1970s Calcutta and is reminded of a Shaivite hermit, Marley becomes a
way in to understanding the East Indian influences on Rastafarian culture
(Prashad, 2001: 87–92).[1] In other situations, different elements may come
to the fore: the wearer of a Bob Marley T-shirt in contemporary Moscow
or Los Angeles may be uninterested in the religious aspects of Rastafarianism,
yet still be deeply invested in the way it symbolizes a philosophical or cultural
alternative to the lifestyle practices of contemporary Western consumer
culture (even if, paradoxically, the availability of the T-shirt is itself entirely
dependent on that culture). Frequently rendered in the contrasting flat tones
characteristic of rudimentary stencilling or screenprinting, Marley's image
often echoes the iconic Alberto Korda photograph of Che Guevara, itself a
globally-recognized symbol of anticapitalist protest.

Of course, as with the example of Che, the wearing of a Bob Marley T-shirt does not necessarily signal a close affinity with these kinds of protest politics. It might alternatively be the case that Bob Marley's countercultural connotations are mobilized to express a more diffuse conception of cool, where what's significant is the way Bob Marley symbolizes an alternative or outsider position to a 'mainstream' culture. Here, a Bob Marley T-shirt can become a tool for its wearer to make a distinction between their own tastes and those of the family or society to which they nominally belong. When, for example, a white European teenager wears a Bob Marley T-shirt, Marley's racial difference can be a significant element of this practice of cultural distinction: to align oneself with racial difference becomes a powerful way of signalling one's own difference. What gets emphasized here are not necessarily any of the particular properties that the image of Bob Marley has, but rather the way in which they come together to create a generalized idea of difference that the wearer is able to associate with her or himself. This is a difference that could be used to signal a range of meanings depending on the particular social and cultural context in which the T-shirt is worn. It might, for example, be a marker of cosmopolitanism

Figure 1.6 © Attila Terdik

set against the narrow parochialism of the local, an explicitly anti-racist statement set against forms of active intolerance and discrimination, or a form of teenage rebellion against parental musical tastes (alternatively, of course, the T-shirt could also be doing the exact opposite, serving as an inter-generational point of symbolic affinity and connection with those parental tastes).

Another set of meanings that may or may not be emphasized by the Bob Marley T-shirt relate to his status as a symbol of drug culture. Bob Marley T-shirts frequently combine his image with the shapes of cannabis leaves; sometimes he is depicted in a haze of smoke; sometimes with a big fat spliff hanging out of his mouth. These associations may draw upon some of the meanings already mentioned – the cool of counterculture, or the important sacramental role of weed in Rastafarian culture – but may use them to express something different again about the significance of cannabis to the wearer's imaginative, creative or recreational life. The text of the T-shirt reproduced in Figure 1.7 clearly combines the psychological and social elements of cannabis consumption (the practice of 'chilling') with an idea of political change (revolution), and in doing so expresses an idea about the inextricability of psychic and material transformation that is also frequently expressed in Bob Marley's lyrics. This interpretation is of course underpinned by further layers of cultural meaning that link race and drug culture, ranging from the romantic association between racial difference and altered mental and psychic states (see Saldanha, 2007) to the fact that dominant stereotypes of petty criminality probably picture your local street-corner drug dealer as a young black man.

The readings of the Bob Marley T-shirt I have just given are of course not the only ones that can be made, and it is not that the T-shirt is confined to meaning only one thing at a time, even if one particular meaning seems to be dominant. To some the Bob Marley T-shirt in Figure 1.3 with the slogan 'one love' might be interpreted as a commitment to anti-racism. To others, it might seem to be a statement of religious or humanitarian equality. Others might interpret 'one love' as a rather empty or anodyne phrase, a 'feelgood' statement that actually doesn't mean very much at all.[2] A further layer of potentially conflicting racial meanings might be opened up by considering the T-shirt's commodity history: where was the cotton to make the T-shirt grown, and who may have been involved in the labour of sewing, printing and distribution? Is it important to the wearer that their Bob Marley T-shirt is 'sweatshop free', and if not do the conditions of its production invalidate its egalitarian message? Alternatively, do the higher prices associated with 'ethical' products mean that a 'sweatshop free' Bob Marley T-shirt is more likely to be a marker of racial privilege, and what kinds of contradiction and paradox does this then open up?

A Bob Marley T-shirt might simultaneously focus all these meanings for different people, or for the same person at different times and in different

Figure 1.7 © Wayne Marshall

places. We cannot arrive at a 'final' or definitive meaning because meaning is the outcome of a dynamic relationship between the object of the T-shirt itself (and the particular characteristics it has – words, images, colours, textures, smells), the person wearing it, and the social and cultural context in which it is being worn (which includes the factor of time as well as space). The fluid interplay between all of these factors is what contributes to the T-shirt's meaning, and if you change one of them you can shift or change that meaning. Meaning is, as we say, profoundly conjunctural: it can never be fixed once and for all because of the unique combination of circumstances that bring it into being.

This does not mean that a Bob Marley T-shirt can simply mean anything at all, or that it can mean anything we want it to mean, for these circumstances are not themselves unlimited, and meaning will stabilize from time to time into certain patterns. As John Clarke helpfully puts it, 'In concrete situations, social arrangements have differing densities, proving more or less resistant to change' (Clarke, 2004: 6). As I have been suggesting, a significant – perhaps the most significant – site for the stabilization of meaning in respect of the Bob Marley T-shirt relates to ideas about race. While they can never be pinned down once and for all, it is possible, from a critical interpretive position, to analyse and interrogate the production of racial meanings in particular conjunctures or 'concrete situations' (see also Moore *et al.*, 2003: 3–4). This process of analysis and interpretation can give us an insight into the cultural formations in which these meanings are given shape. In other words, by thinking critically about cultural artefacts like the Bob Marley T-shirt, we can develop wider insights into how race works in our cultures more generally. That is the project of this book: to explore the cultural politics of race through the critical analysis of consumer culture.

Race beyond racism

Why, though, might we want to understand how race works in our cultures more generally? What is it about race that makes it a subject especially worth thinking about or understanding?

Well, you may already have answered this question by having read this book as far as you have. Race is a fascinating subject. It's not too much of an exaggeration to suggest that we are obsessed by it. Race excites and frightens in equal measure; it is a subject that is incredibly controversial and, as this book hopes to show, it structures and shapes our cultures in profound and important ways.

Despite (perhaps, in a sense, because of) all this, there is often what sometimes seems like a mutual agreement or widespread conspiracy not to understand it better. Weirdly, our cultures work hard not to talk about race or think in detailed ways about how it works. It is as if it is taboo to scrutinize race too closely. More often than not, discussions of race are closed down; things are left unsaid out of a fear of offending someone, 'saying the wrong thing', or, worst, being charged with racism (see Byrne, 2006: 103). The subject of race is frequently considered a 'minefield', and so while it continues to obsess and fascinate, it retains something of an enigmatic character. Nobody quite knows what it is or what to do with it, and so this uncertainty or embarrassment continues (this tendency is even more pronounced in places like the Netherlands, where there is a taboo even on using the word 'race'). You might think that the academic world would be an exception to this, and that we might have created a space in academic books, journals, seminar rooms and lecture halls where race can be explored and interrogated without some of the discomfort and awkwardness that accompanies it elsewhere. This tends unfortunately not to be the case, for the reasons I want to set out now.

The issue that besets a lot of work on race in the academy is less to do with the careful protocols that operate in public discussions, though it's not that these aren't there in academic contexts too. The key issue here relates to a longstanding theoretical commitment that, so often taken for granted and unexamined, has ended up getting in the way of our understanding race better. This is, very simply, the idea that the phenomenon of race is ultimately to be understood and explained by the practice of racism. Racism has for a very long time served as the final guarantee of meaning in race theory: it is what race is so often thought to be 'about'. For this reason, so much of the work that is done on race is blinded to or screened off from its wider meanings. This work simply cannot get to grips with the ways in which race's significance extends above and beyond the question of racism.

One of the reasons why racism has this special status in race theory is because of a belief that racism precedes race and brings it into being. It has become an orthodoxy in thinking on this subject to turn on its head the commonsense self-evidence of race, rightly suggesting that the visual markers we so often use to identify and categorize racial identity are contradictory, incoherent and unstable. This idea that racism precedes race is consolidated by a refusal of what's known as 'essentialist' thinking, the notion that there is no core, essence or foundation to race, and that (as I have already argued) its meaning is therefore to be found in social norms and conventions rather than biological fact. Racists will tend to insist on racial essence: that there is, for example, some kind of 'scientific' proof that different races exist, while anti-racists will tend to demonstrate that what passes for proof and essence is invariably a distinction made in culture, not nature. Questioning and critiquing racial essentialism, we employ very useful concepts like 'racialization' (see, for example, Murji and Solomos, 2005) and 'racial formation' (see Omi and Winant, 1994: 55) to describe the dynamic social and historical processes by which understandings of race are made and remade, rather than being the expression of some biological fact or inner truth of those marked out as racially different. To explore how race operates in different times and in different places helps to reveal this contingency, this sense in which what race means is very much the product of the contexts in which we find it.

While this book is determinedly and unashamedly anti-essentialist and fully committed to a belief in the social constructedness of race, it does not agree with the thesis that racism is at root the only possible cause of or explanation for race. Race is simply more complicated than that. It plays a much wider role in our cultures than just the production of racism. This is not for one second to play down the significance and seriousness of racism, but while racism is always and necessarily going to involve race, race does not always and necessarily involve racism. Even if we go a long way to accepting the idea that some vastly important historical episodes of racist practice (such as European practices of slavery and colonialism) continue in many respects to inform present ideas about race, this is not to concede that those ideas will always and for all time work in the service of racism.

This is quite a controversial position to take, particularly for a person like myself who – racialized as white within a majority white society – benefits (however unwillingly) from the advantages of white privilege. My assertion that we need to understand race beyond racism could accordingly be subjected to a moral or political challenge: surely, it might be argued, it is our critical responsibility to focus on, confront and challenge racism? Isn't this why academics do work on race in the first place, and doesn't a call to think about the meanings of race in excess of racism risk betraying that cause, whatever theoretical advantages it might profess to offer?

While I would agree with the first part of this question – the politics of anti-racism is largely what interests and motivates me too – I want to suggest that anti-racism isn't actually best served by a reduction of race to racism. I want to show in this book how unhelpful, constraining and counter-productive the race-is-all-about-racism position can be. Indeed, I want to show how a perspective that understands racial meanings in excess of racism is actually better equipped to serve the cause of anti-racism. Consider, for example, somebody using race to say something about themselves – as a marker of subjectivity or an expression of identity (practices often erroneously associated mainly with racialized minorities). From a race-as-racism perspective, such behaviours and practices are read, at best, as a reaction to and bulwark against discrimination (by producing and organizing collectivities that can be mobilized in the name of an anti-racist politics), and at worst as a kind of 'collusion' by racialized minorities in reproducing the terms of their own oppression. As Paul Gilroy suggests, an anti-racist analytic trivializes 'the rich complexity of black life by reducing it to nothing more than a response to racism', making black people visible only in the two complementary roles of 'the problem and the victim' (Gilroy, 1990: 208). By forcing our understanding of the personal expression of racial meaning into these stark and unforgiving options, dominant approaches to the study of race are just not capable of coming to terms with all the other things race says and does. Likewise, consider somebody who might be using race to orient themselves in relation to others – as a way, say, of exploring, engaging or living with cultural differences (practices often erroneously associated mainly with racialized majorities). From a race-as-racism perspective, understanding of such behaviour is likewise unhelpfully constrained by recourse to a moral vocabulary only capable of asking whether it has a racist or an anti-racist outcome.

To illustrate this point a little more concretely, let's go back to the example of the Bob Marley T-shirt. If we can think about the racial meanings of the T-shirt only in terms of racism, then we are faced with the rather stark and evidently reductive interpretive choice of deciding whether it and its wearers are exhibiting 'racism' or 'anti-racism'. While race theory's historical focus on dominant power relations, discrimination and inequality can provide important insights here, such a perspective does not allow for an exploration of the full range of things that the Bob Marley T-shirt is doing. Take just the meanings associated with cannabis culture: certainly, a framework that sets up racism as a 'bottom line' is open to analyses that explore the imbrication of race, poverty and petty crime, or the way that stereotyping is involved in the symbolic production of expectations around distribution and exchange, or the ways in which forms of conviviality in drug consumption might operate on the basis of the mimicry and caricature of those marked out as racially different. But what if the racial meanings involved in cannabis culture, in the forms of sociality it organizes, in the imaginative connections produced in the minds of the drug's consumers and so on, cannot be so easily reduced to the theme of racism and anti-racism? What if the racial meanings generated by the Bob Marley T-shirt's drug references exceed these parameters, in the sense, quite simply, that while being in some sense 'about' race, they do not readily lend themselves to an evaluative judgment as to their positive or negative effects? Does someone who's racialized as black and who associates herself with cannabis culture by wearing a Bob Marley T-shirt *have* to be understood as a victim of racism (through poverty or petty criminality or stereotyping), or as struggling against it (through the assertion of identity and belonging)? Does someone who's racialized as white and who associates herself with cannabis culture by wearing the same T-shirt *have* to be understood as a racist (by perpetuating a stereotype of blackness) or as an anti-racist (by expressing solidarity with difference)? Isn't there often so much more going on, so much more to say that's not captured by this morality play that is so keen to assign to social actors the roles of heroes and villains?

Alternatively, consider the example of race and sexual desire: certainly there are ways of reading sexual desire for someone marked out as racially different as a fetishization of race, and a neoimperial form of domination over the other, (see hooks, 1992: 25), but as bell hooks herself acknowledges (ibid.: 39), the eroticism and pleasure wrapped up in the desire for difference do not have to be understood in such terms. From a casual fuck to a long-term relationship, sexual and emotional intimacies with those marked out as racially different from oneself may facilitate forms of 'mutual recognition and discovery' (Dyer, 1997: 7); they may constitute a politics of race and class mutiny that figures as 'the promise of another life' (Obama, 2007: 124) or bring about forms of subjective transformation that in turn produce cosmopolitan social formations (Nava, 2007).[3] Transracial relationships are a large and growing part of contemporary life – in England and Wales the 2011 census shows, for example, that more than a million people self-identify as mixed race (Rogers, 2012), and are accordingly the product of transracial relationships or technologies of reproduction. While it would be ridiculously limiting to think about mixed race relationships in terms of racism alone, it is I would suggest equally implausible to think about mixed race as a kind of racial transcendence or overcoming – that race is such a superficial phenomenon that somehow we stop 'seeing' it when we are in a relationship. Instead, I'd suggest that it's more useful to think about the way in which racial difference can feature as a locus of desire and a significant and longstanding element of what we might find attractive in a chosen partner. While there may be virtue in the anti-racist idea that we're all the same underneath, surely it's also very important to acknowledge that this sameness is not necessarily what draws us to and fascinates us with somebody who's racialized differently from ourselves. Someone's difference can become a feature of how we relate to them: the things we talk about, the music we listen to, the books we read, the family and friendship networks they might bring with them and so on. Given that all these can be inflected by race, there are clearly complexities at work in such relationships that cannot be captured by the paradigm of racism, or (however well-intentioned) the desire for racial transcendence.

I think these examples make it obvious that we need to develop a more expansive critical framework if we are to be in a position to explore in a more sophisticated way the complexities of racial meaning (complexities that might include both racism and anti-racism, but not to the exclusion of all other meanings). Approaches to race that are ultimately focused on racism were developed in the context of twentieth-century societies that for a long time thought of themselves as divided along a single racial line between, say, black and white, or between host and immigrant cultures. Race presented itself as a problem of racism because it didn't appear to be very much more than the issues that arose from a confrontation between essentially different groups, with their own inner consistencies and fixed characteristics. Race would eventually 'go away' because it was thought that immigrants would eventually 'go home' (out of sight, out of mind), or that perceived differences would, alternatively, melt away through adjustive processes of integration or assimilation. In places like Britain, dominant academic approaches to race were initially prompted by mid-century waves of post-colonial immigration, and were accordingly built on the premiss of this kind of frictional encounter or division between two discrete groups.

But race did not go away, and the way that we understand race today has become a lot more sophisticated. There has been a slow but developing realization that Britain and places like it are not and indeed never really were monocultural entities (see Fryer, 1984). To understand race as a binary encounter between one group and another is a simplifying fiction that does not do justice to long and complicated histories of social and cultural diversity. A more developed understanding of the histories of trade and empire does not diminish their implication in racism and human suffering, but it does require us to reconsider the simplified myths of racial homogeneity that are animated by the reductive categories of 'us' and 'them'. The whole point about postcolonial criticism is not about expressing penitent guilt for Western superiority, but about displacing the hierarchies of culture, knowledge and power on which that superiority is built.

To recognize that we are inextricably linked in more complicated ways than we can ever fully describe to a multiplicity of other social places and spaces around the world, and that this has been the norm rather than a recent development in human history, is to expand and extend our understanding of race beyond the fictitious cultural boundaries of the sovereign nation-state (Paul Gilroy's *The Black Atlantic* (1993) is instructive here). It is to oblige us to recognize that 'they' are 'us' and 'we' are 'them' in cultural as well as geographical terms: as this book will demonstrate, race is a creative resource that is dispersed throughout our common global multiculture. As it is commodified and capitalized upon, race becomes detached, in significant ways, from the particular groups and bodies that – in the old, binary language of racial difference – used to guarantee its meaning. While claims of ownership are common, nobody owns race. Though it cannot escape the operations of power, nobody is ultimately in control or in charge. Race is patently no longer *just* a subject fit for discussions around discrimination, poverty and under-achievement. There is more to race than this.

If we can accept that race does not 'go away', and that it is accordingly not the job of a critic to 'get rid of', to transcend or 'see beyond' it, we are also in a far better place when it comes to understanding the ways in which groups and individuals invest in, engage with, and produce racial meanings. We can, in other words, address more straightforwardly the rather obvious sense in which race is a widespread cultural resource used by everybody – minorities and majorities alike – to express an infinitely variable number of different ideas, connections, aspirations, affiliations, fascinations, excitements, sympathies, beliefs, commitments and desires. Race is not always used in racist ways, and though racism can be one of the significant effects of race, it is not the only one.

What about 'ethnicity'?

Now, it would be incorrect and unfair to suggest that the wider meanings of race have entirely escaped critical attention. There *is* a space reserved for these kind of discussions, and that space has tended to be organized by the concept of 'ethnicity'. Because of the aforementioned orthodoxy on the social constructedness of race – the agreement that the meaning of race is to be found in culture not nature, that the essentialist, biological claim on racial difference is a phoney one, that ultimately what tends to be called race does not 'really' exist in the sense that it is imagined to – there has been a tendency to substitute discussions of race for discussions of ethnicity. Ethnicity has become a legitimate and acceptable concept precisely because it references culture, not biology. As a name for the shared experience of language, religion, history, tradition, geography, laws and so on, ethnicity captures what groups of people may have in common without incorrectly suggesting that that shared experience is somehow 'internal' to them. Ethnicity, particularly as it is developed in poststructuralist theory (see Hall, 1996) suggests that identity is not fixed once and for all but that it changes according to time, place and social context. Ethnicity does not describe who we are, once-and-for-all, but rather is attentive to the dynamism of the social. It is, as it is often put, a question not of 'being' but of 'becoming'.

As a technically more accurate description of identity formation than biological essentialism, ethnicity has accordingly come to be used in the place of race, and the concept of race, as noted above, has often been reserved for the discussion of racism. Race and racialization are conceived of as naming ideas and processes that are illegitimate and essentializing, suspect on both conceptual and moral grounds, and deployed from critical perspectives with the objective of challenging or overthrowing them. Ethnicity, by contrast, is often considered a legitimate, anti-essentialist concept, used to describe the differences that people so evidently have, and from which they derive meaning.

There are a couple of problems with this framing, though, that mean it is often not sufficiently open to the broader critical framework I am recommending in this book. The first (and for our purposes, main) problem is that, despite the dynamism and anti-essentialism of the concept of ethnicity, it still has a strong tendency to map culture – if only contingently – onto particular groups and individuals. Ethnicity comes to mean the characteristics that people exhibit or live or possess, and while these characteristics are not written into their biology as in essentialist theories of race, they will tend to be subjected to some test of credibility or authenticity that requires them to 'belong'. To return once again to the Bob Marley T-shirt: discussions of ethnicity here would tend to circulate around an African-Caribbean identity, or the sense in which Bob Marley's ethnicity has parallels or resonances with the ethnic experience of the person wearing the T-shirt. The language of ethnicity is rather difficult to use when we want to discuss, for example, the deployment of the T-shirt as a marker of taste, or cool, or social distinction, or to generate any number of other meanings that are not directly related to a shared cultural identity between Bob Marley and the T-shirt's wearer. Because of this, there is a strong tendency not to talk about these factors at all, or, rather, not to talk about them in terms of ethnicity. There is, in other words, a problem with the use of ethnicity to describe the expression or mobilization of ideas about cultural differences outside of a framework of identity. This is one of the reasons why I am interested in using the concept of race. Race, as I have suggested, can reference a far wider range of meanings that can be mobilized by, but do not have, reductively, to be 'about', particular groups or individuals.

A second problem with the concept of ethnicity is, as has often been pointed out, a tendency for it to be deployed in essentialist terms. While it is possible to foreground the adaptive, impermanent and changeable characteristics of ethnicity, the concept is often treated as if it were fixed and frozen. The UK census, for example, has adopted the anti-racist language of ethnicity, but what is meant by ethnicity in this and a wide range of other official and unofficial contexts is actually an essentialist one: ethnicity is determined by a place or community of origin obtained at birth and expressed in language, cultural affiliation or skin colour. The problem here is that ethnicity is often being used euphemistically. People say 'ethnicity' but they actually mean 'race'. I am not arguing that we should stop using a term like ethnicity – it crops up many times in the following chapters – but simply suggesting that we are not dealing here with a 'bad' and suspect concept (race) and a 'good' and legitimate one (ethnicity); rather, that both these terms are constituent parts of the vocabulary we use to make sense of ourselves and others. The phenomenology of race (the ways in which social actors actually go about using the languages and practices of race) is often messy and confusing, and while from a more 'scientific' perspective terms like 'race' and 'ethnicity' may be used in our cultures incoherently, inadequately or inaccurately, this should not provide us with a reason or excuse not to try to understand how they *are* being used, and to what ends.

One rather unfortunate side effect of the correct insistence that, in biological terms, 'race does not exist' is then the failure to know what to do with those who use the concept, both directly and euphemistically. Because race is a biologically invalid category, it is common in academic discussions to work with the premiss that people who use a language of race do so 'wrongly', and in doing so lend meaning to an idea that we'd be better off just getting rid of. In the worst case (not as uncommon as you might think), critics who take this position adopt the rather patronizing and moralizing stance that if everybody thought about race like they did then racism would disappear. These critics are signed up to an idea of racial transcendence: the idea that race might just 'go away' if we can all agree that it is not 'real'. Usually invested in a narrative that thinks about race as the creation of a particular social and historical moment (of, broadly speaking, European imperialism and colonialism), and which reads the subsequent (postcolonial) histories of race as the continued unfolding of that history, such critics look forward to a future point where those colonial legacies are addressed and accounted for, where wrongs are righted, and where the category of race itself is somehow overcome. From this perspective, race is so tied up with racism that to give it credence as a site of meaning is to perpetuate that racism.

While this is a nice idea, it's also in my reading a bit of a fantasy. Even if practices of European imperialism and colonialism are the most important origin of the modern idea of race (which I think they are, by the way), it's a rather great imaginative leap to think that by doing away with injustice (racism) the idea of race will simply vanish into thin air: Pandora's box is open, and the genie of race doesn't crawl obediently back into the bottle of social equality. As Jamie Sherman suggests, while it is true that race gets embedded in social structures and institutions and can work in the interests of the powerful, it is not something that is mechanistically imposed from 'above' by dominant classes, faceless corporations, governments or an evil media. Race is a feature of our common culture and is 'constructed, performed and authenticated through habits of seeing, hearing, speaking and writing' (Sherman, 2009: 170). People continue to use race to understand themselves and others. Its richness and plurality of meanings is undeniable, and it is stubbornly resistant to the policing of self-deceiving critics who 'know better'. The critical position that thinks the end of racism necessitates the end of race is at a loss to know what to do with race's continuing presence. It is accordingly the argument of this book that it is better to face up to the determined, palpable fact of race, in all its complexity, than to hold on to the fantasy that it can be dismissed or disappeared through education or enlightenment. Race does not go away.

But as I asserted at the start of this chapter, the fact that race does not go away needn't be regarded pessimistically. The fact that we're 'stuck' with race doesn't mean we have to reconcile ourselves to living with something we don't like. The acceptance of race certainly isn't to do with a fatalistic acceptance of racism. It's to do with recognizing that if we want to do away with racism we need to develop a better and fuller understanding of what race does. To try to confront racism without acknowledging the full complexity of racial meaning is to undermine anti-racism and place an arbitrary and rudimentary limit on how we conceptualize it. Rather than impose these limits on our understanding of race, and in doing so grow its mysteriousness, this book sets out to explore and examine realms of racial meaning that a lot of race theory has habitually ignored or passed over in silence. It is the argument of this book that we need to talk about race more, not less, for race is everybody's business. By drawing on the fascinating work of the many scholars who break race out of its premature containment as a function of racism (for I am by no means the first person to be frustrated by these limitations), it is the suggestion of this book that to really understand race we need to range across the disciplinary boundaries that function to keep it in place. Race isn't just a subject for sociology or social policy, or for cultural studies, or media studies, or history or literature, or politics, or psychology or geography, or science studies, or ecology, or anthropology, or whatever. It's a subject for all of these (and more), simultaneously and together.

Finally, this is not, I feel bound to note, to create a fetish of race. Some friendly critics have suggested that the term 'race' is so indelibly marked by a history of slavery, exploitation and genocide that it is necessary for us to develop new terms that do not bring with them all this baggage. While I disagree with this for the reasons I have just set out, I am not obstinately and for all time wedded to the term. It's possible that alternative, less 'loaded' ways might develop for talking and thinking about the patterning of identity, belonging, culture and experience that race currently makes intelligible to us (the observation that race doesn't go away is not and cannot be for all time), but these are as yet underdeveloped in our cultures. The contradictory, imprecise, unscientific language of race is what we most often have. It's the term people use. More profoundly, it's the thing that people mean, even when they substitute for it a more acceptable term like 'ethnicity', or a more abstract term like 'difference'. Race is the messy, mixed up thing we're all talking about. Race is the thing that this book tries, in its partial, incomplete and provisional way, to understand.

Chapter outline

My next chapter will situate *Consuming Race* in relation to key debates in the humanities and social sciences, including theories of consumption, capitalism, imperialism and colonialism. It considers the limitations of some older work on consumption, and sets out five critical positions that provide some new and interesting ways of thinking about the subject of race and consumption. I suggest, firstly, that it can be useful to think about racial identity as a commodity that derives its value from practices of consumption. I then think about 'authentic' culture as necessarily produced through processes of stereotyping and imitation. I argue that the desire to address racialized inequalities through consumption does not escape the circuits of representation and mediation, and that it is increasingly important to try to think about race beyond the binary of 'us' and 'them'. Finally, I introduce the idea of racial metonomy as a way of thinking about how race can be manifested in objects, places, landscapes, animals and plants.

The third chapter of this book engages with a widespread cultural trend away from cosmopolitan consuming practices, and towards an idea of 'ethnically appropriate' consumption. It suggests that in an attempt to identify forms of 'appropriate' white ethnicity in multicultural contexts, some white consumers have found meaning in nostalgic fantasies of domestic femininity. I go on to consider a recent fashion for Nordic culture (from modernist design to 'Nordic noir') among white British consumers, and argue that it too is marked by fantasies of ethnic appropriateness, in this case manifested in the landscape, climate, food, culture and politics of the Nordic countries. The material and symbolic consumption of a Nordic fantasy serves, I suggest, as a point of identification for white people in search of themselves.

In Chapter 4, I consider the way in which non-white subjects may engage with forms of symbolic whiteness in consumer culture. I explore the emergence of the figure of the 'black nerd', and provide a reading of the online Black Nerds Network as engaged in the appropriation of a hitherto 'white' retro culture. Breaking with a longstanding association between blackness and futurity, I suggest that retro style can provide new ways for non-white subjects to symbolically access and engage with the cultural past. I then move on to consider the idea of 'post-black' culture in relation to Barack Obama and the rise of a black middle-class in contemporary North America.

Chapter 5 explores food as an example of cross-cultural consumption. It reflects on how the idea of cultural authenticity is produced and transacted in the history of 'Indian' food in Britain, and moves on to explore the 'post-authentic authenticity' of the Vietnamese sandwich the banh mi. Thinking about the global mediation of contemporary food cultures, this chapter shows how the banh mi is produced through the intersection of Vietnamese, US and UK food cultures. Finally, I consider the phenomenon of 'street food' as a context for the production of culinary authenticity. In all cases, the physical tastes, sensations and artefacts of rich and complex material cultures are drawn on in the expressive performances of identity and difference.

The sixth chapter of this book thinks about the ways in which the cultures of childhood are saturated with race. It begins by considering the long-standing transnational significance of the 'red Indian' in childhood culture, and suggests that it can be read as a barometer of changing attitudes to and investments in ideas about race and cultural difference. I go on to explore the representation of racial diversity on British children's TV, looking at shows like *Teletubbies*, *Waybuloo* and *Nina and the Neurons*. In particular, I explore how and why non-naturalistic shows so often hold onto the visual signifiers of race. The chapter then thinks about how and why animals come to represent racial characteristics, and the way that these are manifested in children's media, toys and games. These provide examples, I suggest, of a two-way transfer of racial meaning between human and non-human life.

I pick up this theme again in Chapter 7, which also considers how animals and plants get caught up in practices of human meaning making. This chapter begins by surveying ecological debates about 'native' and 'non-native' animal species, and focuses in particular on the way in which nature gets defined as outside of human influence. This, in turn, is accompanied by implicit ideas about how plant and animal life is thought to 'belong' to particular spaces and places. Practices of 'natural gardening' bring together people and nature, and an association between human identity and flora and fauna is implicitly informed by ideas of who (and what) belongs within the national space. I consider the iconic position of the red squirrel in narratives of 'British' nature, and make a case for the 'natural' environment as a key site for the production and contestation of racialized ideas of national identity and belonging.

The eighth chapter of this book centres on the stories we tell about race, and explores a range of different sites involved in the production of racial knowledge. This is knowledge that we use to navigate and negotiate contemporary cultures of race. It is my suggestion in this chapter that there is a relationship between particular cultural forms and the characteristics of the racial knowledge that they produce. This chapter starts off by exploring how a fast-paced new media culture obsessively returns to the telling of stories that exhibit and admonish racist speech acts. I go on to discuss popular race novels as a way of acquiring knowledge across the boundaries of race, and how controversies around images on YouTube encourage the idea that there are 'essential' differences between Muslims and non-Muslims. Finally, I consider what 'good' or 'progressive' representations in the HBO show *The Wire* tell us about the characteristics of audience desire.

In my conclusion I consider how this book's argument that we are all enmeshed in the production and reproduction of racial meanings can help us to reevaluate some deterministic metaphors that so often encourage a fatalism in the cultural politics of race.

Chapter 2

Theorizing racial consumption

Theorizing racial consumption

As my introduction has suggested, this book is interested in thinking about race as not something that people 'have', and more a thing that people 'do'. Consumption is a way of thinking about this practice of 'doing' as a material and symbolic engagement with our contemporary culture. Race isn't something that 'goes away', and we're really limiting our imaginative horizons if we think that race can be explained by racism alone. The first objective of this chapter is to flesh out how the following chapters are positioned in relation to some of the relevant debates and traditions in the humanities and social sciences, including theories of consumption, capitalism, imperialism and colonialism. The chapter then goes on to consider the limitations of some older work on race and consumption, before setting out five critical positions that provide some useful ways of thinking about the subject: first, the idea that it is legitimate to think about racial identity as something that can be produced, commodified and consumed in market contexts; second, that we can't 'get rid' of racial stereotypes even if we wanted to, and that our critical job might be to engage with them rather than dismiss them; third, and relatedly, that because race is manifested in the context of consumer culture, attempts to deal with forms of racialized inequality must themselves engage with the politics of consumer culture; fourth, that we really need to recognize that the objective conditions of global racial practice are no longer adequately described (however well-meaningly) by a binary of 'us' and 'them'; fifth, and lastly, that it's very useful to recognize that we're sometimes talking about race when we think we're talking about something else entirely. An idea of racial metonymy, I suggest, is key to understanding where race comes from, and what it does.

How this book understands consumption

As I have already suggested, a lot of thinking about race limits itself to questions of racism, and the consideration of race in the context of consumer culture provides a useful way of opening up to a fuller range of what race does in our contemporary cultures. An everyday or commonsense definition of 'consumption' relates to the purchase of goods and services. This isn't a bad starting point, but it is one I want to extend and expand. As Arjun Appadurai has noted, the process of buying, selling or exchange is often only a brief moment in the social life of things (Appadurai, 1986: Chapter 1). Certainly the moment of purchase can be a significant one, but it is the starting point of this book that we do not stop consuming something when we own it, and we do not need to own something to consume it. The process of consumption encompasses a wide range of activities in which consumption is caught up in human practices of meaning making, where what is consumed gets taken out of old contexts and put into new ones, where those meanings are transformed through use.

Challenging some of the longstanding associations that have often accompanied ideas about consumption, this kind of perspective helps us to recognize that consuming practices are, as Appadurai suggests, 'eminently social, relational and active rather than private, atomic or passive' (ibid.: 31). If consumption helps us to think about the way that social relations are shaped by the objects we desire, buy, use and own, it also prompts us to reassess the idea that objects are the inert and lifeless things we often take them to be. Sure, objects don't speak or interact with us in the same way that other people might do, but this doesn't mean that objects are wholly reliant on people to activate their meanings. Objects, in other words, are not 'switched off' until somebody purposely turns them on. What an object means is not always the conscious and expressed intention of the person or persons who makes, buys, displays or uses it. It can be argued, then, that objects have a certain 'agency' of their own, that is, a capacity 'to make things happen' (Lury, 2011, 57). As Paul Gilroy remarks, the hold that commodities like cars have over us 'reveals how particular objects and technologies can become, in effect, active, dynamic social forces in the material cultures of everyday life' (Gilroy, 2010: 30). Rather than think of meanings as fixed to objects in consumer culture, it can be more useful to think of objects' social value as 'emergent in the way we use and live with them' (Dant, 1999: 15). As Daniel Miller puts it, 'things make people just as much as people make things' (2010: 135). Like the science studies perspective called actor network theory, this attentiveness to the agency of objects helps us to move away from the idea that human subjectivity and identity – our sense of who we are and how we relate to others – is somehow innate to and imprinted on our bodies and our minds, and opens us up to a consideration of how these important markers of who we are come to be made and remade as we interact with people, places, animals and things.

Just as it's not so useful to restrict consumption only to the practice of shopping, neither do I want to limit our understanding of consumption just to material objects. As Jean Baudrillard has suggested, consumption can be thought of as 'an active form of relationship (not only to objects, but also to society and the world)' (Baudrillard, 1996: 199). Though material objects can play an important role in consumption, I am just as interested in the role of images and symbols – in information and representations – as an integral part of consuming practice. My tendency here is to think about 'material culture' as part of a broader category of 'consumer culture' (see Dant, 1999: 32) that is both material and semiotic. This is a very open conception of consumption, and sometimes there is little if anything to distinguish it from a more general category like 'culture' itself. This book is, however, called *Consuming Race*, not *Cultures of Race*, for culture is (like ethnicity) a term often used to describe properties and characteristics that are thought to 'belong to' groups or individuals (hence 'Iranian culture' or 'Asian culture'). Because the objects of consumer culture are ostensibly available to everyone, what consumption has in its favour is a propensity to bring to our attention the idea that culture is not an innate possession. Indeed, from a certain perspective, the fact that we can buy and own commodities works as proof that they are not 'really' ours, because they could just as easily be someone else's. As I suggested in the last chapter, there is a tendency to approach race as if it were a phenomenon that exists and operates prior to consumer culture (this is the case not only with essentialist ideas about biology, racial embodiment and cultural authenticity, but sometimes also in anti-essentialist ideas about the social/political 'origins' of racialization). The really useful thing about consumption, then, is that it requires us to think seriously about how race is produced and reproduced in spaces and places that are sometimes dismissed as trivial, insignificant or (at best) secondary to the 'real business' of race. I will come back to the relationship between race and consumption in a moment.

Consumption and capitalism

Despite the very broad concept of consumption I'm employing here, it is worth holding onto the idea that consumption might provide us with a way of exploring some specific aspects of what it's like to live now in the twenty-first century, in social formations that – notwithstanding their diversity – are increasingly organized in their culture, economics and politics by the precepts of consumer capitalism. Despite its evident failures, the market-oriented organizational model known as neoliberalism remains dominant, encouraging all social actors to conceive of themselves not as citizens, communities or comrades but, first and foremost, as consumers. Practices of consumption, in other words, are currently shaped and structured in consumer-capitalist contexts, and it is useful to recognize the ways in which consumption in turn works to produce, reproduce and develop contemporary capitalist cultures. The production of commodities – goods and services to be bought and sold in markets – has always been an important part of capitalist organization, and commodity production shapes in significant ways how we understand ourselves and relate to one another. What Karl Marx called 'commodity fetishism' (and others later called 'reification') describes the way that capitalism encourages us to lose touch with the dynamism and interconnectedness of human relationships by treating commodities as if they were autonomous of those relationships. The development of consumer societies in the twentieth century further encouraged individualistic forms of belief and behaviour as capitalism played an increasingly important role in producing human needs, with commodities becoming a medium through which people expressed themselves, their relationships and their desires. And so as the market came to play an increasingly significant role in the organization of culture, culture became increasingly important to the organization of capitalism (Jameson, 1991). Consumer culture can accordingly be thought of as the key contemporary site for the production and circulation of values and meanings (Featherstone, 2007), and as a realm for the expression of identity and morality (Bauman, 2007; 2011, Chapter 5). As Celia Lury suggests, the contemporary consumer 'is not invited to be rational or instrumental in their use of products, but instead to employ products in an expressive display of lifestyle' (Lury, 2011: 61). By providing an endlessly novel array of objects and images, consumer culture gives individuals an immense variety of opportunities to explore, define and understand themselves and their relationships. Such practices of identification and self-transformation do not happen as if once and for all, but are part of an ongoing and fluid process of creation and recreation. While in the past expressive possibilities were more limited by the terms of a given ethnic repertoire, consumer culture opens up all cultures to the possibilities of engagement. As *The Communist Manifesto* convincingly argued (Marx and Engels, 1992), transnationalism, cosmopolitanism and xenophilia have all been facilitated by the global development of capitalism.

To recognize capitalism's central role in contemporary culture and acknowledge its capacities for distorting and debasing human relations is not, therefore, to suggest that the subject of consumption is somehow to be dismissed as unworthy of our engagement, or to be used only in a pejorative sense. If the commodity fetish subordinates the human to the market, culture's inscription within the market provides commodities with a potentiality for expressing the human. Acts of consumption have their own cultural politics, and can also serve as a precursor to other forms of political consciousness and organization. Power works in complicated and contradictory ways in consumer culture, and its characteristics demand to be understood rather than rejected out of hand (Banet-Weiser, 2007: 210). While we might have investments in changing them, we cannot specify the terms of the cultures in which we operate. And so while this book has no illusions about the injustices of capitalism, it also does not, in attempting to develop an understanding of contemporary practices of consumption, want to reduce these practices to telling a story about capitalism alone. Thinking back to the example of the Bob Marley T-shirt in the previous chapter should make this easy to understand: although racially-inflected issues ranging from the shirt's commodity history (who made it, under what conditions, for what markets?), to Bob Marley's status as a brand in the commodified genre of reggae music, are in some respects made explicable by an interpretive practice that reads the T-shirt as a 'product' of capitalism, there are a wide range of other equally significant issues – relating to status, identity, affinity, history, taste, politics, culture and so on – that are not always fully and coherently explained by that reading. This does not mean that when we explore these issues the T-shirt stops being a commodity in consumer culture, but it does mean it is not 'just' or 'only' that. As I have suggested, in consumer societies there is an intensification of the relationship between capitalism and culture. In this context it is not only likely that whatever subject we might want to think about will in some sense be framed by capitalism, but moreover that the resources at our disposal to struggle against capitalism will themselves also derive from those same 'compromised' cultural conditions (see Laclau, 1990: 56). As we swim in capitalist culture, there is no absolute critical position that allows us to step outside of capitalism, but that doesn't mean that we're just its slaves (see Hall, 1981: 232). We cede too much to capitalism by attributing to it sole responsibility for the creative and social dimensions of commodities and commodification, those elements on which capitalism depends, but does not and cannot produce for itself (Gilbert, 2008: 109; see also Halberstam, 2005: 12). As Matthias Zick Varul has suggested, resolutely anti-consumerist forms of anti-capitalism are often caught up in parochial and paternalistic fantasies of community that deny the creative and transformative potential of consumer culture (Varul, 2013: 294). Despite the protestations of some commentators who remain invested in its principled refusal, it is evidently quite possible to develop critical engagements with consumer culture that do not result in the mindless celebration of capitalist oppression. Even under a changed economic regime, many of the of the ways we relate to one another through images, ideas, objects and practices would still continue, albeit in new forms: in this sense, even if capitalism came to an end, consumption would not.[4]

Imperial and colonial legacies

Also requiring a degree of critical sophistication is our understanding of the role played in the cultural politics of race by the history of European imperialism and colonialism and the culturally segregated racial formations that were typically their product. Any understanding of contemporary acts of racial consumption needs to acknowledge the particular importance of this history in giving shape to the meaning of race over the last five hundred years or so. 'Imperialism' is a way of talking about the way that territories outside Europe were often violently taken as European possessions. State and commercial interests in Portugal, Spain, Belgium, Germany, Britain and France (among others) all built overseas empires, and were involved in the extraction of goods and raw materials and the brutal exploitation of slave or indentured (forced) labour. Empires were kept in place by military and economic means, and frequently involved the settlement (or colonization) of land. European imperialism went hand in hand with the development and expansion of capitalism, and it was accordingly on the back of this wealth that consumer societies first developed (for a more detailed account in relation to the politics of representation, see Hall, 1992). Despite the fact that anti-imperial struggle led to the formal dismantling of most European empires by the middle of the last century, imperialism and colonialism continue to have an important bearing on understandings of race in contemporary culture. As Mimi Sheller suggests in her book *Consuming the Caribbean*, the economic and political dominance of European states that was produced through imperialism and colonialism continues to be felt in the relationships between the West and the global South: mobile flows of consumption – from goods such as sugar and coffee to human bodies to texts, images and other cultural products – continue to provide direct and indirect linkages between 'overdeveloped' and 'underdeveloped' worlds (Sheller, 2003: 3–4).

The academic field known as postcolonial theory was developed in the latter half of the twentieth century as an attempt to make sense of the complex ways in which the political and economic practices of imperialism and colonialism were also wrapped up in the production of discourses (that is, ideas, beliefs and attitudes that frame a particular subject or problem and shape the ways in which it is interpreted). One of the most influential texts in postcolonial theory is *Orientalism*, written in the late 1970s by Edward Said. Said persuasively argues that imperial and colonial distinctions between East and West, between Occident and Orient, came to be defined through Orientalism, a style of thinking and a body of knowledge manifested in texts, images and objects (Said, 1995). Though it took the East as its subject, Orientalism was a Western artefact – it represented the East for Western audiences – and as such became a mechanism for exerting power and domination over the East as the cultural logic of imperial and colonial projects. Neither Orientalism nor the East or the West it describes are 'real' entities; they are representations, and their importance is a symbolic one. By expressing an idea of irreconcilable cultural differences, Orientalism provides a rationale for Western imperialism and simultaneously shores up a fictive idea of the West's cultural and territorial integrity (in actuality neither as distinct as is often supposed even within the theory of Orientalism itself (Bryce, 2013)).

The important point here is not that imperialism and colonialism precede and in doing so determine a set of beliefs and orientations like Orientalism, or alternatively that those beliefs and orientations set out the conceptual ground for subsequent practices of imperialism or colonialism. Rather, it is that they are inextricably part of the same social and historical processes. What sometimes get separated out as the 'material' or the 'economic' and the 'ideological' or the 'cultural' are inextricably linked and simultaneously co-produced. Anne McClintock's classic study of 'commodity racism' offers a useful example of the interwoven character of the material and the semiotic. McClintock describes how in late Victorian Britain a surplus of materials produced in the colonies (oils to make cleaning products, cotton clothes to keep clean) stimulated the development of a large consumer market for the domestic commodity of soap. Advertisements for this new commodity were often framed in a dominant imperialist language of white superiority and black inferiority, drawing on and reproducing longstanding racial associations (whiteness with cleanliness, enlightenment and civilization; blackness with dirt, ungodliness and nature). It was accordingly the case that a commodity that was developed and produced as a result of Victorian imperialism also worked to reinforce the belief system that perpetuated a racist distinction between black and white. Reaching mass audiences and thereby communicating ideas about race to a far wider population than ever before, the consumer spectacle of soap marketing 'could package, market and distribute evolutionary racism on a hitherto unimagined scale' (McClintock, 1995: 131). Commodity racism hereby represents the convergence – or, alternatively, the irreducibility – of the materiality of the commodity and the ideas and beliefs that are associated with it. In McClintock's analysis, domestic consumer culture is inextricably linked not only to imperial practices, but also to the ways of thinking that accompany it.

While the history of imperialism and colonialism remains of immense significance to this day, it is important that we do not allow our contemporary moral rejection of these practices to short-circuit our understanding of the complexities of contemporary racial formation. Although it is absolutely right to point out that practices of imperialism and colonialism were wrapped up in a view of the world that is reductive and pernicious, too often the fictitious, binary logic exemplified by Orientalist thinking ('East' versus 'West', 'us' versus 'them') is confused in weaker postcolonial critiques for a description of the objective terms of any encounter with cultural difference. Though Said's book is very much interested in the way in which the legacies of Orientalism continue way after the formal dismantling of empires and on to the present day, he is rightly dismissive of the 'dogmatic slumber' (Said, 1995: 327) of applying its framework as if it described all possible relationships and representations on an East–West/North–South axis. Adherents of this mechanistic practice of thinking-by-numbers will invariably position Western subjects as imperialists and abusers, and non-Western subjects as exploited victims. It is my suggestion here that it is possible to retain an understanding of the uneven global distribution of power and privilege while at the same time working to unpick and complicate the often essentializing distinctions between 'us' and 'them' that otherwise simplistically turn Orientalism inside out (see also Young, 1995: 5).

Likewise, this is a perspective that needs to be brought to bear, too, on encounters and representations on a smaller cultural and geographical scale. As I argued in the last chapter, supposedly critical work that can only understand difference *within* contemporary multicultural social formations as involving the racism of white people and the brave resistance of non-whites does nobody any favours. This is not to deny the possibility of white racism and non-white resistance but at the same time it is not to treat it as a foregone conclusion, an anti-critical and ahistorical position which turns everyone into the puppets of the racial categories to which they are assigned. Certainly we can think of racism as something that exists beyond the intentions of particular social actors (in a racist society white anti-racists will, for example, still benefit from the privileges of whiteness), but to acknowledge this should not lead us towards a fairy story that can only deal with the subject of race in terms of victims and perpetrators. As I argued in the previous chapter, the reduction of race to questions of racism is to artificially restrict our understanding of the complexities of racial meaning. The example that the sophisticated work of Said and McClintock provides is of the necessity of thinking about race in the context of ever-changing configurations of social, cultural, economic, political, technological and ecological life. While practices of racial consumption may repeat or echo imperial, colonial or historically racist dynamics, they may also provide contexts where the struggle against them may find expression too. More likely, they will be host to their adaptation, modification and transformation according to the conditions of the present: as I have discussed at length elsewhere, one defining characteristic of race in our contemporary cultures is the hegemony of anti-racism. In order to understand race today we need to understand the complexities and contradictions of a situation where racism occurs in contexts where most people think of themselves as anti-racist (Pitcher, 2009; 2011). Later on in this chapter I will consider in a little more detail the importance of understanding racial consumption beyond the dynamics of 'us' and 'them'.

Race and consumption

We need a similarly developed understanding of the complexity of relationships when we come to think about race and capitalism. Again, this requires us to resist the urge to reduce one term simply to the origin, cause or explanation of the other. While of course in a racially segregated context like Jim Crow America, consumer culture served as a tool and expression of racism, it also provided a context for its contestation (see Davis, 2007 and Micheletti, 2003). Different times and places have seen different configurations of capitalism and race. Against the rather facile position that capitalism is intrinsically racist (or, as has been argued more recently, anti-racist), it is important to be attentive to the particular social and cultural formations in which race and capitalism are both operative (see Pitcher, 2012 for a detailed version of this argument). This is going to be especially important when, as in this book, the objective is to try to think about racial meanings in excess of both racism and anti-racism. As per the relationship between capitalism and consumption, this again requires us to be sensitive to the way that capitalism informs, structures and shapes practices of race without suggesting that it 'determines' them in some straightforward and inflexible sense.

The spectre of capitalist determination is at work in some influential but now rather dated takes on race and consumption. Take, for example, Henry Giroux's discussion of the famous late 1980s and early 1990s advertising posters by the Italian fashion brand Benetton (Giroux, 1994). To Giroux, the campaigns' adoption of issues-based images feeds off their controversy for promotional ends while packaging, taming and denuding them of conflict. Difference, he writes, is seized upon by capital 'in order to create new markets and products' (ibid.: 15). This is an activity of exploitation and containment, accentuating 'a warmed-up diet of liberal pluralism and harmonious consensus' (ibid.: 16) that serves corporate interests by denying 'radical possibilities' (ibid.: 18). In apparent conflict with his acknowledgement of representation and consumption as sites of political struggle (ibid.: 27), the fact that these campaigns were commercial enterprises seems to preclude the possibility that they might simultaneously have some meaningful political purchase. In Giroux's analysis, 'ideas that hold the promise of promoting social criticism are insinuated into products in an attempt to subordinate the dynamics of social struggle to the production of new lifestyles' (ibid.: 15). The notion that 'the production of new lifestyles' might itself constitute some form of 'social struggle' seems, somewhat arbitrarily, to be ruled out. In his discussion of two racially marked images (the torso of a black woman suckling a white baby; a black and white hand handcuffed together), Giroux rather perversely argues against the logic of controversy that would surely seek to challenge or undermine dominant representations of race by insisting that both images reproduce racist stereotypes: the first image, he argues, reproduces the 'imperialist coding' of 'the black slave/wet nurse or mammy'; the second 'reproduces the racist assumption that social issues regarding crime, turmoil and lawlessness are essentially black problems' (ibid.: 25, 26). Besides shifting product, Giroux is unable to accept that these posters can do anything other than consolidate dominant racisms because he refuses to entertain the possibility that an advertising campaign might manifest anything other than a reactionary racial politics.

Susan Willis likewise tends to answer in the negative the question she poses in the title of her article 'I want the black one: is there a place for Afro-American culture in commodity culture?' (Willis, 1990). While Willis's more sophisticated argument recognizes that it is possible to engage with 'consumer society in a more complex way than to simply point out its racism' (ibid.: 86), she reads consumer culture as historically closed off to African Americans, and subsequently open to them only through the process of mimicking white norms, whereby African Americans become the 'replicants' of whites. Strategies adopted by African American artists to subvert and play with the commodity form provide a critical commentary on commodity culture, but cannot express a coherent African American cultural identity because of the degrading and dehumanizing nature of consumption. Willis's position, in other words, is so invested in the negative and corrupting dimensions of consumption per se that questions of race and consumption are always figured negatively: African Americans are either disadvantaged from being excluded from consumption altogether, or their inclusion is subject to their degradation by the inherently damaging nature of capitalism. Though Deborah Root's book *Cannibal Culture* provides a different focus on the relationship between race and consumption, she too comes to similar conclusions. Root's emphasis is on 'the commodification and consumption of difference' (Root, 1996: xi), exploring attempts in the West to perceive other cultures through practices of consumption. In her reading, Western culture consumes difference in a self-referential mode, and she uses the metaphorical figures of vampires and cannibals to draw out an affinity between acts of consumption and colonial violence and authority (ibid.: 18). With parallels to Giroux's take on the subject, consumption to Root is an act of control, providing an encounter with cultural difference that neutralizes its otherwise critical ambivalence (ibid.: 69).

While all three arguments I summarize here have some valid and useful points to make about the inequalities of power and privilege that consumption can consolidate, they also share a rather less helpful desire to maintain a clear distinction between valued ideas and an inherently corrupting capitalist culture. For Giroux, the distinction is between the representation of racial difference as a form of anti-racist political struggle and the ruthless promotional operations of a multinational corporation. Although he allows for the possibility of the complication and interpenetration of these two elements insofar as capitalism preys on and depoliticizes anti-racism, their interrelationship is asymmetrical because in Giroux's reading capitalism always wins out. To Willis the differential positioning of white and African-American people in US society is reproduced in consumer culture, which is ruled out as a medium for the production of social equality. To Root, the consumption of difference is a one-way process that follows the model of Western colonialism, and as such continues in the realm of culture and consumption an imperialistic legacy. It is not clear whether Root considers a non-exploitative encounter with cultural difference to be possible, but her valourization of what she calls 'earth-based societies' (Root, 1996: 204) suggests that the renouncement of consumer culture is likely to be a necessary precondition of it. According to these arguments, socially progressive or uncorrupted forms of anti-racist representation (Giroux), African-American culture (Willis), and encounters with cultural difference (Root) are all impossible within consumer culture.

It is the position of this book that these arguments cannot give a full picture of the relationship between race and consumption. Certainly they provide their own insights and describe some important critical positions, but they are too hasty to close down the potential in consumer culture for race to do anything other than perpetuate existing injustices, inequalities and regimes of representation. All three arguments are in some respects prey to the interpretive tendency I called into question in the previous chapter of reducing the question of race to the problem of racism. Over the next few pages I want to introduce five alternative theoretical perspectives that can help us to think differently about the relationship between race and consumer culture, and to get to grips with some emergent possibilities in the politics of racial consumption. I want first to suggest that forms of culture and identity can legitimately be produced through practices of commodification, and that this does not cheapen or render them invalid. I will then explore some ideas about authenticity and stereotyping that ask us to think critically about some taken-for-granted assumptions about how we understand racial difference. Discussing some of the literature on 'fair trade', I will briefly think about challenging inequality through consumption. I will then question the divisions and distinctions between West and non-West that very often inform understandings of the cultural geographies of difference. Finally, I will introduce the idea of racial metonomy as a way of thinking about the interrelationship between the human, animal, organic and inorganic in the production of racial meaning.

Identity through consumption

The argument I want to make first derives from the writing of Jean and John Comaroff, who have had a longstanding research interest in the theme of racial consumption. The Comaroffs, who use the term 'ethnicity' to talk about the resources of cultural identity, suggest that scholars have tended to shy away from thinking about the relationship between ethnicity and consumption because culture has tended to be thought of as the antithesis of what is commercial. Commodification is often conceived of as a 'selling out' of culture, depleting its authenticity and reducing its value. Take, for example, the commonly-derided traveller-bag friendly tacky trinkets to be found in any tourist destination (that is, pretty much anywhere in the world). These tourist goods are usually regarded by all but the most credulous as the product of a 'tourist gaze' (see Urry, 2002), that is, the faked-up simulation of culture designed to satisfy the consuming needs of visiting tourists. The mass-production of ethnic commodities is accordingly often thought to destroy and despoil the cultures they purport to represent.

What the Comaroffs argue is quite the opposite. From the production of tourist crafts and the wearing of 'traditional' dress to the running of ethnic-branded casinos and the marketing of nation-states, the Comaroffs suggest that 'mass-circulation reaffirms ethnicity [. . .] and, with it, the status of the embodied ethnic subject as a source and means of identity. Greater supply, in other words, entails greater demand' (Comaroff and Comaroff, 2009: 20).

The imaginative and conceptual leap that the Comaroffs make in reevaluating the status of the ethnic commodity is central to the argument of this book. It is only by holding to the idea that culture is something that happens outside of capitalism that its commodification can be taken to ruin or reduce it. If we think about this for a moment, it becomes clear that it is a perspective that often comes bundled up with some rather dubious ideas about social geography and race: it is precisely because dominant ideas about Western culture (and particularly white Western culture) so closely associate it with the capitalist system that there is a desire for there to be 'other' people, in 'other' places, existing outside of it. It is, indeed, a rather patronizing position that reinforces a hierarchical distinction between 'us' and 'them' by suggesting that 'we' live in a commercial, inauthentic, capitalist culture and 'they' somehow live outside of it. Once we remove this expectation (which is actually very similar to the desire that structures the 'tourist gaze'), then the logic of the Comaroffs' argument becomes clear: because nobody lives outside of capitalist social formations, and because culture is a site of value (a particularly important one in contemporary capitalism), it is surely to be expected that, to a greater or lesser extent, the resources all people use to shape their sense of who they are – as individuals and as communities – are also going to be the resources of consumer culture. Cultural difference is increasingly commodified at the same time that commodities are becoming increasingly cultural – the stuff of feeling and experience (ibid.: 144; see also Baudrillard, 1996: 201; Lazzarato, 2013). The Comaroffs' argument applies as much to the corporate nationhood of 'Britishness', whereby forms of identity and belonging are encouraged through the production of cultural attachments of citizen-stakeholders to the nation-state (Comaroff and Comaroff, 2009: 117–38) to the San people of southern Africa, whose commodified performances for tourists have provided the material for their recognition (by themselves and others) as sharing a common culture (ibid.: 86–116). Cultural commodification and the development of identity as a corporate category – one that can operate like a brand or an entity that can 'own' ideas, practices, materials or products – hereby develop hand-in-hand. See, for example, Smith (2010) for an illustration of the way individuals, corporations and rival nation-states are drawn into a dispute over the symbolic ownership of yoghurt.

Once we move beyond what might be termed a rather romantic attachment to the idea that culture and identity happen outside of capitalism and commodification, we are no longer held back by the idea that these processes somehow represent the betrayal of or estrangement from a 'true' identity. Rather, it is through an engagement and interaction with the materials of consumer culture that a 'true' identity emerges. We cannot make a distinction between the producers and consumers of culture because to produce is also to consume: we are part of the audience of our own ethnic performances (Comaroff and Comaroff, 2009: 26). If this kind of perspective seems counter-intuitive, it is probably because the claim that identity makes is often implicitly an essentialist one – the idea that 'things have always been this way', that a certain practice is longstanding or even 'natural' to us, our families and our communities. As I have already discussed, the ideas we have about who we are and where we're from are often made in essentialist terms, and an attentiveness to the 'constructedness' of these claims is an important step in understanding identity in the context of consumer culture. Contemporary forms of Aboriginal Australian identity, for example, are usefully understood as the product of a capitalist regime whereby legal challenges over the ownership of land are only recognized on the basis of a commodified claim to 'indigenousness' (see Povinelli, 1998). Though the Comaroffs focus on the more corporate dimensions of ethnicity, their insights have parallels to the way that, in consumer culture more generally, identity is conceived as a personal property. When individuals are incited to 'sell themselves' in job interviews or on dating sites, it is clear that we are dealing with self-identity as 'a kind of *cultural resource, asset or possession*' (Lury, 2011: 26). The forms of identity that we describe using the terminology of ethnicity, cultural difference and race are thus increasingly implicated in consumer culture. Racial identities are, as Paul Gilroy suggests, 'composed by complex attachments to varieties, brands, styles, and objects of consumption' (Gilroy, 2010: 8). In Rivke Jaffe's discussion of 'ital chic' in contemporary Jamaica, it is through the consumption of environmental, ethical and health-branded products that middle-class consumers are able to make a claim on Rastafari culture. In Jaffe's analysis, is only because ital chic is woven into a globalized consumer culture that it is able to channel symbolic affinities with 'local' tastes and traditions (Jaffe, 2010).

Encountering difference, encountering ourselves

The second theoretical strand I want to introduce as an important component of this book begins by focusing on how we go about the process of understanding and relating to others, and then considers this process in relation to how we understand ourselves. The Comaroffs' argument provides a useful starting point here because the model of the commodity already opens us up to the idea of some kind of encounter – classically, commodities don't exist outside of markets, and markets are by definition places of transaction and exchange. Racial identities are, like all identities, inherently relational in the sense that identity is defined through difference: we understand who we are in relation to who we're not. While this idea seems on the face of it fairly straightforward, it prompts a question that is rather harder to answer: if we need to know others in order to know ourselves, what are the terms of this encounter? In short, how is it that we know what we're not? This is a question that Fredric Jameson deals with in an essay on cultural studies where he asks us to think about what it is that goes to make up a group's cultural identity. He suggests that:

> No group 'has' a culture all by itself: culture is the nimbus perceived by one group when it comes into contact with and observes another one. [. . .] in this sense, then, a 'culture' is the ensemble of stigmata one group bears in the eyes of the other group (and vice versa).
>
> (Jameson, 1993: 33)

Jameson highlights the idea here that cultural identity is not simply relational, but moreover that the knowledge we have of another group will always be inadequate – never a 'complete' understanding, but one that is necessarily shaped by the impossibility of attaining something like full knowledge. Jameson suggests that because our idea of another group is necessarily based on a generalization from particular contacts and experiences, this will always result in the production of stereotypes, insofar as relations between groups 'must always involve collective abstractions of the other group, no matter how sanitized, no matter how liberally censored or imbued with respect' (ibid.: 35). Rey Chow embroiders on this idea in relation to the problem of representation, suggesting that because by definition one cannot get to the 'truth' of another culture, what she calls cross-ethnic representation 'is a process in which the acceleration and intensification of contacts brought by technology and commerce entail an acceleration and intensification of stereotypes' (Chow, 2002: 63). It is not possible, therefore, simply to get rid of or to 'correct' stereotypes, for when we 'challenge' stereotypes, we are simply replacing them with other stereotypes. Stereotyping is not best understood as involving misrepresentation because it is a necessary device 'fundamental to the representation of one group by another' (ibid.: 54). Summarizing her position, Paul Bowman suggests that:

> Chow's point is that rather than trying to expel stereotypes from the realms of representation, perhaps we need to acknowledge that there may be no getting away from stereotypes – that stereotyping may actually reflect an inevitable aspect of 'culture'.
>
> (Bowman, 2010: 9; see also Dyer, 2002: Chapter 3)

This acceptance of the necessity of stereotyping is a useful way of thinking about the terms of the encounter with cultural difference. While it is of course possible to understand our relationship to difference through stereotypes as harmful or destructive (by consolidating the apparent differences between 'us' and 'them'), it is alternatively possible to think about the engagement with stereotypes as part of a process that disrupts the apparent integrity of those differences. If we don't engage with difference, the integrity of that difference remains intact and the stereotype is not questioned as a stereotype. While the consumption of racial difference works through stereotypes rather than 'true' representations (which in truth do not actually exist), the process of engaging with stereotypes offers us the possibility of recognizing them as such. An engagement with stereotypes does not offer up the possibility of transcending or getting beyond them, for there is no immediate 'truth' being hidden by the stereotype waiting to get out, but what it does offer is a process in which the activity of engagement makes the stereotype in some sense one's own. While the stereotype never really 'belonged' to the other group, the process of engagement can help to make this apparent to us.

Consider, for example, the anxiety that often accompanies the engagement with objects, practices and representations that are not thought of as 'our own' (say, to pick a crude example, the use of chopsticks in a Chinese restaurant by someone who normally uses a knife and fork). People will often worry about whether what they're doing is correct, or appropriate, or even whether what they're doing is somehow exploitative of the culture (and, by inference, group) with which they are symbolically engaged. One way of reading this anxiety is that there really is a 'correct' way of doing things that is closed off to us when we don't 'belong' to the culture in question: we do not know the protocols, the languages, the etiquette involved, and this increases our self-consciousness and consolidates the sense in which we feel like strangers to that culture. Alternatively, this anxiety can be understood as being produced by the absence of a fundamental underlying truth to a culture or a particular set of cultural practices. While what we took to be a 'real' culture seems neither as coherent or stable as it appeared to be from outside, we mistakenly read this as the fault of our engagement, rather than an intrinsic characteristic of culture itself. The clumsiness and uncomfortableness that are so often produced by an encounter with cultural difference are an effect of the boundary-crossing nature of that engagement, not our intrinsic incompatibility with it (sure, we can use chopsticks more or less competently, but this is something anyone with a hand and a brain can learn to do). Though we might desire to 'transcend' the stereotype to get to something more 'real', the practice of cultural engagement can reveal a culture's stereotype to be the most stable and substantial thing about it. While of course our discomfort can have the opposite effect (working to shore up our outsider status and thus the apparent integrity of the cultural difference encountered), we might alternatively say that it can help us to reveal the extent to which perceived differences are an effect of, and do not precede, our encounter with them. From this perspective, while consuming race does not make race disappear, it can help to reveal its contingency, that is, the mistakenness of taking the irreconcilable fact of race for granted. 'Is that all there is to it?', we might at last exclaim to ourselves, as what seemed to be the impressive edifice of a sovereign culture dissolves before our eyes. This brokering of differences is one that is arguably facilitated by the kinds of equivalences between identities that become available in the dynamics of a mass-mediated consumer culture (see Jameson, 1993: 37).

This way of reading cultural differences as produced through relationships of encounter and exchange requires us to move away from ideas about culture as the pure and discrete property of any specific group or individual. The Comaroffs' argument helped us to refuse the idea that culture is something that takes place outside of capitalism, and therefore that we cannot make a meaningful distinction between authentic and inauthentic culture on the basis of its commodification. The implications of Jameson and Chow's discussions likewise require us to reassess our understanding of cultural authenticity. It is not only other cultures that are necessarily understood through stereotypes, but according to Jameson this is how we relate to and understand our own culture too, for the idea of being in possession of a culture is an idea that is itself formed through the creation of a boundary separating it from other cultures. Other cultures, in other words, provide an impression of what lies outside our own culture, and in doing so play a crucial role in giving shape to our understanding of our own culture. When we speak of 'our own' culture, this is 'the recuperation of the Other's view of us' (Jameson, 1993: 33). Both 'our' culture and 'their' culture are accordingly built on this mutual interaction, transacted through the material of generalization and stereotype.

This perspective is of course troubling to anyone who takes culture (whether their own, or anyone else's) for granted, yet it provides us with some very useful tools for understanding practices of racial consumption, which we can now think of in terms of infinitely complex processes of engagement, exchange and negotiation where seemingly permanent or longstanding forms of identity and meaning are in actual fact the dynamic, contingent products of those processes. While the conviction that culture is something we 'have' is hard to shake for people who have never been estranged from it, the experiences of people who get categorized as 'mixed race' can often offer some insights into these processes. With some parallels to the experience of transgender people who have an understanding of their own gender identity that is in conflict with the gender to which they have been assigned by others, the experience of being 'mixed race' will often disturb the 'naturalness' of the idea of culture as possession and in so doing reveal the constructedness of processes of identification. People positioned as 'mixed race' are faced with conflicting categories of racial identification, and as such the taken-for-grantedness of racial identity is thrown up into the air. What other people might think of as an unproblematic expression of who they are is revealed to be the assemblage of a complicated series of behaviours, practices and associations. Like the anxiety involved in engaging with difference noted above, 'mixed race' people are made conscious of what – after Judith Butler (1990) – we might call racial performativity: the sense in which racial identity is not a set of stable and fixed characteristics but is the product of practices of racial performance. In the same way that gender identity does not precede imitation but rather is the *effect* of the imitation of gender identity (Butler, 2006: 261), it is through the performance of race that race comes into being. The experience of being 'mixed race' accordingly highlights something that is true of all racial identities, and underlines the importance of what I am calling racial consumption as a means by which race is performed on an ongoing basis, through our inter-actions with one another, mediated through the expressive material and immaterial contexts of consumer culture.[5]

For an example of racial performativity, take Iain Condry's discussion of Japanese hip hop. While Condry recognizes that the 'blackness' of hip hop is key to its cultural meaning in Japan, the Japanese 'borrowing' of US hip hop does not render that process inauthentic. Certainly, Japanese hip hop is an imitation of US hip hop, but only in the sense that hip hop, like all musical genres, works through imitation (Condry, 2007: 648). There is nothing fundamentally different between, say, the way an African American person develops their expertise as a rapper and the way that a Japanese person becomes skilled at the same activity – both develop their talent through the emulation of sounds and rhythms and styles. Similarly, Bakari Kitwana's exploration of white Americans' love of hip hop suggests that there is no easy answer to the question 'when does Black youth culture end and the packaged imitation of Black youth culture begin?' (Kitwana, 2005: 121). This is because imitation and appropriation can function as vehicles of respect and exchange even as hip hop simultaneously reinforces and upends racial stereotypes (ibid.: 162). To extend this a little further, neither is there a fundamental difference between these processes and the way that culture works more generally. All culture is produced through forms of imitation. No culture springs, as if by some spontaneous magic, from the 'heart' or 'soul' of any particular group of people. Culture is learned and practised and, like with the learning of a musical instrument, competencies can be developed, elaborated, polished. It can, like the 'instinctive' fingers of a skilled musician, become like 'second-nature'. But the ease and facility with which a culture might be performed does not prevent it from being a learned property. 'Second nature' does not make something 'nature'; it is not possible for culture to 'belong' to anyone.

This is not to argue that when we use race to 'say' something about ourselves or about others these meanings are empty or random; simply that those meanings do not derive from anything more longstanding or substantial than our collaborative layering of racial performances. In Kitwana and Condry's discussions of hip hop, ideas about cultural authenticity are clearly in operation because authenticity is still a locus of value, but authenticity is defined and experienced in the context of consuming practice; it does not exist in advance of this. And so forms of cultural authenticity can derive from ostensibly inauthentic sources. Mary Crain writes, for example, about how 'native' Ecuadorian women in Quito's domestic service and tourist economies self-consciously adopt certain 'traditional' ways of behaving and dressing to appeal to their employers (Crain in Howes, 1996: 125–37). These women, in David Howes's gloss, 'have proceeded to "occupy" and exploit the very stereotypes that were intended to dominate them' (Howes, 1996: 13). It is not simply that the perceived authenticity of cultural difference can be manufactured (see Watts and Orbe, 2002), but that cultural authenticity itself can be produced by practices of commodification and consumption. As Paul Bowman suggests, the artefacts and practices of Japanese martial arts 'are produced and consumed as if authentically ancient culture, when in fact they have been deliberately produced: conjured up, exported, (re)imported and consumed' (Bowman, 2010: 47; see also Joseph, 2012). Reversing dominant understandings of authenticity and consumption, Sean Kingston makes a convincing case for cultural authenticity as the product of the marketplace. Though the value of 'Authentic Primitive Art' 'dried up when it was perceived as no longer being authored by the primitive, but by the Western system of commodities' (Kingston, 1999: 345), authenticity can be reclaimed and reinscribed through these selfsame processes. The value of some forms of 'authentic' folk art have been revived through the motif of corrupted authenticity: consider for example the excitement among collectors, curators and contemporary visual artists like Grayson Perry for Afghan 'war rugs' (see Cahill, 2009), where a supposedly traditional craft form combines symbols of 'authentic' folk culture with references to military hardware and media spectacle (see Figure 2.1). In Chapter 5, I discuss some of the dynamics of what I call postauthentic authenticity which give an indication of how definitions of the authentic find expression in the context of postmodern consumer culture.

Defetishization/refetishization

A third and related theoretical strand I want to introduce here – using some of the literature on charity and 'fair trade' – relates to attempts on the part of consumers to engage with some of the racialized inequalities made visible by consumer culture. Contemporary consumers are often *reflexive* consumers, and are very much aware of and sensitive to unequal distributions

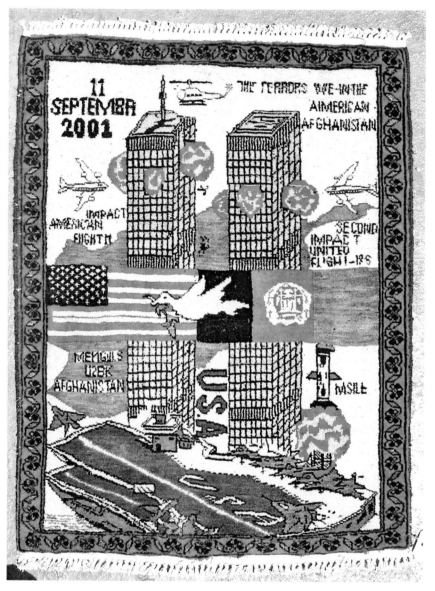

Figure 2.1 World Trade Center War Rug from Afghanistan (2002). © Kevin Sudeith

of wealth, power and privilege that are still so often organized along racial lines. I accordingly want to touch on the way in which forms of consumption are informed by and in dialogue with patterns of racialized inequality.

It is the norm rather than the exception that the goods that we buy will have had a long and complicated journey – from the harvest, mining or processing of raw materials to the assembly of components, to the often convoluted practices of packaging and repackaging, sale and resale – that precede their appearance in our shops or on our web browsers. Many of the things we buy have been to places we have never been and will never go, and will have passed through the hands of innumerable others whose anonymity is sealed by the process of commodification. As noted earlier in this chapter, the idea of the 'commodity fetish' was developed in order to understand the processes by which the social characteristics of commodities are concealed from our view. This process is material as well as conceptual, for the mark of the mass-produced commodity is its standardization and interchangeability. While consumer goods will still often rely on the dexterity of human minds, eyes and hands to construct and produce them, the mark of human contact is intentionally erased from view. Fingerprints are wiped away and imperfections are trimmed off by real people impersonating impersonal machines. Objects are sealed into transparent plastic bags that work like amniotic membranes so that their contents appear to be born, fully formed, in the act of their unwrapping.

It is an awareness of these anonymizing processes that produces in consumers a concern that they might be doing some harm to someone, somewhere, along the line. Practices of fair trade provide ways of thinking about the transnational connectedness of consuming practices, ways of making apparent the connections that already exist between ourselves and people in different spaces and places, and of making connections – sometimes involving new forms of exchange, commitment and obligation – that work against the anonymous logics of commodification. As Michael Goodman suggests, the moral economy of fair trade goods 'stitches consumers to the very places and livelihood struggles of production via embedded ethical, political, and discursive networks' by providing 'space for the re-appearance of producers and the material, social and economic conditions under which those commodities are produced' (Goodman, 2004: 893, 900).

In his reading of the Divine chocolate brand, Matthias Zick Varul notes how fair trade's practice of making visible the product's producers and conditions of production simultaneously involves their 'romantic commodification' (Varul, 2008: 659). By fulfilling the romantic desires of consumers invested in a rich imagery of 'agricultural and artisan producers in Latin America, Sub-Saharan Africa and South Asia', the discourse of the cosmopolitan fair trade consumer thus 'feeds on the identifiable otherness of the producer' (ibid.: 661, 668), meaning that fair trade's attempts to dispel commodity fetishism wind up creating a fetish out of products as the bearers of cultural difference. The commodity fetish is hereby not destroyed but, in Goodman's reading, subject to a 're-working [. . .] to the advantage of those involved in fair trade' (Goodman, 2004: 902). The positions taken by Goodman and Varul are useful in their recognition that the endurance of the fetish, as products continue to focus meanings, does not in itself invalidate or undermine the politics of fair trade. Clearly, practices of defetishization – perhaps better conceived as involving 'a fetish for defetishization' (Binkley and Littler, 2008: 552) – are still subject to processes of representation and mediation, and these practices do not somehow escape regimes of racial representation, even if they are intended to challenge global inequalities that are in part organized along racial lines. Although, in Varul's analysis, fair trade is in itself not capable of reconfiguring a continuing global imbalance between First and Third worlds, it nevertheless 'bears evidence against the moral power of capitalism', and in doing so keeps alive the visibility of that global imbalance to contemporary consumers (Varul, 2008: 674).

Similar points can be made about the ways in which practices of charity make visible racialized inequalities, and particularly how acts of giving involve the orchestration of emotional attachments and symbolic exchange between consuming subjects and the objects of their sympathy. Does, for example, the figure of the 'development celebrity' facilitate an important emotional work of bearing witness by proxy, or are such forms of intimacy wrapped up in the narcissism of self-recognition (Goodman and Barnes, 2011; Chouliaraki, 2010)? Is a meaningful kind of transnational connection developed by Western Muslims who donate to organizations like Islamic Relief and Red Crescent, or is the idea of diasporic solidarity more a function of a Western desire for such connections (see Werbner, 2002)? The terms by which distant others are identified and known are certainly often double-edged. Take, for example, the international marketing campaign ran by the French multinational Danone for its Volvic water brand. Promising '1L for 10L', the Volvic campaign stated that for every litre sold a further ten litres of drinking water would be provided via investment in wells in a number of African countries. While such a campaign might be subject to criticism or praise according to empirical criteria (What did it deliver? Who did it help?), its symbolic aspects are perhaps harder to unpick: does the act of purchase placate the guilt of wealthy consumers who might more usefully have drunk tap water and exercised their moral discomfort through alternative charitable or political routes? Does '1L for 10L' express to the consumer something significant about the inequalities of the global economic system, or alternatively does it suggest that life is, literally, cheaper elsewhere? Does this scale say something about the relative value or significance of the human lives that it represents: by setting up an idea of tiny gestures with magnified effects does it suggest that, while starting off with less, the recipients of such aid have intrinsically lesser needs? Does it, in other words, serve to justify the very inequality it supposedly sets out to remedy?

These kinds of ambiguities and contradictions are widely recognized in the debates around charity and fair trade, and I do not have space to do justice to their complexity here. My interest in flagging them up is really just to make the point that attempts on the part of consumers to engage with global inequalities (that are themselves frequently racialized) do not, as a rule, facilitate in any straightforward sense the removal of those inequalities (which are often vast, with multiple causal factors), but they do have an important bearing on making those inequalities legible – understandable – to consuming subjects. What such knowledge *does* is a very difficult question to answer, and an analysis of any particular case might record some ambivalent or conflicted outcomes. For the purposes of the present argument, the key point is that this knowledge is just as constructed or mediated as any other. Consumers do not arrive at some underlying 'truth' when they engage with racialized inequalities through acts of consumption. Rather, they facilitate engagements with a different set of stories or representations of racialized difference (some of these stories are the subject of Chapter 8). While, in other words, we may be invested in removing some of the barriers of racial distinction, the activities we undertake in order to do so can work to consolidate or reproduce those barriers in new and different ways. This is not to suggest that such activities are necessarily without value, but simply that the fact of our desire for a particular outcome does not in itself bring that outcome about. There is no way of short-circuiting the complexities and ambiguities of consumer culture in order to arrive at some elemental conception of racial justice, and the pursuit of redistributive agendas must occur through, rather than against or over the top of, circuits of representation and mediation.

Consuming race beyond 'us' and 'them'

A fourth important perspective I want to advance relates to the ubiquity of capitalist culture. As this chapter has already argued, we live in a moment of history where the economic system called capitalism organizes and influences humankind more extensively and intensively than ever before. Given this fact, it no longer makes sense to say we live in capitalist societies, as if these societies were autonomous and independent from one another, for our social worlds cross over and extend beyond individual nation-states. Our social formations are, in other words, inherently transnational. While capitalist norms, values and practices differ from place to place, capitalism provides the vast majority of people in the world today with a shared experience not only of trade, money and markets, but also of a common capitalist culture. Consumer culture is accordingly a way of describing all those practices by which social groups and individuals relate to themselves and one another in the context of a globally dominant consumer capitalism. Even critical orientations to globalized cultural forms are themselves shaped by those forms, for the 'observer and observed are inside the same loop' (Shire, 2008: 14–15). While capitalism has developed at different rates and intensities, it is most useful to think of consumer culture not as a specifically European or Western phenomenon, but as involving 'contact zones, the exchange of goods and knowledge, and processes of incorporation, emulation and assimilation in a transnational space' (Lury, 2011: 83). Indeed, such a reading is sensitive to the continuities between contemporary consumer culture and a colonial modernity where the political and cultural practices of race were part of an 'international regime of racial rule' (Hesse, 2011: 160).

In this book I am particularly interested in thinking about consumer culture from a transnational perspective not because I think it's possible to transcend or overcome the particular social, geographical and institutional conditions of its composition. I am writing this book in south east London: I understand and speak mainly English, and I watch TV and browse the web in this language too. The examples I draw on over the following pages will inevitably be patterned by all these factors, and many others too. Thinking about consumer culture transnationally is not to do with denying our own personal, partial, limited experiences of the world, but rather of recognizing that 'the local is always already organised by global forces, institutions and structures that play an essential role in the dynamics of specific situations and circumstances' (Szeman, 2006: 204). Moreover, it is to do with making a commitment to understanding processes and practices of consumption in such a way that does not reproduce some of the long-standing but often profoundly inaccurate conceptual distinctions that derive from thinking about consumer culture as a particularly Western phenomenon. Attempts to think critically about European and American culture have frequently been invested in the idea that there are spaces and places in the world untouched by the problems and issues that affect the West. An unfortunate side effect of this way of thinking is that it tends to reinforce the idea that there are somehow longstanding, innate, developmental or 'essential' differences between 'the West and the rest' (Hall, 1992). Without diminishing some of the differentials of power, privilege and prestige that are frequently in operation, this book sets out to contest these kinds of distinctions. It seeks to problematize and complicate the idea that there are certain groups of people in the world who are 'producers' and others who are 'consumers' in the same way that it seeks to problematize and complicate the idea that there are certain groups of people in the world who are *either* 'racialized' (usually understood as the victims of racism) *or* 'racializing' (usually understood as the perpetrators of racism). The starting point of a transnational take on consumption is that there is no 'us' and 'them' in consumer culture. However unequal, we are all participants in a globalized consumer capitalism. We are all consumers and we are all producers just as we are all positioned and produced in discourses of race. Our desire for origins, authenticity and roots, alongside the practices that seek to locate and uncover them, are all shaped by contemporary consumer culture (see Halter, 2000; see also Miller, 2010: 32).[6]

The kind of perspective I am recommending here does not set out in any way to diminish the absolute horrors of slavery, the inhuman abuses of imperialism and colonialism, and the racisms that were and remain their potent legacy. As I have already suggested, these events and practices provide an unavoidable context for all contemporary understandings of race. It is true, too, that the denial or the diminishment of the significance of these events and practices remains a key feature of contemporary race politics, and that it can therefore be very damaging to embrace ideas about the transcendence or overcoming of racism in the present that are predicated on the avoidance of this legacy. In the British context, this is a tendency that Paul Gilroy characterizes as a 'postimperial melancholia', involving the diminishment, denial and forgetting of that history (Gilroy, 2004: 98), fostering an inability to understand, or come to terms with, 'the political-cultural effects of the end of empire' (Schwarz, 2011: 4). It is in acknow-ledgement of these distorting conceptual conditions of the postimperial present that I am making the case for a need to think beyond the dogmatic certainties of a simplifying postcolonial critique. The process of 'forgetting', to use that metaphor, can be just as much implicated in selective forms of remembering as it is in the straightforward refusal to remember. As Gilroy and others have convincingly argued, one reason why it is difficult to properly face up to the history of empire is because of feelings of 'paralyzing guilt' towards it (Gilroy, 2004: 108). This guilt will frequently motivate and find a home in postcolonial critique itself. An investment in a judgment as to the absolute evils of imperialism produces a moral position that allows a kind of disconnection from that history. The recognition that imperialism was a 'bad thing' can accordingly absolve us of the need to think about it too closely. The same is true of racism: to self-identify in anti-racist terms is ostensibly a way of confronting racism, but it can just as easily be a way of avoiding responsibility for it (for more on this, see Pitcher, 2009: 11–19).

It is my suggestion here that it is on some level the acceptance (even the 'success') of the critique of empire, colonialism and racism that can stand in the way of a better understanding. The designation of absolute wrong produces a moral clarity that is often harnessed to 'explain' all questions of race. It is under these circumstances that the guilt-driven enthusiasm to embrace the 'correct' explanation – to indict imperialism and racism – can block our apperception of the efflorescent complexity of race. The very thing that motivates a moral and critical impulse is what prevents a more nuanced engagement with it. To understand the postcolonial present we need to move beyond analytical categories that were developed in the first moment of decolonization. It's not that racism has vanished or that there aren't practices that we might usefully identify as colonial or imperialist, but rather that our critical engagement with these practices needs to be informed by and developed out of the social, cultural and political conditions of the present.

Take, for example, the issue of popular culture mediating symbolic relations between global North and South: once upon a time, it might have made some sense to frame this discussion in terms of a Western cultural imperialism: in terms of the imposition of culture from core to periphery, on the governmental power of Western models, on the massive inequalities of technological control and thus the chronic one-sidedness of representational practice. But to cleave to this framework now is to give a falsely static reading of non-Western cultures, as if they have somehow remained trapped in an earlier century. The people who inhabit contemporary South Asia, or Africa, or Latin America, are no longer just the nameless, passive victims of Western cultural imperialism (as of course they never really were), but also at least in part visible co-participants in an interactive, technologized, self-reflexive, global media culture. US hip hop and Indonesian Indo pop are part of the same transnational space of media production and consumption. If we want to think about social, economic and cultural inequalities, we need to understand how they work in precisely this context. This might mean (shock horror!) that it might be harder than it used to be to divide the world up between evil perpetrators and exemplary victims.

Racial metonomy

The fifth and final perspective I want to flag up in this chapter is the idea of racial metonomy. As I suggested in my introduction, the widespread obsession with race is frequently accompanied by a conspiracy not to talk about it. Taboos and embarrassments don't mean race goes away, but they do mean that when we're actually talking about race, we're often ostensibly talking about something else. Metonomy is simply the name we give for the act of substituting one word, idea, object or image for another. To use a clear and obvious example of this: in 2012 plans by the state-owned Horniman museum in Forest Hill, south east London, to extend its alcohol licence for public events were met with protests by local residents who, according to the front page headline of the local freesheet the *News Shopper*, remembered the '"pandemonium" when 20,000 jerk chicken fans descended on the premises in 2009' (Chandler, 2012). Nowhere in the newspaper report complaining of street brawls, gridlocked roads and 'drunks roaming the streets' is the subject of race mentioned, yet in its description of '[h]ungry masses [. . .] craving a taste for spicy Caribbean food [. . .] tempted by Reggae Reggae Sauce founder Levi Roots [. . .] and [black British TV presenter] Floella Benjamin' (ibid.), a strong association is nevertheless established between the Caribbean cultural origins of jerk chicken and the reportedly inappropriate behaviour of some of those who attended the 2009 festival. It is accordingly not unreasonable to suggest that a racial subtext underlies the protests, or the reporting of them, as the Horniman's suburban-residential setting is deemed an inappropriate location for high numbers of 'jerk chicken fans'. Whether these fans are themselves of Caribbean heritage is perhaps beside the point: what seems to be the problem is that they are the enthusiastic consumers of Caribbean culture. Though the Horniman's nineteenth-century ethnographic collections are curated and framed in terms of London's multicultural demographics (its website boasts of 'the first permanent exhibition in Britain dedicated to African art and culture'), local residents' reports of 'chaos' and 'pandemonium' suggest a desire to limit the celebration of Caribbean culinary culture.

'Jerk chicken', in this example, becomes a metonym for Caribbean culture, which might in turn be said to stand in for people of Caribbean heritage. In other words, the reluctance to name race results in its metonymic substitution. Another similar example: my old hairdresser, whose professional identity is very much shaped by a taste for lo-fi indie music, once confessed to me that he can't cut hair to R&B, and that if R&B is ever playing in the shop I should leave because he'll likely stab me with his scissors. In this case, my hairdresser's dislikes are a way of expressing an aesthetic that draws on a familiar caricature of R&B as commercial and 'commodified' which in turn depends on a symbolic rejection of blackness (see Bannister, 2006: 86). This racialized positioning clearly utilizes metonymy to provide an aesthetic content (the imputed characteristics of different musical styles) through which my hairdresser's difference can be expressed: in this example, both R&B and indie music are metonymic carriers of racial meaning. This book is full of racial metonyms: in Chapter 3, ideas about place and landscape become substitutes and ciphers for race. In Chapter 6, taboos around race and childhood culture mean that racial difference figures as species difference in children's toys and media, while in Chapter 7, wild animals and plants are stand-ins for discussions about human identity and belonging. It is arguably the case that race has always lent itself to a metonymic reading, slipping between human identities, plant and animal species, objects, qualities and characteristics: the language of white and black have, for example, for centuries been capable of shifting from nouns to adjectives and adjectives to nouns (see Dalal, 2002: Chapter 8).

Racial metonymy helps us to understand that 'other things' do not just operate as 'stand-ins' for race, but that, more significantly, they can function to carry and produce racial meanings independently of the groups and individuals we so often presume that they name. This takes us back, then, to the key point I sketched out in the introduction: race is not a property or identity that people 'have'. Race is a device we use to organize a wide range of meanings relating to notions of belonging, to behaviour, to particular attributes, qualities and characteristics, to ways of relating to and interrelating with one another, to our felt needs, wants, curiosities and desires. While these meanings will typically be indexed back to particular groups or individuals, it is a mistake to position those groups or individuals as their origin. They are not. Race's discursive fluidity means that it informs and shapes the totality of our cultures, and we must accordingly look to our cultures as a whole to find the 'answers' to race, learning how to let go of the fetish of racial embodiment. Race is something we all 'do' almost all the time. Its problems and satisfactions are problems and satisfactions for us all. The following chapters in this book attempt to read and interpret some of the ways in which race 'works' in our contemporary cultures. They do not present definitive arguments; they each just try to develop some ideas about how we might think about the way we're all wrapped up in this strange thing called race.

Chapter 3

Ethnic appropriateness
White nostalgia and Nordic noir

Against cosmopolitan consumption

It is a commonplace of our times that life in the twenty-first century brings with it a greater degree of social and cultural interconnectedness than ever before. From the operation of the global economic system, to the ways in which knowledge and understanding are shaped by new media technologies, to the increasing facility with which those who can afford it may travel about the planet, even the most provincial of locations is caught up in a global network of culture. Besides a working internet connection, there's not, for example, anything to stop a Yoroba Muslim getting into Swedish-composed Korean pop music, any more than there's anything to stop us doing the Google search that instantaneously delivers to us their blog about it. The subject position of the cosmopolitan consumer is available to more and more people, and it is hard to envisage the possibility that this trend towards increasing diversity will slow any time soon: even the most dramatic descriptions of cultural eclecticism from a few decades ago now come across as quaintly parochial (see Lyotard, 1984: 76). While it is increasingly normal to embrace a culturally plural global culture, there is, however, evidence that some people are moving in what seems like the opposite direction. In the context of globalization, it is possible to identify a stepping back or retreat into ideas about culture that refuse or react against these kinds of interconnections. This chapter sets out to think about one example of this apparent retreat, namely a trend in contemporary British society among middle-class white people towards the consumption of an explicitly 'white' culture.

The first way of understanding this apparent retreat into whiteness is as a criticism of the 'excesses' of cosmopolitan consumption. In an early 1990s study of the collection of 'primitive' African art among affluent whites in New York, David Halle suggests that cosmopolitan consuming practices tended to correlate with a Democratic politics, serving in part as a symbolic protest against racial segregation (Halle, 1993: 406). 'Primitive' art, given aesthetic currency by early twentieth-century European avant gardes, accordingly operated as a way for affluent whites to signify their disposition towards a 'progressive' race politics. We can now see a certain embarrassment towards and retrenchment of such practices. This is reflected, for example, in contemporary attitudes towards the collection and display of historical or heritage objects, where there is a greater sensitivity towards the contexts of appropriation and a reckoning of the symbolic violence involved in presuming the legibility of cultural difference (Naidoo, 2005: 36–7).

High art and heritage are not the only areas in which we can find evidence of a turn away from cosmopolitan consumption. It can also be discerned in more everyday consumer practices, and this chapter will focus on the way this turn is negotiated and resolved in the consumption of housewares, furniture, fiction and food. Of central importance here is not only the idea now held by some consumers that the practice of consumption involves the exercise of power and control over that which is being consumed, but moreover that there are limits to the capacity of consuming practice as a way of understanding, relating to and engaging with cultural difference. There are, in other words, aspects of culture that cannot be simply bought and sold. There are limits to what money can buy, and it is an error to assume that culture can be acquired like a can of beans. Such critical positions (which of course are based on quite a narrow view of consumption as simply a commercial activity) will often highlight the vulgarity of cosmopolitan consumption and the lack of care given over to the ostensibly profounder activities of dialogue, interaction and exchange. This critique of consumption as a way of knowing or understanding is sometimes accompanied in more academic debates by a reckoning of whiteness as central to the process of consuming difference. Though unmarked as such, the cosmopolitan or multicultural consumer is, it is said, an implicitly white one. It is accordingly whiteness that organizes and gives value to consuming practices. The white subject is a 'subject without properties' (see Dyer, 1997: 37–8), a dominant position that takes its own perspective to be a universal one, and from which others are made to be representative of their own particularity. The partiality or ethnocentricity of whiteness therefore goes unexamined, while those who are excluded from its privileged position are subject to its imperial scrutiny: what, after all, is 'difference' different from if not a white norm?

A second way of understanding the retreat from practices of consuming difference among white people (which in some respects derives from the first) relates to the reducing value of such practices. Because processes of increased interconnection and exchange make it far easier than it once was to be a cosmopolitan consumer, there is ostensibly less to be gained from an engagement with difference. While to a twentieth-century countercultural traveller an 'authentic' Moroccan kaftan or an Indian sitar might have served as a badge of adventurousness and self-transformation, their easy availability to the package tourist or casual ebayer somewhat diminishes that value.

If we think about consumption as a way of establishing and maintaining class identity – particularly among those whose hold on such a position is more symbolic than economic (Featherstone, 2007) – then the consumption of cultural difference by middle-class white people is no longer necessarily a particularly effective way of accruing cultural capital. Indeed, I want to suggest in this chapter that while it may once have been the case that an openness towards difference served as a mechanism of distinction, it is now just as likely the critique of that openness – and in some respects its self-conscious rejection – that produces symbolic rewards for the consumer. The refusal to engage in certain practices of cosmopolitan consumption, to draw a limit to one's consuming practices, has come to be valued in itself. Ecological imperatives play their part here: holidays that do not involve air travel and diets that do not incur food miles are part of a wider valorization of that which is local or native (in Chapter 7 I explore some of the horticultural implications of this).

A third factor that has arguably influenced the trend away from cosmopolitan consumption is an effect of the process of commodification itself. As discussed in Chapter 2, Comaroff and Comaroff have suggested that in order to extract value from its sale, culture effectively becomes the legal possession of the individuals and groups who can claim it as their own (Comaroff and Comaroff, 2009). I want to suggest that this commodification of culture has accordingly led the development of more distantiated relationships with cultural difference. The value of cultural difference as a form of self-transformation is reduced because one's engagement with difference confirms and consolidates the specificity or uniqueness of those to whom it belongs. The cosmopolitan consumer can no longer take that difference and make it their own because it would constitute a disrespectful appropriation – effectively a theft of culture. The terms of engagement become shaped by these precepts, so that respect for the integrity of the other's difference becomes of primary concern in the contemporary cultural economy. In inverse proportion to this, there opens up a space whereby value can be derived from engaging with one's own ethnic specificity. As Marilyn Halter suggests, the 'roots phenomenon' – ethnic celebrations, interest in genealogy, travel to ancestral homelands, ethnic artefacts, cuisine, music, literature and language – is itself facilitated by the circulation of cultural commodities in the contemporary marketplace (Halter, 2000: 5). The logic of cultural commodification thus not only encourages, say, people of Latin American heritage to engage with 'indigenous' versions of Brazilian or Argentine culture, but also for white people to engage with and develop their own forms of cultural specificity. We are all encouraged to exhibit culturally appropriate ways of behaving, practices that by definition do not cause offence to or misrepresent others because they can only work to make us more like ourselves. It is accordingly the critique of cosmopolitan consumption – of the imperial, excessive or insensitive engagement of white people with cultural difference – that leads to the identification and development of the white subject positions I want to explore here. No longer suffused with false universalism, white culture takes its place alongside and in supposed equality with other forms of culture. This chapter accordingly concerns itself with some of the ways in which people who are racialized as white in contemporary Britain are invited to engage in what we might call 'ethnically appropriate' forms of consumption.

It is worth noting that anti-cosmopolitanism is best seen as a tendency within a transnational consumer culture that, as I have already suggested, also facilitates forms of cosmopolitan interconnectedness, contact and exchange. I am making the case here for one particular way in which consumers navigate contemporary culture, and the claims I want to make in this chapter should be considered in the knowledge that there are always parallel cosmopolitan tendencies at work (see, for example, Olesen, 2010). As is commonly recognized, the contemporary recognition and celebration of the local is itself a function of a globalization, and both cosmopolitanism and its critique demand to be understood as elements of the same social and political conjuncture (for some reflections on these dynamics, see Bradotti *et al.*, 2013).

Chromatic nostalgia

Feelgood narratives of multicultural pluralism have for a long time drawn on a chromatic imagery, conceiving of the ways in which racial diversity brings 'colour' to a bland or monochrome cultural landscape. I want to begin by considering the way in which an apparent retreat into whiteness is likewise figured through the metonymic link between race and colour. Consider the following comic reflection by the anthropologist Daniel Miller, who laments:

> a gradual leaching out of colour and print from the world of clothing in London. Just as in Rushdie's story [*Haroun and the Sea of Stories*], it is as though somewhere there is a vast hole through which colour and print is leaking out, leaving an increasingly grey, brown and black world of clothing that makes for a drab, colourless environment [. . .] I feel personally affronted by this assault, since I too suffer from this same affliction. When I started lecturing I was still wearing a bright orange jersey and a necklace of shells retained from my fieldwork in the Solomon Islands. But I was already looking like an anachronistic *hippie*. Of course, being a hippie was itself merely conventional to that time, and I have shifted with all the subsequent movements towards the colourless. [. . .] About the most exciting possibility left for me to discover is a new shade of grey.
>
> (Miller, 2010: 35)

Miller's description of the withdrawal of colour is clearly inflected by the critique of cosmopolitan consumption I have just outlined. Personified in the figure of Miller himself in his 'orange jersey and necklace of shells', a culturally eclectic style moves from fashionability to unfashionability, and Miller is left to reconcile his cosmopolitan desire – rendered as a taste for 'colour' – with the norms of a culture in which this colour no longer has a place. Miller is so regretful of this cultural shift because he takes it personally – he is the 'hippie' wearing the ostentatiously 'different' shell necklace (perhaps referencing the historic practice of using shells as currency in the Solomon Islands, and thus also signifying to his anthropology students the existence not just of cultural difference but of alternative systems of economy and trade). This is not a sartorial transformation that Miller desires or approves of (hence its dramatic presentation as an 'affliction'), yet it represents a demand that culture has made and which Miller is obliged to fulfil. The important point here is that the aesthetic shift that Miller describes is not a critique of cultural difference per se, but relates to the inappropriateness of Miller's sartorial choices as a white academic. The place and period Miller describes – London over the last thirty to forty years – is otherwise characterized by an undeniable move in the direction of greater social and cultural pluralism. Despite continuing racisms, London has become more diverse and in the main more comfortable with that diversity. What's less acceptable, and which Miller's reflection sums up so nicely, is someone like him – a middle-aged, middle-class white person with high levels of cultural capital – dressing in an ethnically 'inappropriate' fashion.

While it would be incorrect to extend this observation to white people in general (an African-American aesthetic, communicated through multi-national sports brands, is after all near-ubiquitous among urban and rural teenagers alike the world over), there is among certain demographics a clear trend towards ethnically appropriate forms of dress and behaviour. This is, I want to argue, to do with more than simply the conservatism of middle age. Middle-class investments in whiteness are being produced not through intentional racism, but through the criticism of inappropriate or excessive cosmopolitanism. This is done not out of a rejection of multicultural social formations, but rather an attentiveness to their abiding cultural logic of ethnic appropriateness. To understand this trend, we need to start thinking about the resources of 'ethnic' whiteness beyond the cultural politics of the far right, or as projected onto abject individuals and communities (as 'chavs' or 'white trash') as a way of externalizing the morally troubling phenomena of racial inequality (Wray and Newitz, 1997).[7] In Wray and Newitz's argument, the class politics of 'white trash' are the outcome of an ostensible anti-racist consensus where 'bad' whites become the scapegoat for racism. Similarly, I want to suggest that the precondition for the development of middle-class forms of ethnic whiteness is the ideological dominance of pluralism and cultural diversity. It is in part out of a perceived need not to misrepresent, caricature or in some other way deal inappropriately with difference that we can best understand this kind of 'return' or 'retreat' into whiteness.

One interesting cultural site to explore the metonymic link between race and colour is provided by the UK homeware and fashion retailer The White Company, a largely internet-based mail order business which at the time of writing employs around 1,000 people, with just under 40 UK stores or concessions, and a handful of franchises in the Middle East. It should be noted from the start that as with most of the examples in this book I'm not interested in making any glib and facile charge of racism here. As is the case with any contemporary business of its size and standing, the company presents itself in explicitly multicultural terms, and there is absolutely no reason to doubt the company's commitment to its own declaration on the 'white life' section of its careers webpages that 'diversity and inclusion are key to our success' (The White Company Careers, 2013a). Neither – to avoid other potential misreadings – am I suggesting that The White Company's white customers are somehow motivated by racism, or that the business is somehow closed off to non-white consumers. All this notwithstanding, it is nevertheless the case that The White Company has an interesting aesthetic that articulates discourses of chromatic whiteness to an aspirational lifestyle that can be read in relation to the 'retreat' into an ethnic whiteness I want to explore in this chapter.

The White Company's dominant representational mode is, first and foremost, an undeniably nostalgic one. Though its print catalogues feature products set in uncluttered neutral spaces that could be taken for contemporary boutique hotel rooms, there is a notable absence of technology – no TVs, laptops or telephones. Baths feature more prominently than showers, logs burn in open fires and candles provide ambient lighting. A 'classic white shirt' is described as being reminiscent 'of Audrey Hepburn's in "Roman Holiday"' or as giving a 'vintage Victorian feel' (The White Company, 2012a: 114). Reproduction bins, buckets and jugs are 'inspired by traditional enamelware pieces we found in vintage shops' (The White Company, 2013a: 94). Children's toys are made of wood, and take the form of 'traditional' items like soldier skittles, alphabet blocks, rocking horses and 1950s racing cars (The White Company, 2012c: 138–41), while little girls are dressed in 'vintage fairy jersey nightwear' in 'frilled empire styles', as they pose holding books with black-and-white illustrations (The White Company, 2012b: 157). This historically indeterminate (but mid-twentieth-century oriented) 'old fashioned' styling enables The White Company to develop ideas about the circumstances of production, providing it with an 'artisan' distinctiveness that sets it apart in a 'mass-produced' present. As one 'PR friendly' enthusiast of the company has blogged, The White Company's

Florence chest of drawers suits our style perfectly [. . .] we're all for statement pieces that *say things about us* rather than mass-produced things [. . .] I sometimes think I should have been born in the Victorian era where things were prettier and pieces were celebrated for being unique.

(G. Mills, 2013)

This is also, it hardly needs saying, a model of retro femininity: the two 'Mens' pages in the Winter 2012 catalogue are in case of confusion labelled 'perfect gifts for the men in your lives' (The White Company, 2012b: 39). The absence of 'modern' technologies is paralleled by the virtual absence of references to the world of work. Typically, The White Company catalogues feature young white woman lounging around daylight-lit high-end interiors wearing nightwear and bedsocks. The world of The White Company is a world of leisure: a pair of tortoiseshell reading glasses sit atop the open pages of some French literary fiction; writing paper and a black and gold pen nestle on crisp white Egyptian cotton bed linen (The White Company, 2013a: 18, 26). Though The White Company appears to sell itself as the province of women from a super-rich leisure class, its demographic is necessarily a more popular one than this. Its founder's back-story, prominently featured on the company website, expresses a kind of class insecurity in her autobiographical search for white homewares:

It all began in 1993 . . . At the time, the few white items I could find and afford were somehow all such cheap designs and of average or poor quality. All the gorgeous high-quality ones I loved were only to be found in the designer departments and of course, with the designer label came the snooty sales assistant and the high price tag!

So I set on a mission to create a company that specialised in supplying stylish, white designer quality items for the home that were affordable.

(The White Company, 2013b)

This text clearly positions The White Company brand as facilitating its customers' own aspirational desires, and provides us with a strategy to read other elements of its aesthetic. When the Winter 2012 catalogue describes Christmas as involving the consumer in 'juggling lots of hats – present buyer, host, party planner and chef' (The White Company, 2012b: 17), it seems clear that the presentation of leisure activities as work provides a sublimated version of a more mundane roster of 'real' work, childcare and housework. When the Spring 2013 'Utility Room' feature suggests that 'We all dream of having a special room in the house dedicated to domestic order' (The White Company, 2013a: 94) it is obvious that this is a 'dream' in the fantasy sense, and that there isn't really going to be much spring cleaning going on with a £10 bar of soap. To read The White Company retro-feminine aesthetic in terms of aspiration and fantasy is, as I am suggesting, to read it as opening up a consuming space where the obligations of 'real' life are temporarily screened off from view. Fantasies about endless leisure displace the obligations of a more mundane existence, where the operative gender regime promises harder work and fewer rewards.

But what, precisely, is the place of whiteness in this aspirational fantasy? One model is provided by Angela McRobbie's reading of the retro burlesque of the American performer Dita Von Teese, who suggests that such performances invoke a norm of nostalgic whiteness (McRobbie, 2009: 43). As I have just suggested, the concerted historical references in The White Company aesthetic encourage an interpretation where the past provides a refuge from the demands of the present, and it would not be implausible to suggest that The White Company articulates some kind of nostalgia for a now-lapsed mythological 'white' culture thought to have existed before Britain felt the effects of postcolonial immigration. This might be considered to be part of a broader nostalgia for 'simpler' times, where racial diversity features alongside technology and women's entry into the workplace as aspects of the contemporary world that The White Company aesthetic shields from view. Such a reading is plausible so long as this nostalgia is not read in too literal a sense as necessarily motivated by an explicit and intentional racism. As in Joanne Hollows's reading of the appeal of ideas of domestic femininity to contemporary women, The White Company facilitates an embrace of a nostalgic whiteness as a site of fantasy, and a means of exploring identities 'that may not be realizable, or even desirable, outside of fantasy' (Hollows, 2006: 113). It is not, therefore, that the consumer of The White Company aesthetic literally wants to return to a 'whiter' past, any more than she really wants (or indeed thinks it possible) to give up working or to reject the advances of feminism for endless afternoons in bedsocks. In Hollows's analysis fantasies of domesticity play a role in symbolically resolving some of the competing demands (centrally, between career and motherhood) that beset contemporary femininity. The fantasy of domestic life gives working women the opportunity to make up in the realm of the imagination for a way of living that the time constraints of employment do not permit. In an analogous way, I want to suggest that the fantasy of nostalgic whiteness provides the customers of The White Company with a reasonably coherent means of understanding and orienting themselves in the racial context of the present.[8]

As I have already suggested, in multicultural social formations there has developed a demand for white people to exhibit 'ethnically appropriate' ways of living. While the cosmopolitan appropriation of cultural difference once provided a model for white consuming practices, the demand to exhibit sensitivity and respect towards difference has led to a requirement for white people to develop a sense of their own 'ethnic' distinctiveness. There is a thorny problem here for the subject position of whiteness, that 'subject without properties': what is the cultural content of a racial identity that has until now largely existed as the unnamed and unmarked centre of racial normativity, and which is now being required to define *itself* when it has hitherto only defined itself in contradistinction to racial others, a manoeuvre that is no longer available to it? In the case of The White Company, it is precisely an idea of the past that helps to give shape to what we might call the cultural content of whiteness. Though there is a large overlap between this past and the period of the British Empire (so that race as a theme is by no means absent), it nevertheless describes in the popular imagination the idea of a territorial Britain undisturbed by the presence of racial difference. Albeit erroneous, such evocations draw on the still-resonant mythology that Britain was once, at some point in the past, a 'white' nation. It is therefore the case that a symbolic return to and recovery of the cultural content of the past is a way of filling up the otherwise empty shell of the white subject. Because this is an idea of white culture 'before' the presence of racial difference, it does not present the otherwise troubling problem of being defined by an antagonistic relationship in proximity to that racial difference (as might the insistent whiteness of the far right). Rather, it is a loosely naturalistic conception of culture, an idea about the norms and conventions of a white culture that might have operated prior to postcolonial immigration (for more on the articulation of race and nature, see Chapter 7). The fact that The White Company's version of nostalgic whiteness is historical but not historically specific (it does not, for example, provide a 'period' look) makes it an indeterminate temporal space, allowing the past and present to commingle in an aesthetic that is 'classically modern', neither 'cutting edge' nor 'too traditional' (The White Company Careers, 2013b). Whiteness occupies a space to some extent outside of time, and like the perennial fashion discourse of 'timeless' and 'classic' looks promises never to go out of date. As such, The White Company allows the consumer to construct for them- selves a contemporary white identity that draws on an idea of what white people might have been up to 'before' the now problematized detour of cosmopolitanism. In our multicultural present, this fantasy of nostalgic whiteness is not, therefore, best understood as a protest against racial differ- ence and an assertion of white supremacy, but an attempt at solving the problem of white identity in a postcolonial context (though as I will go on to show there is a sense in which the embrace of whiteness *can* serve as a marker of positional advantage in economies of race). The imaginative return or retreat into an historical whiteness is an attempt to occupy a subject position that does not symbolically depend on a relationship with non- whites. It is, in other words, an idea of racial autonomy that presupposes the coexistence of racial others.

Into the white

The White Company is not the only context in which an answer is provided to the question of what might constitute 'ethnically appropriate' ways of living for white people. In this next section, I want to give further attention to the colouration of whiteness, and in doing so trace the contours of a more geographically-oriented fantasy of whiteness that can be found in a vogue for the culture of the Nordic countries that has developed in Britain over the last five years or so. Often figured in the British context as 'Scandinavian' (which technically describes just Sweden, Norway and Denmark), I employ here a more geographically expansive reference to Nordic culture, which includes Finland, Iceland and wider territorial possessions. This fashion for Nordic culture can be discerned across a wide range of cultural forms, from the food of the Danish restaurant Noma (named 'best restaurant in the world' in 2010, 2011 and 2012 by British magazine *Restaurant*), to the global fashionability of the Swedish Kånken backpack, dubbed 'the ultimate in utilitarian cool' (Hemma Magazine, 2011). British designers of kitchen accessories have drawn on a typographical signifier of 'Scandinavian cool' by adopting the 'gratuitous umlaut' (Booth, 2013). The front page of the *Guardian*'s travel section exclaims 'Scandimania! Head north for the coolest spots on the planet' (*Guardian*, 2011), while the weekly news magazine *The Economist* claims that 'the land of the bland' has been transformed into 'a cultural powerhouse' (*Economist*, 2013). Since October 2010, London's Earl's Court exhibition centre has hosted an annual two-day Scandinavia Show, showcasing 'Scandinavian design, travel, lifestyle, fashion, culture and food' (Scandinavian Show, 2012). The field of popular literature has seen an explosion of interest in Nordic crime fiction (dubbed 'Nordic noir' or 'Scandy lit'), on the back of the British publication in 2008 of Swedish writer Stieg Larsson's *The Girl With the Dragon Tattoo*, and its sequels. While Larsson's books became Hollywood movies, we have also seen a developing interest in Nordic crime television: *Wallander*, *The Killing*, *Borgen* and *The Bridge* have all developed avid, if niche, followings on UK terrestrial TV. Promotional material for the two-day Nordicana literature and film festival in June 2013 entreated cultural consumers to 'join us for all things Scandi cool and Nordic noir' (Nordicana, 2013). Finally, posters that appeared in my local park in 2012 advertising training sessions in 'Nordic walking', and the subsequent sight of dozens of enthusiastic perambulators, confirmed for me this fashion for all things Nordic. Though contemporary interest in Nordic culture is by no means solely a British phenomenon, I want to speculate in what follows on the ways in which Nordic culture resonates with white British audiences. In particular I want to explore the sense in which the consumption of Nordic culture is shaped by ideas about the relationship between geography and culture, fulfilling a desire for an 'ethnically appropriate' white culture by mapping the cultural coordinates of whiteness.

I want to begin this exploration of Nordic fashionability in the field of interior design, and in particular the taste for 'mid-century modern' furniture from the Nordic countries. Second-hand Danish furniture has a particular following, and named vintage designers command high prices in boutique shops like London's Two Columbia Road (twocolumbiaroad.co.uk), at 'pop-up' 'vintage and modern design shows' (modernshows.com) and at second-hand furniture warehouses (designsofmodernity.com). The first point I want to make here is that despite being positioned as a manifestation of modernist internationalism, a contemporary taste for Nordic design seems to be marked by the shift this chapter is describing away from cosmopolitan aesthetics. There is an interesting disparity between the presentation and contextualization of contemporary and historical versions of Nordic interior and furniture design. While the emphasis in contemporary retro aesthetics has a tendency to read Nordic design in terms of a unifying modernist aesthetic – functionality, flat tones, absence of decoration, simplification of form – a survey of historical sources paints a more culturally eclectic picture. *Decorative Art 50s*, a recent reprinting of a 1950s British-based survey of design trends, demonstrates how Modernist designs of the period often drew on and were styled with references to 'ethnic' art (primarily African and oriental) and non-Western locations.[9] Like the work of fellow designers from other geographical regions, Nordic design from the 1950s has a cosmopolitan flavour: an interior subtitled 'Corner of a Finnish living-room' features a drawing of an 'African' woman (Fiell and Fiell, 2008: 160); a wall unit in smoked oak and pine by Danish designer Knud Juul-Hansen supports a white sculpture of a hippopotamus (ibid.: 191); a hand-print fabric design, titled 'grotesque' and based on African masks, is by Swedish textile designer Maud Fredin-Fredholm (ibid.: 269). There does not appear to be any special relationship between Nordic design and these African references – they seem to be part and parcel of the broader modernist aesthetic that Nordic design was a part of. We might suggest, then, that one feature of the recent retro revival of Nordic design has been an editing out of the cosmopolitan elements that have subsequently come to be thought of as tasteless and embarrassing.

A reformed, culturally streamlined Nordic design aesthetic is accordingly now anchored more firmly in the imaginative social geography of the North. To the retro consumer, it provides a discourse of consumption that is secure in its whiteness. Faced with the question of how to furnish their houses in a post-consmopolitan context, I want to suggest that white British people are drawn to a Nordic style in order to conform to the protocols and expectations of 'ethnically appropriate' behaviour. Though as I have already suggested the impetus for this particular symbolic journey is a function of the demands of our current, multicultural moment, it is built on associations

– between whiteness and northernness – that have a long association. As Richard Dyer notes, while the geographies of whiteness are plural, 'North European Whiteness' and the people that it indexes ('Anglos, Teutons and Nordics') are the most securely white (Dyer, 1997: 12). A chromatic whiteness connects and affirms the analogy between identity and landscape: northerly places are marked by a literal whiteness (of snow and ice) and cognate characteristics (the cold, cleanliness, hardness) that the Romantic imagination simultaneously attaches to the bodies that dwell within them.[10] A journey towards the North therefore becomes a journey of increasing purity, a distillation of the qualities of whiteness. If we follow Dyer's seductive suggestion that whiteness finds its apotheosis in death, then the Nordic countries stand as the last bastions of inhabitable whiteness before the horizonless disorientation of the total whiteout.

Positioned at the furthest point on this spectrum of whiteness, we can think of Nordic interiors as both a protection from and an expression of the geographical and climactic extremities of whiteness. Such a reading is often made and thereby reinforced in commentary on Nordic design that makes frequent reference to the influence of nature, geography and quality of light. In her reading of Scandinavian style as a landscape-influenced folk tradition, design writer Ingrid Sommar describes a 'light and pallid' palette 'favoured by the inhabitants of the frozen north [. . .] the opposite end of the spectrum to the rich, deep tones of the Mediterranean countries' (Sommar, 2003: 7). The experience of living in whiteness is said to refine perceptual sensibilities, such that like the apocryphal variety of Inuit words for snow, Scandinavians can, in Bradley Quinn's estimation, 'detect many more colours and subtle nuances in snow than do those living in more temperate climes' (Quinn, 2003: 99). Like a straight-faced version of Daniel Miller's ironic excitement about discovering 'a new shade of grey', Quinn enthuses that 'Scandinavians' perception of white encompasses a range of fine gradations' (ibid.). In Sommar's view, the unity of people and landscape has a genealogical dimension, and that:

> To understand the durable simplicity that has developed in the north – characterised by clean lines, practicality, craftmanship [sic] and democratic ideals – you have to go back many centuries to the peasant societies that originally dominated the region, and which made a powerful contribution in shaping the culture of the Nordic countries.
>
> (Sommar, 2003: 6)

What is interesting here is not so much the claim to Nordic ethnicity but the sheer eclecticism of the qualities that are organized and explained by that claim. In Sommar's analysis, simplicity, practicality and craftsmanship are conjoined with 'democratic ideals' as defining elements of Nordic culture. This easy conflation of design and democracy – echoed in Sommar's later claim that in 1930s Scandinavia, 'good design was an obvious democratic right' (ibid.: 7) is arguably facilitated by the Nordic countries' reputation, cultivated both at home and abroad, for their development of social democracy and the welfare state, a theme to which I will shortly return.

A parallel and interrelated conception of social and aesthetic inheritance constitutes a dominant discourse in Nordic design, at least in its international-facing publicity. The English language website of the company Muuto, for example, presents quotations from its designers on the meaning of 'new Nordic' design: to Jonas Wagell, 'Nordic design is rooted in social values about functionality and accessibility for all. Simplistic materials and moderate forms reflect the Nordic soul'. Louise Cambell similarly suggests that Nordic designers have 'inherited the thrill of rational thinking, the joy of detail, and the strive [sic] for good craftsmanship from our predecessors', while the studio 'Whatswhat' highlight 'the evolution of a common heritage' (Muuto, 2013). Making similar connections between history, geography and design practice, the design and interiors website ferm LIVING 'favours honest materials that craftsmen have used for millennia', and claims that its designs 'remain rooted in the Danish soil' (ferm LIVING, 2013).

The repeated connection between landscape and aesthetics produces a highly consistent portrait of a Nordic temperament. Psychological dispositions and ethical, social and spiritual values are shown to be the simultaneous product of a place and the ideas and practices it generates. This corporate model of Nordic ethnicity is, I want to suggest, precisely what has given Nordic style such a strong purchase in a contemporary British context. Discourses that circulate around Nordic design provide, as with The White Company, a strong conception of a 'fitting' ethnic whiteness, a kind of originary or ur-whiteness that is apparently untroubled by the proximity or experience of cultural difference as per contemporary Britain. This is again, of course, a fantasy, but it is an attractive one in the sense that it appears to provide a solution to the demand to uncover an acceptable way of being white in the context of multiculture. Nordic white culture is a form of whiteness that is perceived as simply the 'natural' expression of people behaving in 'appropriate' ways in the social and geographical contexts they find themselves in. It is a fantasy model of what white people are like when left to their own devices.

When boring becomes fashionable

Nordic whiteness does not only provide a symbolic place of origin to 'fill in' the cultural content of whiteness in multicultural Britain. It also describes a set of values and beliefs that position it socially and politically. Ostensible descriptions of design objects and furniture, because they are so strongly inflected by ideas about the human and environmental contexts of their conception and construction, become descriptions of the qualities of an ideal whiteness. An interiors article in the *Guardian* magazine from 2011, titled 'Handy Scandi' and subtitled 'It's official: we're in love with Scandinavian design', can, like the quotations from Nordic designers noted above, be read as a portrait of an ideal white subject position. Consider the following passage:

> The Nordic countries – Norway, Sweden, Denmark, Finland and Iceland – have an unpretentious approach to design, in contrast to that often elitist world. Furniture is clean-lined and useful, made from often plain, natural materials such as bare wood, sheepskin, leather and wool. Design, in the Scandinavian tradition, provides emotional comfort and enriches daily living. It is not about style over substance, or status symbols – in fact, distaste for showiness is palpable.
>
> (Thompson, 2011)

While this is ostensibly about Nordic design, there is of course a slippage between aesthetic and human qualities: 'unpretentious', 'useful', 'plain', 'natural' might all serve as descriptions of the Nordic model of cultural whiteness. There is a recuperation of qualities here, for there is a longstanding insecurity in the cultural imaginaries of whiteness that – faced with the exoticism of difference – conceives of itself as 'boring'.[11] We might say that the contemporary Nordic model facilitates a rebranding of whiteness, giving new life to a subject position by redefining negatives as positives. As Thomas Winther, director of the 2012 Scandinavia Show puts it, 'We have a reputation for being chilled out and sophisticated and yes, a bit boring – but boring has become fashionable' (Woods, 2012). This re-evaluation of 'boring' is certainly what appears to be going on towards the end of the quotation from the *Guardian*, where 'substance' is valorized over 'style', 'status' and 'showiness' in the production of cultural artefacts (accordingly providing a model of how they should be consumed). This configuration of whiteness as reserved and modest can, to follow the suggestion of Roopali Mukherjee, be understood as a form of 'inconspicuous consumption', allowing whites to maintain a degree of racial distinction from a black culture that has appropriated – in the aesthetics of 'bling' – some of the accoutrements of high-class luxury commodity consumption (Mukherjee, 2011: 186). Consider, in relation to this, fashion journalists' framing of a 'white' look as a key fashion trend for winter 2012–13: 'this is all about the antithesis of bling' (Jones and Seamons, 2012). Despite figuring a social-geographical retreat into whiteness, the Nordic model should accordingly not be seen as representing the isolation of its subject from the conditions of racial diversity, but rather as developing a positional advantage in a racial economy where less is more.

This association of Nordic whiteness with the characteristics of inconspicuousness and modesty also has strong ecological resonances.

In a 2010 article for the *Observer*, Norwegian-born journalist and presenter Mariella Frostrup writes:

> Now that flying in food from around the world is increasingly frowned upon, it seems the perfect moment for Britain to embrace our northerly connections, our food's shared roots, ingredients and influences. Recreating Tuscany is so 1990s; instead I'm all for herring and line-caught fish, cloudberries and blueberries, crayfish and coldwater prawns to brighten up my dinner table.
>
> (Frostrup, 2010: 37)

In contrast to the inappropriateness of the 1990s vogue for Italian cuisine, an explicit link is hereby made between Britain and the Nordic countries on the basis of their 'shared roots, ingredients and influences'. In so doing, British consumers can also fulfil an ecological imperative to consume sustainable and seasonal produce: 'We don't', accords Trina Hahnemann, food writer and author of *The Nordic Diet*, 'need to look to Italy or Thailand for food ideas' (Seal, 2010: 39). An ecological theme is present, too, in much of the design material that references a Nordic or modernist aesthetic: the website of the East London contemporary furniture, lighting and homewares company Haus claims that 'Our goal is to choose carefully the things we live with, and to keep them for a long time. We would rather have a few "good" things. This seems to make sense both economically and ecologically' (Haus, 2013), while the Danish/Dutch homewares company 95% declares its motto to be 'Buy Once, Buy Well!' (95percentshop, 2013). The recycling practices involved in the purchase of 'upcycled' or 'vintage' furniture likewise appear to accord with a model of environmental consumption, particularly when the objects of consumer desire are constructed out of materials like tropical hardwoods that might now be considered ecologically unsustainable (for a more detailed consideration of the relationship between ecology and economy in austerity culture, see Bramall, 2013).

It is my suggestion, then, that the Nordic model of whiteness is articulated to ideas about ecologically sustainable production, and to notions of consuming in a modest and appropriate manner. The white subject is a virtuous subject too. Again, I think it's possible to read this in terms of racial positioning, either in relation to perceptions of the more expressively ostentatious consuming practices of non-whites (as a critique of 'bling') or in a wider geopolitical sense where a sensitivity to environmental issues becomes a badge of Western identity against the uncontrolled polluting activities of a rampantly industrializing global South. It should hardly need saying that my suggestion here is not that ecological subject positions are somehow closed off to non-white people in Britain (and the same goes in respect of a taste for Danish furniture, cloudberries or crayfish). It is simply that the valorization of the Nordic countries in contemporary Britain lines up so many apparently indissoluble elements (geography, climate, history, nature) as involved in the longstanding production and development of a 'people' and their tastes, beliefs, values, practices and products that it is hard not to read the desire for Nordic culture in racially exclusive terms.

White noire

There is as I have suggested one further element lurking in the contemporary British fascination for Nordic culture, and that is a romanticized reading of the politics of Nordic social liberalism and social democracy as produced out of the same 'natural' combination of climate, geography and culture. While debates within the Nordic countries focus on the decline or passing of social democracy, it is nevertheless the case that 'Nordic exceptionalism' (Browning, 2007) continues to have currency on the international scene. Nordic countries figure prominently in books like *The Spirit Level* (Wilson and Pickett, 2010), where they provide a model of societies with lower rates of social inequality. Despite the fact that the literary, cinematic and televisual genre of 'Nordic noir' repeatedly and insistently presents a version of social democracy as in decline or as rotten to the core, the egalitarian possibilities of Nordic societies remain attractive in the British context. In the estimation of Jakob Stougaard-Nielsen, 'Scandinavian crime fiction is to a large extent shoring up the bygone values of national, welfare state and family cohesiveness under [. . .] a new global regime' (in Thomson, 2012). Stougaard-Nielsen reads the woolly Faroese jumper worn famously by Sofie Gråbøl as Sara Lund in *The Killing* as a symbol of the 1970s 'golden age' of the Danish welfare state, and to British audiences a nostalgic idea of social democracy arguably holds a particular allure in the context of economic recession and austerity politics. Nordic social democracy symbolizes a solution of sorts to the ongoing economic crisis. It is a solution that is essentially extra-economic, in the sense that Britain does not possess resources in raw materials to develop equivalent levels of wealth to its northerly neighbours. Instead, it is a solution based on notions of social organization, social liberalism and social equality that derive, as per the descriptions of Nordic design as the product of landscape and climate, from the qualities of Nordic culture – and by association, from the qualities of whiteness itself. This is paralleled by processes within Nordic countries that have encouraged the reinterpretation of political struggles as forms of cultural expression: as Ferruh Yilmaz argues of the Danish case, the Danish welfare system becomes a cultural construct, the product of 'native' values and secured through the maintenance of cultural homogeneity (Yilmaz, forthcoming). When Henrietta Thompson writes that our attraction to Scandinavian design increases 'the more uncertain the world looks' (Thompson, 2011) it is clearly the ideas, beliefs and values that design objects represent that provide a solution to or escape from uncertainty, rather than the objects themselves.

In the context of widespread pessimism in respect of social and political solutions to British decline or 'an upwardly mobile future for self, society and world', a Nordic model promises a 'return to roots, to fixed identifications that are immune, in principle, from social change' (Freidman, 1997: 71). Like the embrace of ancient northern European history by English black metal fans, consumers of Nordic design are also looking for somewhere to belong 'in the post-industrial age of hypermobility' (Lucas *et al.*, 2011: 290; see also Hage, 2003: 50).

If we turn to consider the explicit race politics of the Nordic countries, it could be said that on the face of it these present a rather more ambivalent picture for white identificatory practice: global outrage over cartoons of Mohammed published in the Danish newspaper *Jyllands-Posten* in 2005, and the mass murders in Norway in 2011, mean that the Nordic countries figure as sites of conflict and controversy in respect of their politics of race. While even the most casual observer of the political rise of the likes of the Danish People's Party, the True Finns, the Norwegian Progress Party and the Swedish Democrats is unlikely to position the Nordic countries as sites of aspiration, it is arguably the case that the abiding mythology of Nordic social liberalism retains a special place in British racial imaginaries. The example of the Danish Mohammed cartoons is a case in point: while both (closet) racists and anti-racists were able to line themselves up in support of or in opposition to the cartoons' publication, there was arguably a larger proportion of people for whom the idea of Denmark as exemplary of liberal freedoms served as the primary reference point for understanding the controversy. However inflated, and however much betrayed by a range of recent xenophobic immigration policies (particularly in Denmark), the Nordic countries' socially liberal reputation continues to signify, even if in truth this 'militant liberalism' (Lægaard, 2009: 318–9) is actually a shell for Islamphobic racism.

What the Danish cartoons controversy makes evident is the way a socially liberal identity – in this case circulating around a fundamental commitment to the principle of freedom of speech – is produced through its opposition to Islamic protest. As with other instances of where the causes of gay rights or women's rights 'become articulated to the nation and used as markers of European, Western or "civilizational" superiority' (Gunkel and Pitcher, 2008), a 'liberal' or 'progressive' identity is given coherence through the proximity of Islamic difference (for more on this, see Chapter 8). The putative expression and maintenance of Nordic social liberalism accordingly becomes a way of cohering the values of a 'tolerant' secular whiteness even as it engages in forms of intolerant distinction. While it was once arguably the frigidity of domestic sexual culture that was the implicit point of contrast for British ideas about the sexual freedom and openness of the Nordic countries, these too are now measured against the perceived conservatism and repressiveness of Muslim culture. Even as they are mobilized to illiberal and intolerant ends, the myths of Nordic tolerance and social liberalism continue to exert a hold on dominant cultural imaginaries, bolstering Conservative Prime Minister David Cameron's call for 'muscular liberalism' in relations with Britain's Muslim community (Wintour, 2011). The illiberal exercise of liberalism hints at qualities of excessiveness or extremity that perhaps bleed over into fascist and crypto-fascist forms of whiteness (Dyer, 1997: Chapter 6).

It has been my suggestion here that the Nordic countries have provided a model of white culture that resonates with contemporary British audiences. The material and symbolic consumption of a monocultural Nordic culture is informed by the notion that it somehow represents an 'originary' or 'ideal' way for white people to live, think and behave. A strong association is developed between, on the one hand, the non-human conditions of natural landscape, climate and qualities of light, and on the other the ethical, political and spiritual values of the Nordic peoples. A racialized idea of whiteness articulates these elements together, binding and rooting together blood and soil, and serving as a point of identification for white people in search of themselves. Middle class white people can forge in the idea of Nordic culture their relationship to fashionable ideas about environmental sustainability and to a socially liberal world view, in part through their distinction from polluting and illiberal racial others. Like the indeterminately historical model of white identity provided by The White Company, the consumption of Nordic culture provides an appealing set of cultural coordinates to orient white identity in multicultural contexts where (as part of the injunction to be true to themselves) everybody is called upon to behave in an ethnically appropriate fashion.

These symbolic returns to white roots, or to a purer, more elemental whiteness, are made in the context of economic crisis and political pessimism. They are not future-oriented transformations of the self, but forms of retreat where one's object is to become more like oneself. While interrogation of cosmopolitanism's imperial tendencies is a very important critical manoeuvre, respect for difference has now become a premiss for disengagement from it. Rey Chow uses the term 'coercive mimeticism' to describe the cultural obligation placed on 'ethnics in North American society' to 'resemble what is recognizably ethnic' (Chow, 2002: 107), and we might suggest that the critique of cosmopolitan whiteness has produced conditions where white people too are encouraged to exhibit this kind of self-mimicry as a condition of their belonging. This tendency is by no means an absolute one, and it is of course in conflict with a wide range of hybrid and cosmopolitan cultural forms, but it remains troubling in the sense that it follows and thereby strengthens the apparent differences in culture that set us apart from one another: ethnicity hereby hardens as a marker of identity and we all begin to dress ourselves in the right manner, eat the right things, give our kids the right names and dream the right dreams as appropriate to our respective ethnic categories. As Paul Gilroy has suggested, 'the urge to dismiss preemptorily the prospect of any authentic human connection' across the supposedly absolute and impermeable lines of identity can mean that '[t]imid and selfish responses are often justified in the name of complexity and ambivalence' (Gilroy, 2010: 66). Rather than all of us becoming prisoners of our 'own' culture on the basis of its necessity and inevitability, the examples of 'ethnic' white culture examined in this chapter have been shown to involve profoundly imaginative investments, immersed in fantasy and desire. Like many such cultural returns, there is nothing 'natural' about their figuration of cultural origins. There is, in other words, no reason why we should have to be thinking like this.

Chapter 4

Engaging whiteness
Black nerds

Engaging whiteness

This chapter, like the last, sets out to explore the consumption of forms of whiteness. But while the last chapter placed its focus on white people's fantasies of ethnic whiteness, here I want to explore the engagement of non-white subjects with ideas about whiteness and white culture. Because the basic logic of racism positions whiteness in a place of dominance within a cultural hierarchy, there has been a longstanding suspicion in critical work of non-white engagements with whiteness. From discussions of caste to practices of skin lightening, it is sometimes said that the desire for whiteness in cultures outside the West represents a form of self-denial or even self-hatred – a mechanism of racism – as the power of whiteness is perpetuated as an aspiration and a norm. The attraction of a white Western aesthetics in Japanese culture has, for example, long been linked to fears of cultural isolation and developmental inhibition: identification or engagement with white culture hereby becomes a way of 'catching up'. Whether or not cultures have had direct experience of Western colonialism, it can be convincingly argued that the power of whiteness continues to be felt across the globe, as dominant tastes and representations continue to be shaped by a desire to become white, or at least to assimilate the supposed qualities and characteristics of white culture. According to Frantz Fanon, the power of whiteness is such that non-whites internalize an inferiority complex (Fanon, 1986: 13) which maintains their continuing subordination. One political response to this overdetermining power of whiteness (of which, incidentally, Fanon did not himself entirely approve (Fanon, 1967: 17–27), has been the valorization of non-white identities in an attempt to restore some kind of balance. This approach has also been attempted within Western nation-states with white majorities: in the mid-twentieth-century US, 'black pride' and the assertion that 'black is beautiful' became, for example, one way of attempting to dislodge a racist aesthetics from cultural dominance.

In a valuable essay on black hair composed in the late 1980s, Kobena Mercer sets out some of the conceptual limits of these kind of discourses, and in particular the ways in which they tend to produce a rather essentializing conception of black styles in which what is considered 'natural' is given precedence over the 'artificial'. In his insistence that 'hair is never a straightforward biological fact' (Mercer, 1994: 100), Mercer refuses an implicitly racialized binary of nature and culture, and defends the legitimacy of treated and 'artificial' styles against the criticism that they represent some kind of capitulation to a dominant white aesthetic. For Mercer, black styles need to be understood as produced through syncretic and creolizing processes that represent a creative engagement with – but not the victory of or assimilation to – a dominant white culture. A black cultural politics may therefore take place both 'in and against hegemonic cultural codes' (ibid.: 121). Mercer's insights can be applied to more contemporary global trends for hair relaxing, straightening, wigs and weaves, particularly among people of African heritage. While of course it's always possible that individuals might harbour an internalized racism, this is by no means a foregone conclusion of any adopted style or fashion, however ostensibly 'white' it may appear to be.

What an argument like Mercer's frees up is the possibility of reading culture in its broadest sense as a space where racially-marked identities, fashions and styles may be tried on, adapted and reworked by anyone, without a sense in which those identities, fashions and styles necessarily bring with them a set of stable or predetermined meanings. Such a perspective obviously accords with the basic orientation of this book: as I have already suggested, it is more productive to think about race less as a possession that people 'have', and more a thing that they 'do' in acts of creative consumption. While it does not follow that we can simply 'be' anyone we like (because in culture we are positioned by others as much if not more than we position ourselves), it remains the case that culture is inherently dynamic. Though the mobile resources of race are not equally available to everyone (see Skeggs, 2004: 1), it remains the case that no racial meaning is fixed as if for all time, but is always subject to reworking and reconfiguration as the signifiers of meaning (words, texts, images, objects, ideas, places, practices) are assembled and reassembled in ever new ways by cultural actors. Signifiers that are assigned a particular racial meaning are not indefinitely 'tied' to it even if that meaning happens to be retained as a longstanding memory or trace, for an 'original' meaning is necessarily modified in the context of its reworking (for more on this, see Pitcher, 2011). In thinking a bit about the way that certain signifiers of whiteness are engaged with by non-white subjects, this chapter therefore sets out, like Mercer, to move beyond a critical framework that would read this practice as a capitulation to white dominance or supremacy, and instead tries to consider how non-white articulations of white culture can provide new ways of doing and being black. Because of the examples it uses, this chapter will employ the now conventional use of the term 'black' to describe identities that make some claim on an African heritage.

Black nerds

The idea of the nerd has followed an interesting cultural trajectory since its mid-twentieth-century US origins. From its initial status as the antithesis of hipster culture (in 1950s America, it appears to have been synonymous with 'square'), the nerd was transformed by the rise of computers and information technology, taking on a subcultural status and for the first time becoming a positive and even aspirational term: it is no coincidence that the first Apple Macintosh computer was released in the same year (1984) as the comedy film *Revenge of the Nerds*. Since strongly associated with computer and gaming culture, the idea of the nerd has gone mainstream. The obsessive, single-minded pursuit of skill or expertise that partly defines nerd culture can now be switched on and off such that we can be nerdy about one particular set of enthusiasms without compromising our popularity or social skills (see, for example, Patton Oswalt's lament about 'Boba Fett's helmet emblazoned on sleeveless T-shirts worn by gym douches hefting dumbells' (Oswalt, 2010)). Jocks and hipsters alike: now everyone positively *wants* to be a nerd.

An element of continuity in the nerd's trajectory from square to hip is its normative positioning in terms of sex/gender and race: the nerd still remains in many instances both male and white. Though the mainstreaming of nerdhood has allowed for some limited female claims on a nerd identity, male privilege continues to be explained away by coding the obsessive characteristics of the nerd as innately masculine. In racial terms, it is the nerd's associations with a lack of physical strength or sexual presence that mean that the nerd has been implicitly conceived as the antonym of a dominant black identity. Despite the fact that it's now cool to be a nerd, the cerebral, introverted and clumsy characteristics of nerdhood may nevertheless still be understood as unhealthy, even pathological, and in this sense they can be read as expressing on some level the racialized anxieties of a white Western modernity in fear of having lost touch with some ineffable human freedom (see Bonnett, 2000, Chapter 4; White, 2013; Nakamura, 2008: 100). Ron Eglash's article on the subject captures something of this worry in Brian Eno's striking definition of a nerd as 'a human being without enough Africa in him' (Eglash, 2002: 52). Dominant Western representations of south and east Asian culture – drawing on fantasies about innate intelligence, the significance of education, Confucian values or otaku culture – have opened up some cultural space for Asian nerds, and longstanding stereotypes of brainy Jews are fed by the anti-Semitic paranoia that computer technologies are at root some kind of nebbish conspiracy. And so while nerds don't have to be white, the least likely candidate for nerdhood remains a black male.

And yet, like a racial version of the 'rules of the internet' rule 34 ('If it exists, there is porn of it – no exceptions' (see TV tropes, 2013b)), the structural improbability of black nerds means that black nerds are necessarily with us (Eglash includes in this category Malcolm X, the character Steve

Urkel from *Family Matters* and sci-fi characters played by Samuel L. Jackson). Of course the necessity of the prefix 'black' in the naming of black nerds itself foregrounds their unusualness and exceptionality: the black nerd has become the intentional subversion of a racist stereotype of blackness where physical strength and a large, insistent penis are attributes of a subject equivalently lacking in intelligence, culture and sophistication (see also the discussion of Omar Little in Chapter 8). Because this stereotype of blackness is developed by the same culture that produces the white nerd, there's a sense in which these identity positions help to bring one another into being: white nerds make unnerdy blacks, and vice versa. To name the black nerd is therefore to name something that is both outside of – and at the same time a part of – a dominant regime of racial representation. The idea of the

Figure 4.1 Black Nerds Network logo. © Ochuko Ojiri

black nerd draws on existing understandings of both blackness and nerdishness to unpick the underlying racial logics of both.

The internet-based group Black Nerds Network originated in the UK and continues to have a presence on a number of social media sites (see links via blacknerdsnetwork.com). In its inaugural press release, the Black Nerds Network set out an origin story where 'two self-confessed Nerds' express their frustration 'that the African/Caribbean people were the only community that would promote and celebrate (outwardly anyway) a "ghetto lifestyle"'. As a result of their dissatisfaction with what they saw as the self-imposed limitations of dominant urban black identities, 'they decided to promote the very simple idea that it's good to be a NERD!!' (Black Nerds Network, 2006). The connotations of whiteness that are borne by the idea of the nerd permit the black nerd access to an area of culture that has hitherto been largely closed off to black subjects. Although the characteristics of nerdishness might appear to be superficially derogatory, they generate novel opportunities for self-expression for the self-identifying black nerd otherwise tied to an impossibly narrow repertoire of sporty, urban or ghetto cultures. Rather than understand a black engagement with whiteness as a form of self-hatred or self-betrayal, it's more useful to think about it as a way of engaging with and disturbing (or 'queering') the underlying logics of racial formation.

Pitching itself as 'aimed at book-reading, fashion-thinking, kite-flying nerds', the Black Nerds Network's press release sets out a long list of things that 'we like', classed as '70's – 80's retro to present day'. The Black Nerds list mixes high fashion culture references with popular and low-end fashion brands; it combines UK TV nostalgia with references to African and

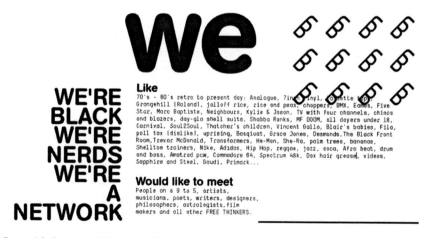

Figure 4.2 Screengrab from the Black Nerds Network press pack. © Ochuko Ojiri

Caribbean culture; it lists anachronistic technologies alongside black musical forms. The Black Nerds Network's list does not, therefore, represent a straightforward claim to a cerebral blackness designed (as was 'black is beautiful') to challenge a stereotype. A precise generational reference (to 'Thatcher's children') provides a key to reading an otherwise eclectic list: there is a sense here of an attempt to describe something of the specific texture of growing up black in 1970s and 80s Britain – hence references to the global children's toy and media franchises He-Man and Transformers juxtaposed with *Desmonds*, the first black British sitcom, or the way in which what might be termed 'credible' international black figures like Jean-Michel Basquiat and Marc Baptiste are namechecked alongside rather less renowned British artistes like the family-based pop group Five Star. While there are sufficient references to technology and high culture to justify the 'nerd' tag (the Amstrad PCW, the designers Charles and Ray Eames, a museum exhibition about interior furnishings), there are also ample references to a more 'classic' repertoire of black cultural references that prevent us from reading the black nerd as in denial of 'his' blackness. Indeed, the Black Nerd Network seem to be making a claim on nerdiness as an intrinsic component of late twentieth- and early twenty-first-century black British experience. While Ron Eglash is concerned in his more technocentric reading of black nerds that nerd identity remains uncool, and so continues to close science and technology off to black students who otherwise risk the charge of 'acting white' (Eglash, 2002: 59), the Black Nerds Network suggest a move in keeping with the mainstreaming of nerd culture that reconfigures the uncool as part of cool, retaining the associations between whiteness and nerd identity, but using these 'white' resources to forge a new kind of black.

The whiteness of retro

They do this, primarily, through the trope of retro fashion. One way of reading retro is that it involves the ironic recuperation into cool of things that have become uncool. In their references to the early personal computer the Sinclair 48K, or to day-glo shell suits, the Black Nerds Network express an interest in once fashionable things that fell into technological or sartorial obsolescence. They recognize that the destiny of all cool things is to become uncool, which in contemporary retro culture always implies the possibility of their resurrection, if only as objects of nostalgia. In the last chapter, I made a reading of the retro nostalgia circulating around The White Company as strongly shaped by an implicit whiteness, and I'd suggest that the whiteness of retro nostalgia is very much part of its meaning and appeal for the Black Nerds Network too. As an expression of nerdhood, retro culture facilitates a kind of 'racial cross-dressing' (Lott, 1999), presenting a different way of being black or of 'doing' blackness precisely because (and not in spite of) its implicit association with white people.

Retro culture is a particularly potent resource here precisely because of the longstanding association between blackness and futurity. Narratives of anti-racism typically conceive of racism as having been overcome over time, and will tend to counterpose the (bad, racist) past with the (good, post-racist) future, with the present situated somewhere between the two. Black identity has itself been informed by this framing, and has arguably been caught up in a similarly future-oriented teleology.[12] A negative effect of all the positive connotations of a black future is not so much a denial of the presence of black people in the past, but rather the unavailability to black subjects of certain orientations to the past. Black people have a status as the interpreters or custodians of a specifically black history, but little purchase on pasts without this theme or focus.

Consider, in British culture, the fate of the celebrity David Dickinson, of the daytime TV shows *Bargain Hunt* and *Dickinson's Real Deal*, whose skin tone is the frequent subject of jokes about fake tan. While Dickinson's Turkish-Armenian ancestry would likely be read in racial terms were he an expert on, say, Middle-Eastern cuisine, it is arguably the fact that it is because Dickinson's shows centre around antiques that his appearance is read in terms of an (aberrant) whiteness. This is hardly surprising, given the unofficial role of antiques shows' 'heritage capitalism' (Pham, 2010) in producing racially exclusive narratives of identity and belonging.[13] While established struggles in respect of black history and museum curating mean that the past is no longer entirely a white artefact (see Littler and Naidoo, 2005), the realm of antiques (as compared with that of, say, non-Western art and craft) has tended to be conceived as a largely white world. Though retro culture's focus on mid- to late-twentieth-century history makes it more open to an engagement with material culture that is more evidently marked by cultural diversity, I want to suggest that its subjective orientation towards the historical (rather than the explicitly black historical) has also remained the province of whiteness. To be the kind of person who is into retro culture, in other words, is still, in the main, to be white (Baker, 2013: 114).

In this respect, the consumption of and engagement with retro culture can be thought of as an example of a broader historical omnivorousness that might be said to be characteristic of a white subject position. The satirical blog Stuff White People Like communicates a sense of this in its entry '#116 Black Music that Black People Don't Listen to Anymore':

> If you are good at concealing laughter and contempt, you should ask a white person about 'Real Hip Hop.' They will quickly tell you about how they don't listen to 'Commercial Hip Hop' (aka music that black people actually enjoy), and that they much prefer 'Classic Hip Hop'.
>
> 'I don't listen to that commercial stuff. I'm more into the Real Hip Hop, you know? KRS One, Del Tha Funkee Homosapien, De La Soul, Wu Tang, you know, The Old School.'
>
> (Stuff White People Like, 2008)

Though this sketch is perhaps a little overhasty in denying a relationship between black people and an explicitly black musical heritage (for classically, one way of doing black has always been to claim a relationship to some kind of historical legacy of blackness), what Stuff White People Like captures so nicely is a sense of the way in which historical (here 'classic') objects become a resource for a certain kind of white subject. It communicates a sense in which for this subject the historicity (or 'pastness') of cultural forms – and in this example explicitly black cultural forms – opens them up to practices of appropriation and recuperation.[14] The past – including the 'black' past, is assimilated to and becomes in a sense the property of the whiteness that makes such a universalizing claim upon it. Within this historical matrix there is considerable symbolic advantage to be gained by black subjects who are themselves capable of making precisely this sort of 'white' claim on the past. As I have already suggested, the Black Nerds Network's engagement with a retro aesthetic represents just such a manoeuvre. The Black Nerds Network do not limit themselves to the nostalgic revival of historical objects marked or defined by their blackness (soca, Dax hair grease, iconic TV newsreader Trevor Macdonald) but combine these with elements of a mainstream and implicitly white culture (Kylie and Jason, She-Ra, TV with four channels). In lining up the former alongside the latter they are the curators of a kind of cultural equivalence. In one respect, this just communicates the banal experiential truth that She-Ra or four channel TV were, like Trevor Macdonald, all elements of popular multiculture in late-twentieth-century Britain, but it nevertheless makes an important claim that subverts the tendency to racial essentialism in the classification of historical artefacts (in short: Kylie and Jason are part of black culture too!). The Black Nerds Network are accordingly able to open up a different way of performing blackness through the occupation of the universalizing, eclectic and hitherto white subject position of the retro consumer, able to access and redeploy the entirety of the recent past rather than just the small portion of it that is circumscribed and classified as 'black culture'.

The Black Nerds Network are of course not alone in their adoption of a retro style – similar orientations to the cultural past can be seen in the super smart 'preppy' look that won black British rapper Tinie Tempah the GQ award for 'best dressed man' in 2012, or Kanye West's 'very avant-garde prep look' that later morphed into his 'emo-nerd stage' (Deleon, 2013), confirmed in its nerdiness by West's eclectic blogging on architecture and design (Freeman, 2009). While Asha Best reads the insertion of non-whites into the retro revival of mid-twentieth-century hipster culture as producing an ahistorical fantasy of racial transcendence (Best, 2012), it's possible to read counterfactual histories of race in more radical terms as involving the occupation or colonization of historical material cultures from which non-whites were once excluded, and in doing so developing 'alternative histories' (Samuel, 1994: 114) as part of a black cultural politics. Certainly, the resources of retro style are not equally available to all black people (there is in particular an entanglement with class and cultural capital that I will shortly examine further). There are also risks for black subjects engaging in practices that move onto 'white' territory – including the possible charge of inauthenticity or self-betrayal – but of course there are simultaneously risks associated with investing in an idea of 'pure' or 'authentic' blackness, not least in consolidating a marginal and limiting repertoire of legitimate tastes, desires and aspirations. The Black Nerds Network demonstrate a productive tension between ideas of white and black. They make us uncertain as to who might be borrowing from, absorbing or appropriating whom (are they doing 'white' in a 'black' way, or 'black' in a 'white' way?). In so doing, they exemplify an ambiguity that explores and expands the possibilities of blackness.

Post blackness

Because the idea of race is so often used to understand and explain the characteristics of being human, and because these characteristics are so often divided up in racialized binaries (like that of nerdy whites and physical blacks) that have in the context of our racist societies tended very much to work in the favour of white people (even with all its negative associations it's clear that the nerd is a figure *appropriate* to our postindustrial technological present), it should be nothing more than a statement of fact to recognize that the struggle against racism necessarily involves the kind of reworking of categories that I have just described. In other words, if white and black are in a mutually constitutive binary then the resources for reworking blackness will *necessarily* be marked by their whiteness (and vice versa). The point is not that the ostensible resources of whiteness have to remain the 'property' of whiteness (even if it is their whiteness that has made them valuable to black cultural actors). In such manoeuvres, characteristics of whiteness and blackness are mixed up in such a way as to upset and undermine both. Yet investments in the maintenance and policing of racial essences are similarly strong among anti-racists and racists alike. Relatedly, there remains a suspicion among some of the more explicitly politicized exponents of a black cultural politics towards new articulations of blackness. As I have argued at some length elsewhere (Pitcher, 2010), the 'betrayal' felt by some contemporary defenders of the US civil rights movement in response to Barack Obama's election as the first black president is founded on a refusal to accept the legitimacy of a 'post-black' model of black politics (Marable, 2009). While it is important to register the political losses involved in post-black politics – not least the decreasing power of a black narrative of critical oppositionality as black politics has moved from the margins to the mainstream – this should I suggest not blind us to the significant symbolic gains that Obama's presidency represents for the cause of US anti-racism.

In terms of the argument of the present chapter, it is worth emphasizing the extent to which Obama's political ascendancy has necessarily involved the appropriation of or engagement with hitherto 'white' subject positions. The position of the US presidency has in much of American history served as a symbol of de jure or de facto white supremacy, and so in the most striking and obvious sense the fact of a black man in the White House is precisely to do with occupying a subject position that has hitherto been unequivocally marked by its whiteness. Obama's status as 'a black man who doesn't conform to the normal scripts for African-American identity' (Appiah in Derbyshire, 2008) can likewise be thought of in terms of a claim on certain tropes and characteristics of whiteness: it is not inconsequential that, as a lifelong fan of comic books, sci-fi and an exponent of 'Jedi mind meld' (see Peterson, 2013), Barack Obama is frequently described as a nerd.

As has been widely recognized, the most significant event in the context of Obama's presidency was not his appeal to black voters, but the fact that for the first time in history white Americans were able to break with 'the one ironclad rule in American racial politics' and cast a majority vote for a black candidate (Marable, 2009: 4). This, too, might be understood in terms of a reconfiguration of blackness involving the selective and strategic appropriation of 'white' orientations, not least of which is the desire to exhibit a progressive race politics, for it was in significant part white people's desire to express their anti-racism that put Obama in the White House: we might say that Obama's skill in playing with whiteness was precisely what allowed white Americans to desire him as a black candidate. Though one way of reading this is as a careerist capitulation to a white political agenda, where Obama becomes 'not a black leader but an American leader who happens to be black' (Jones, 2008: 123), a subtler interpretation might begin by recognizing that new ways of doing and being black will necessarily involve forms of trespass onto a hitherto 'white' terrain. While more longstanding tropes of black politics do not risk the charge of inauthenticity or betrayal, their secure isolation from the terrain of whiteness potentially describes a limit to their critical potential. Rather than interpret black articulations of whiteness as undermining black subjects, we might read such practices as involving the valuable colonization (and thus transformation) of a dominant racially exclusive political culture.

It is particularly in the US context that it seems relevant to extend the interpretive frame of post-black politics to describe, in a broader sense, the features of what we might call post-black culture. In comparison with other Western states, the US has by far the largest and most established black middle class, and it is in the context of a significant rise in the number of black people graduating from university, taking on professional and managerial jobs, and accruing political and economic power (Mukherjee,

2011: 178) that there have developed increasing anxieties about the meaning of blackness more generally. In the same way that a black politics can no longer claim a status of critical oppositionality external to and uncompromised by a mainstream white culture (if indeed it ever really could), black culture in the US can no longer be thought of in singular terms. Once united in its diversity by an explicit, omnipresent and almost blanket racism, the black experience in the US has to an extent been dispersed by the rise of its middle class. While (as is true for first-generation middle-class subjects more generally) upward black social mobility is still often marked by working-class affiliations (Rollock *et al.*, 2013), there has nevertheless been a great diversification of the ways in which black culture is manifested. With this rightly have come anxieties (what is black culture now, in all its diversity?), political challenges (how do we continue to challenge racism when everyone agrees it's a bad thing?), and responsibilities (including acute moral questions for the US's black middle classes about their role in challenging or perpetuating forms of class inequality that simultaneously cleave along racial lines). Yet such problems are symptomatic of a historical moment where, in the words of one commentator, 'the definitions and boundaries of Blackness are expanding in forty million directions – or really, into infinity'. While this doesn't mean the end of blackness, 'it means we're leaving behind the vision of Blackness as something narrowly definable and we're embracing every conception of Blackness as legitimate' (Touré, 2011: 12).

It is in the context of this new and confusing proliferation of black identities that some commentators have suggested the possibility of a 'post-racial' moment (Huffington Post, 2013). While it should be clear this is a reading I do not support (as I argued in the introduction to this book, race does not go away – it expands and proliferates even under conditions of increasing equality), what the idea of the post-racial seems so often, however inadequately, to be groping towards is this sense in which the old scripts for racial identity are from the perspective of the twenty-first century looking increasingly thin and threadbare. Though episodes like the killing of Trayvon Martin remind us of the horrific ways in which US society continues to sanction and justify racism (for racist articulations of race have not somehow magically gone away), it is at the same time imperative to register the ways in which the shifting, complicating and diversifying status of blackness means that those old scripts are, in certain circumstances, disintegrating under the weight of their own contradictions. It certainly seems likely that the kinds of engagements with and deployments of whiteness that this chapter has described will become an increasing feature of black identities. The subject position of the black nerd and its relationship to retro culture is to be most usefully understood as an expansion of the terms of expressive possibility in black culture, partly based on a claim to the ownership of and belonging to the material and semiotic substance of the common cultural past. While there is an element of truth to the accusation or lament that this is the betrayal of an earlier moment in black identity (marked by a common experience and the greater sense of community and belonging that goes with it), this betrayal has been a necessary part of the shifting status of blackness in our contemporary cultures. Away from the US and UK, in other contexts and for other reasons, non-white versions of 'white' cultural forms also become channels for community, identity and self-expression: from Mexican emos (Grillo, 2008) to Batswana metalheads (Banchs, 2013), these are not ways for non-white people to express self-hatred or to deny their cultural specificity, but rather to forge new ways of being themselves.

Chapter 5

The taste of race
Authenticity and food cultures

Food and its cultures of consumption arguably provide the most visible and 'everyday' context for encounters and engagements with difference. Indeed, it is this very ordinariness that has often led critics to question the significance, depth or sincerity of crosscultural culinary consumption. While food tends to be recognized as an important resource for migrant and post-migrant communities in maintaining a conception of culture and transacting relations with an idea of 'home' (see, for example, Mankikar, 2005), the racial politics of crosscultural engagements with food and food cultures tend to be regarded with less seriousness. Perhaps it is the very ease with which food is picked up as a medium of cultural engagement that fuels such estimations: while it is true that we do not approach different food cultures unthinkingly (taste is so often a matter of education; the technologies and apparatuses of consumption so often require a degree of preparation and training), there is nevertheless a sensual immediacy to the practice of eating that does not require the effort that goes into, say, understanding a new written or spoken language. It is no accident that in the British context an 'ethnic' food is a component part of that well-worn list of the superficialities of multicultural display ('saris, steel bands and samosas').

As a package for cultural difference, food can also be said to reinforce dominant racial hierarchies of production and consumption. Lining up non-white producers to attend to the desires of white consumers, food can be said to describe a commodity and a service, not a relationship among equals. The preparation and sale of food become one of the few available commercial avenues for those who have been forced into self-employment by poor job prospects and workplace racism (Möhring, 2008: 135). As such, the commodification of culture to be swallowed down or spat out does not necessarily make food an ideal medium for establishing the terms of cultural equality and exchange.

Even if we accept that there is a degree of truth to both these assessments, food retains a remarkable status in our cultural formations that makes its racial politics hard to dismiss. Take the food we buy in supermarkets: while particular ingredients are sometimes ethnically unmarked, pretty much all processed food products – from readymeals to dips, condiments, spices, pickles and sauces – are understood, presented and sold as deriving from particular traditions among particular people in particular places. Although the conventions of global capitalism mean that nearly all the food for sale goes through complicated and transnational logistics of processing, production and packaging, only some of it gets marked out as 'belonging' to regionally or nationally conceived ethnic groups. Multinational food producers organize their brands accordingly (Associated British Foods, for example, manufactures both the Chinese 'Blue Dragon' and Indian 'Patak's' brands), and supermarkets are laid out according to ethnic categories, displaying aisles and aisles of ethnically themed products to provide one's meat, fish or vegetables with the desired cultural qualities, to be washed down with an ethnically appropriate brand of beer.[15] While it is therefore fanciful to imagine that one's purchases have anything more than a symbolic connection to their putative ethnic origins (despite the best efforts of promotional materials that continue to market brands like Patak's as family businesses), the interest in and desire for 'ethnic' foods demands to be understood as involving something more significant than just the patronising indulgencies of feelgood multiculturalism or the cynical manipulations of multinational marketeers. In twenty-first-century Britain, the massive and rapid success of the multinational South African-based Mozambican-Portuguese franchise Nandos among culturally heterogeneous urban populations shows that ethnic food cultures can provide a shared space of consumption. The example of Nandos shows how ethnically marked food can produce a range of different cultural resonances – providing Muslim consumers with Halal meat; reminding another customer of 'Caribbean food' (Sawyer, 2010) – organized, in contrast to the example at the end of Chapter 2, around the culturally unifying force of spicy chicken. Even if, in other circumstances, commodified ethnic difference is sometimes like a seasoning or spice livening up 'the dull dish that is mainstream white culture' (hooks, 1992: 21), it is useful to think about what this process of 'seasoning' might be all about. Could there perhaps be more going on here than just a relentless search for novelty in the midst of majoritarian cultural stagnation? Does the consuming subject really have to be white, and does her or his consumption of 'ethnic' foods necessarily have to be marked by the expression or denial of their own difference, as determined from the central point of some imaginary white culture?

Though this chapter will not be able to fully answer these questions, what I want to take seriously here is an idea of food as a mode of engagement with cultural difference. To consume 'ethnic' food – that is, food that is marked out as deriving in some sense from outside one's own immediate cultural context – can, even if it is done regularly and without much excitement or ceremony, nevertheless be understood as a meaningful practice, with important somatic and symbolic aspects (see Highmore, 2008). In often minor and unexceptional ways, I want to suggest that one becomes different by taking into one's body something that is itself marked out by difference. The activity of relating to and engaging with difference is not just a positional one – like a political affiliation – but is a form of situated practice, an 'everyday "doing"' (Amin, 2012: 93). The process of swallowing down is an intimate physical act, and its meaning is rarely a straightforward one: does it suggest control (the conquering of difference), self-transformation (the internalization of difference), or is it to do with cosmopolitan familiarity (a facility with difference)? Does it suggest adventurousness, cultural omnivorousness or sophistication? Solidarity or fellow feeling? An escape from one's own culture, or from the mass-produced commodity culture that it symbolizes? While all of this depends on the contexts of consumption, it is invariably the case that one key factor in the consumption of ethnic food relates to the circulation of ideas about authenticity. By focusing on a consumer desire for authenticity, this chapter will explore the symbolic terms of its production and supply, from the poetics of British-Indian cuisine to the international fashion for 'street food' via the Vietnamese sandwich called the banh mi.

Authenticity and contingency

As I suggested in Chapter 2, to get to grips with what authenticity is and how it works it is useful to think about authenticity not as an unchanging quality that particular things have or don't have, but rather as something that gets defined and redefined in the context of consuming practice. As soon as we remove the requirement that there is some kind of essential 'truth' to any culture or identity – that, in other words, we are always dealing with different and competing versions or performances of cultural truth – we can see how authenticity becomes simply a trope or resource to be called upon in the attempts of social actors to secure their own association with a particular idea of the truth. To recognize this is not to reduce the truth value of any culture or identity, but simply to acknowledge that what we take for a cultural truth is not the expression of an interior essence of a person or gesture, object or practice, but a quality of a particular version or performance of culture in a particular time and place. What appears to be true at one particular moment may in time accordingly lose its truth value, or what was once designated false or inauthentic may find itself re-evaluated and recuperated as authentic and true in a different context.

If this is the case with the performance of culture, so it is also true of the activity of its consumption. While the consumer of cultural difference is positioned differently to those who symbolically 'own' that culture, the act of consumption can likewise be seen as a performance that can be done more or less competently, more or less well. The fact that the qualities of truth and authenticity can phase in and out for the producers and consumers of culture alike does not undermine these qualities, but reveals them to be the product of dynamic and ever-changing cultural formations. Culture and identity are in this respect very much like fashions in clothes or music. This is not to trivialize them, but to reveal something useful about how they work. In fashion discourse, the designation of what is fashionable is subject to constant revision, but this doesn't detract from the fashionability of whatever happens to be fashionable at any particular moment – it doesn't become less fashionable because everyone knows it probably won't be fashionable in six months or six year's time. Likewise the perceived truth or authenticity of a manifestation of a particular culture or identity doesn't become less true on the basis that its claim on truth is a contingent one. When a particular cultural practice or object is thought to be authentic, it really is authentic, even though its hold on authenticity will not be ever-lasting. While, unlike with the world of fashion, we tend to be less ready to admit to the impermanency of the truths that we hold to, this is arguably because they help us to invest in an idea of ourselves (and others) that is reasonably stable and permanent: to admit to the contingency of cultural truths is to face the disturbing and exhausting possibility that we are always necessarily hard at work defining and redefining who we are.

It can be interesting to explore in more specific terms the relationship between fashion and cultural authenticity – the question of how particular manifestations of culture become fashionable, and how they go out of fashion – because doing so can help us to think about some of the variety of elements involved in the evaluation and designation of cultural truth and authenticity across time and place. Take for example the popularity of South Asian ('Indian') restaurants in Britain. As Elizabeth Buettner explores in her account of this multi-billion-pound industry, the practice of 'going for an Indian' can be read as an index of changing attitudes to cultural difference in modern Britain. While the earliest Indian restaurants catered to the tastes of former colonials reliving their memories of the Raj (Buettner, 2008: 872–3), postwar Britain saw the expansion of curry house culture, patronized both by South Asian immigrants and increasing numbers of white British customers, serving as the focus, among other things, of middle-class culinary adventurism and racist post-pub homosociality. Buettner notes that by the mid-1970s and early 1980s the development of uniform menus (appealing firmly to 'British' tastes) and décor (most notoriously, red flock wallpaper) was being subjected to criticism by food writers and curry afficionados on the basis of its standardization and inauthenticity (ibid.: 881–3). At the moment, in other words, that there developed a mass audience for the culturally hybrid form of the British-Indian curry, elite consumers came to signal their distinction through their insistence on more 'traditional' and regionally specific forms of Bangladeshi, Pakistani and Indian cuisine. A new type of restaurant has come to be developed where 'new Asian entrepreneurs' challenge:

common British conceptualizations of an undifferentiated Asian population and culture and assert distinct national, regional, class, and religious backgrounds. With restaurants as their stage, South Asians perform their own acts of ethnic absolutism that work against reconfigurations of Britishness that include curry as much as they undercut notions of a monolithic diasporic culture.

(ibid.: 872)

With parallels to 'the mutually constitutive nature of intolerance and multicultural celebration' (ibid.: 901), the reworking of South Asian cuisine in Britain therefore facilitated both a greater attentiveness to the particularities of cultural difference at the same time as signalling a conservative retreat into 'ethnically appropriate' forms of cultural display, a trend that has many parallels in the cultural politics of race in Britain (for more on this, see Chapter 3). The rejection of the dominant postwar mode of British Indian cuisine continues to reverberate in contemporary British food culture. A Tripadvisor review remarks of 'a tastefully decorated' Peterborough restaurant '[w]hat a nice change from flocked wallpaper' (Tripadvisor, 2013), while another restaurant review site notes of a restaurant in Wolverhampton that 'Modern Indian restaurant Bilash has chucked out the chintz and foregone the flock wallpaper to great critical approval', going on to remark that:

You'll find familiar items like chicken tikka on the menu and the signature Goan tiger prawn masala has won awards, but it's the inclusion of dishes such as Hyderabadi byriani and lal mass (a hot lamb curry from Rajasthan) that are rarely seen outside of the Subcontinent that makes Bilash such an interesting prospect.

(Britain's Finest, 2013)

Amidst this evident thirst for a more authentic (meaning culturally specific) version of South Asian culture we can discern a certain nostalgia for a now passed cultural form. Contributors to a discussion board thread on the subject lament the passing of restaurants where, as one poster remarks, 'the waiters wear waistcoats and bow-ties. There's a fish tank. It's virtually pitch black and infinitely looped sitar music'. Another responds 'Oh lovely memories of the Koh-I-Noor and the Shis on Gibson St Glasgow circa early 70s', adding his memories of 'Red flock wallpaper and huge pictures of the Himalayas and awful music' (Digital Spy, 2013). Such sentiments – nostalgic for their own kind of authentic experience – open up a space for the inevitable return of flocked wallpaper in establishments confident enough in their market position that its irony will not be misunderstood (see Harman, 2012).

It is not simply that the meaning of genuine or authentic Indian food changes over time, but that different cultural actors involved in both production and consumption sides of the Indian catering industry are engaged in complicated relationships with the idea of authenticity, and for a variety of reasons. Authenticity is what connects the manufacturers of 'Indian' products (according to their promotional material, Unilever trade brand Knoor Patak's supply over 75 per cent of UK Indian restaurants) with British South Asian restaurant owners seeking to make their product distinct, with a wider group of consumers whose expectations of authenticity are shaped by those restaurant experiences, alongside a wide range of other influences (cook books, TV shows, trips to Goa or Utter Pradesh) that all seek to define and capture the truth of Indian cooking. While the claim to authenticity is a claim to permanence, the object at the centre of this dance of curry house culture – authentic Indian food – is constantly changing. The desire for authenticity necessarily reproduces the germ of dissatisfaction and inauthenticity in its search for new versions of the authentic, because to identify one rendition of the truth is often to invalidate other versions of it. Though like the operation of fantasy in psychoanalysis, the idea of authentic Indian food might actually conceal an absence – ultimately, the non-existence of authenticity – (see Grosrichard, 1998), the search for and contestation of the truth itself produces a kind of cultural resource that services the interest and desire of consuming audiences.

This audience is of course consuming far more than food itself – they are consuming different aesthetic orientations or relationships to culture – and thus social orientations to or relationships with people of South Asian heritage. Buettner notes the irony that a developing taste and respect for Indian food in Britain – and indeed the assimilation of Indian food as a marker of British national identity – has been accompanied by the suspicion and persecution of British Muslims, who are overwhelmingly those who prepare and present it (Buettner, 2008: 891). However superficial or selective these orientations or relationships are, those who make and serve Indian food remain signifiers of its authenticity, though as Theodore Bestor suggests in his description of Latino chefs passing as Japanese in a US sushi restaurant (Bestor, 2005: 18), phenotypical difference can serve as the ethnic guarantee of what are in fact some rather novel combinations of food and culture.

Authenticity plays a part, among other things, in organizing the availability and importance of ingredients and the technologies of their preparation and presentation. Authenticity determines the relative capital of South Asian cuisine within the wider sector of food production. On a crudely economic level, the idea of authenticity keeps the juggernaut of this multi-billion-pound service industry going. In British food culture, where as I have suggested most food products are in some sense packaged as 'ethnic' food, it is not too much of an exaggeration to suggest that the cultural currency of authenticity is the central factor that organizes what we eat, and how we eat it. Without the trope of authenticity even those Glaswegian nostalgics would have nothing to reminisce over.

Post-authentic authenticity

A more recent food fashion provides further insights into the ways in which authenticity catalyzes the consumption of ethnic food, and demonstrates that contemporary food culture is not only global in its identification of places of origin, but also in terms of the trajectories of its mediation. We can use the banh mi (*bánh mì*), a type of Vietnamese sandwich in a rice flour baguette, to show some of the intricate ways here in which authenticity is negotiated, contested and achieved.

One of the most interesting things about the banh mi, and what makes it a useful case study, is the sense in which it departs from the most common model of culinary authenticity. While the authenticity of many ethnic foods is based on an implicit mapping together of food origin and human origin (the idea that 'this is how they make dal in the Punjab' usually means 'this is how they have always made dal in the Punjab'), the banh mi is from the start a 'fusion' food, bringing to the fore the way in which it developed through the interaction of Vietnamese and French food cultures from the mid-nineteenth to the mid-twentieth centuries, during the period of French colonialism in Indochina. Certain elements (the baguette, pâté, mayonnaise) are understood as French, while others (meats, coriander, daikon) are framed as having a Vietnamese 'origin'. The banh mi therefore exemplifies what we might call a 'post-authentic' authenticity: its claim on authenticity is not as if 'for all time', but as a more temporally specific assemblage of influences and ingredients. What is novel about the framing of the banh mi is not that it is a cross-cultural production per se, but that this is a quality that is intentionally foregrounded in its presentation. Foods we might think of as having more static genealogies may have a less well-known cosmopolitan history: that authentic Punjabi dal will likely contain tomatoes ('originally' from South America) that make it is as much of a 'fusion' food as the banh mi. Indeed, the fact that the 'French' baguette is marked as non-Vietnamese while the coriander ('originally' from the Mediterranean region) is understood as a Vietnamese ingredient demonstrates that even the banh mi's cultural hybridity should be recognized as the product of 'constructed geographical knowledges [. . .] constructed from within the spaces of material culture and not from some Olympian viewpoint above them' (Cook and Crang, 2003: 115). Like the implicit understanding of the profound 'impurity' of human differences that runs throughout this book, the designation of a food's supposed 'origin' needs to be understood as a symbolic claim rather than a description of natural/biological fact.

The existence of explicitly post-authentic foods like the banh mi demonstrate how there is no sense in which the theoretically contradictory demands for novelty and truth need actually be in conflict, because there will always be ever-new ways to make an authentic claim. What's most important, in the case of the banh mi, is that it expresses a primary relationship to contemporary Vietnam. This is what the US journalist Walter

Nicholls emphasizes in his 'positively Proustian' description of eating the sandwich in Falls Church, Virginia:

> As I taste the pork liver pâté, ham, cilantro and pickled radish, I close my eyes and I'm cruising the Mekong Delta at Dawn in a funky long boat, as I did a dozen years ago, just south of the city of Can Tho.
> (Nicholls, 2008)

Like the reviewer of London restaurant Bánhmì11 who remarks that 'Perhaps this review isn't being very fair, considering I'd just returned from a three-week trip to Vietnam' (Yelp, 2012), the mark of an authentic (and therefore good) banh mi derives from its apparent similarity to the version made and sold in Vietnam. To trace the banh mi's path to popularity in the West is to tell a familiar story where culturally adventurous early adopters 'discover' the sandwich in cafes and restaurants run by and for members of the Vietnamese diaspora, in this case on the West coast of America (see for example La Ganga, 1988; Hansen, 1991). With the increased popularity of the banh mi and its crossover appeal to a more mainstream demographic, Vietnamese people continue to provide a guarantee of the product's authenticity, as if there is a direct correlative between specific qualities of the food and some kind of ethnic essence; as if there are unlearnable secrets to its preparation that cannot be written down in a recipe. As 'Becky H', comments on an article chronicling the arrival of the banh mi in Ann Arbor, Michigan:

> Vietnamese girl here . . . I've been disappointed by every banh mi I've ever had in Ann Arbor, especially when they're not made by Vietnamese people who grew up making/eating them in Vietnam [. . .]
>   You can get good, legitimate banh mi in Madison Heights, MI, about an hour's drive away. There is a large Vietnamese community there.
> (Webster, 2012)

It is precisely this essentializing connection that implicitly reads 'good, legitimate banh mi' as the expression of 'good, legitimate Vietnamese people' that gets broken as the popularity of the sandwich increases. By 2013, the London-wide café chain Eat were selling chicken banh mi; I spotted a meatball interpretation on sale in the departure lounge of Helsinki airport, and the US supermarket chain Publix had started selling a version of the banh mi renamed the 'Asian BBQ pork sub' (The Daily City, 2013). While one commenter on this Daily City story writes 'This is pretty ridiculous. How about buying the real thing from Orlando's many locally owned and operated Vietnamese shops?', another draws ironically on the discourse of the 'gateway' drug, remarking 'Maybe this will be a gateway sammich that will lead them to the local banh mi spots in Orlando' (ibid.). This later reckoning of the inauthentic banh mi as a station on the path to authenticity demonstrates how the perception of the mainstreaming of ethnic food is still indexed back to the Vietnamese disapora as a community of origin. Despite the fact that the banh mi is from the start understood as a post-authentic 'fusion' food, it appears that any further modifications of the dish will tend to be read as a selling out or dilution of its authenticity. It is unlikely that the proprietors of the restaurant Eat Ban Mi in Austin, Texas, are trying to make much of a claim on authenticity with their determinedly Southern 'Tex-Asian' banh mi range, which includes for $7.65 the 'What's up Cowboy!', filled with 'Beef brisket marinated with Daniels "Yee Haw!"' (Eat Ban Mi, 2013).[16]

Street food

One element that seems to cement the perceived authenticity of some recent contextualizations of the banh mi has been its reworking as 'street food'. Again taking the lead from the banh mi's trajectory to popularity in the US, and in particular the fashionability of 'food trucks' (featured on Canadian and US TV shows like *Eat St.* and *The Great Food Truck Race*), from around 2010–11 the banh mi was widely and comprehensively 'discovered' by the British food media. Attention was focused on Bánhmì11, which began life as a slickly run stall on London's Broadway Market: '[t]hey are already huge in New York and Sydney', writes *Telegraph* reporter Bee Wilson, '[t]his looks like [the] next big thing in sandwiches, the next panini' (Wilson, 2010). Despite having been available in Vietnamese cafes and restaurants in London since at least the late 1990s (see Time Out, 1999), the 'street food' reinvention of the banh mi, assisted by the media-friendly narratives of authentic Vietnamese home cooking presented by Bánhmì11's Van Tran and Anh Vu to celebrity chefs Jamie Oliver and Nigel Slater (*Jamie's Great Britain*, 2011; *Nigel Slater's Simple Cooking*, 2011), seems to have cemented the sandwich's status as an authentic foodstuff. Indeed, the signifiers of street food appear to guarantee the truth status of the banh mi even when it is prepared by those who do not make an ethno-preneurial claim on a Vietnamese identity (see Comaroff and Comaroff, 2009: 51). Serving his sandwiches from the back of a bright yellow three wheel 'vietvan' (in imitation of an autorickshaw or tuk-tuk van), the south London-based trader David Parkin has, according to one reviewer, assembled enough signifiers of street food to confer 'an equally authentic experience' to that of eating Asian street food (DailyCandy, 2011). As has been shown in a study of Australian restaurants in the US, consumers continue to prefer their own fantasies of cultural difference even when presented with a supposedly 'more accurate representation' (Wood and Muñoz, 2007: 250). In the same way that the imitation of racial characteristics is sometimes more convincing than the 'real' thing (see Bonnett, 2006), an awareness of the presentational and performative conventions of street food is what really expresses the 'truth' of the banh mi to its authenticity-hungry consumers, who of course only really desire the (temporary) fulfilment of their own culinary desire.

Used adjectivally, the connotations of 'street' reference more than just a place you might get rained on. Like the other great racial euphemism 'urban', 'street' stands in a contemporary British context as a term not only for the social geographies of non-white culture, but more specifically for practices by which minorities might consolidate the truth of their racial performances. Drawing implicitly on the familiar injunction in transnational hip hop culture against cultural betrayal (keeping it real, not selling out), the characteristics of 'street' reference an unaffected connectedness to an idea of cultural origin, and are bolstered by older meanings in which the street is conceived as a place of ordinary or working-class identity. In whichever case, 'street' stands for authenticity, and as part of the phrase 'street food', it is an authenticity made foreign. 'Street food' takes us away from culturally naturalized forms of outdoor food consumption (say, the burger van or ice cream van), and becomes associated with the idea that people eat differently in different places. To eat street food is therefore not only to vicariously travel to another place, but to take one out of oneself and incorporate some of the qualities of that place. Despite the transnational forces that allow street foods to cross continents and cultures, the locatedness of the street (its adjectival streetness) roots it as the authentic product of that foreign place of origin. The associations with non-white and working class authenticity mean that street food is not the property of cosmopolitan elites, but people who are imaginatively rooted in place as the inhabitants of those foreign streets. Street food therefore defies and denies the fact of its own radical recontextualization, for it remains somehow tied to the social-geographical specificity it references so emphatically. Theodore Bestor notes that the global ubiquity of sushi does not diminish its status as 'Japanese cultural property', for globalization 'grows the franchise' (Bestor, 2005: 17). Similarly, the world of hypermobile global capitalism that creates the possibility of street food is precisely what street food symbolically denies in its insistence that immobility is truth.

'Street food' and its cognate terms do a fair bit of work for the London restaurant chain Wahaca which brands itself as selling 'Mexican market food'. While it has two quasi-mobile 'Mexican Street Kitchens', Wahaca is a largely indoors affair. As if to compensate, as its website records, Wahaca commissions work from 'street artists' to decorate its restaurants, and runs a 'Wahaca Street Project' which sponsors a Mexican charity for children 'whose parents live and work on the street', and has 'the aim of giving back to the streets from which we have taken so much inspiration, enjoyed so many flavours and met so many wonderful characters'. Mexican markets, where 'nothing is allowed to go to waste', become an inspiration for the restaurant's 'attitude for reusing and recycling', and Wahaca's glasswear is 'blown in the traditional way but using only recycled glass'. The street food aesthetic organizes Wahaca's interactive flash-based website, where weather-worn crates of fruit are stacked against the image of an exterior wall of peeling paint and flaking plaster, onto which plays the animated shadow of fast-paced salsa-style dancers. In one section (see Figure 5.1), a virtual five centavos coin will rouse a sleeping drummer, while a further coin will 'shut him up'.

It is by these and other means that Wahaca simulates that ubiquitous touristic fascination with the mundane materiality of foreign places, vicariously providing the consumer with an experience of Mexican street life. The authenticity of the Oaxaca drummer is cemented by his creative act of sonic terrorism, mimicking the minor economic exploitation that is a component part of the tourist experience. Indeed, there is a sense in which the promise of new culinary experiences that a brand like Wahaca thrives upon is always accompanied by the same kind of insecurity that is produced by strange and unfamiliar places: the possibility of being ripped off or sold a pup is in this respect a marker of an authentic experience, an ambivalence of trust that parallels the ambivalence of culinary experimentation: am I going to like this? Is it overpriced? Is it going to make me ill? Success in the rite of culinary experimentation provides the consumer with confidence and worldliness – the feeling of being able to thrive outside of their ordinary.

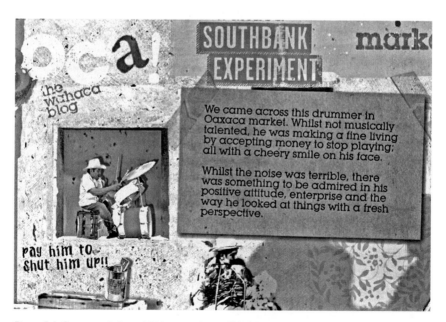

Figure 5.1 Screengrab from Wahaca website. © Wahaca

Failure confirms their cultural immobility. While consumers and restauran-
teurs are respectively invested in having and producing authentic experiences,
the risk of inauthenticity, the frisson of the 'street', and the possibility of
exploitation are a necessary accompaniment to and guarantee of that
authenticity (one might consider in a similar light the terrors of 'gap year'
travel as an intrinsic element of that rite of passage into global bourgeois
adulthood).

From this kind of perspective, what gets wrapped up in the idea of
authenticity has in actuality very little to do with the prosaic detail of how
certain foods are grown, prepared and served in Mexico, Vietnam or
wherever (firstly, practices differ; secondly, who cares?). What authenticity
signifies at the most elemental level is a food or cuisine's foreignness or
otherness: it stands as a symbol of what one is not or does not know. In
Ben Highmore's psychoanalytic reading, the consumption of foreign foods
replays the crucial developmental role of eating in the practice of subject
formation as the means by which we distinguish between ourselves and a
world that is 'not me' (Highmore, 2008: 389–90). In abstract terms, the
difference that is mobilized in ethnic food consumption might provide us
with a way of cohering characteristics of our own identity in relation to
ethnic others, but what is perhaps most interesting about this process is the
sense in which it brings with it the tastes, sensations and artefacts of rich
and complex material cultures that we draw on in the expressive performance
of who we are.

The notion of authenticity as expressing difference rather than verisimili-
tude again undercuts a conception of cultural truths as existing independently
of the desire to discover them. It moves us away from the notion that the
consumption of 'ethnic' food is about experiencing the 'reality' of different
cultures and the places and people they represent, and towards an idea of
consumption as a creative medium of exploration and transformation. It is
less an ethnographic survey of literal differences, and more an adventure
through imaginative possibilities. While, as noted at the start of this chapter,
such practices leave themselves potentially exposed to the charge of
reproducing racial hierarchies and inequalities (particularly in the sense that
they are structurally dependent on maintaining differences as such, and so
holding onto an investment in retaining the other in its otherness), it is at
the same time worth recognizing the sense of openness, experimentation
and self-transformation that is also at work here. Certainly the search for
culinary authenticity can have some culturally conservative tendencies, but
the desire that motivates the consumption of difference is not necessarily
one that reduces and constrains. Although this will not ordinarily admit
to the underlying contingency – and ultimately, the non-existence – of
authenticity, the relentless and never-ending quality of the search for it
provides plenty of opportunities to rework and reform the stories we tell
ourselves about food and culture (see, for example, Duruz, 2011). When,

as in the Australian context, supposedly 'British' foods like sausages and fish and chips signify a racist backlash against multiculturalism (Newman and Gibson, 2005), it's clear there's still politics to be found in a bowl of dal or a banh mi.

And on occasions when the contingency of authenticity does get revealed – when a version of the authentic betrays itself and exposes the inauthenticity that is always a part of it – we are potentially in a position to develop a more sophisticated understanding of cultural difference, and a profounder relationship to the putative bearers of that difference. To be aware of or even be troubled by the inauthenticity of an engagement or encounter with difference (to see, for example, the ways in which the other is constructed to serve the self) can become a means by which we might give more care and attention to the terms of that crosscultural relationship. It can help to reveal something closer to the objective conditions of our relationship with racialized others. This is a scrutiny or openness that precisely does *not* lead to the discovery of a truer or more authentic culture, but one that encourages us to engage with and relate to the desire that produced our interest in the other in the first place. To turn our desire for difference back upon itself does not reveal the truth of the other (that mysterious quality that we can never quite put our finger on), but rather its opposite: it reveals that the other is just as inauthentic as we are.

Chapter 6

Race and children
From anthropomorphism to zoomorphism

The innocence of children

One of the most frequent clichés about race is the one about the innocence of children. Children, we're often told, aren't racist. You aren't born racist. It's an idea that's true enough, but only in the very general sense that language and the meaning that comes with it are developed over time. Certainly, children aren't born racist, but neither are they born with the ability to ride a bicycle or make carrot cake. These, like racism, are learned practices. The insistence on the innocence of children in discussions of race positions race as the product of a corrupted adulthood because of the close association that gets made between race and racism. We don't like to think of children as prejudiced, and so are reluctant to grant them the ability to think in racial terms. But it has been the argument of this book that a tendency to reduce the meanings of race to questions of racism is an over-hasty one, because race does other things too. Rather than hold onto the fantasy of childhood as a somehow race-free zone ('my kids don't see race'), it's interesting to think about the ways in which ideas about race are produced and reproduced in children's media, games and toys.[17] Racial enculturation, the practice of learning about race, is just as much a part of growing up as any other significant element of human culture, but our eagerness to pretend that it doesn't happen (or to want it not to happen) means that we sometimes learn about race by proxy. As this chapter will go on to demonstrate, we're sometimes talking about race when we think we're talking about something else entirely.

If we can agree that childhood is not somehow cut off from the rest of the world, then we must accept, too, that children's toys, books and games are involved in the production and reproduction of cultural norms. It is through the images and objects of childhood that adults provide children with ideas and aspirations, with models of how to think and behave. Children draw on these resources to make sense of the world, developing a picture of who they are by identifying with (or not identifying with) the personalities, situations and relationships they encounter and develop in the context of play. Forms of play like 'make-believe' are accordingly not an escape from the 'real' world, but a way of locating ourselves within it. This is, for example, why the political debate over gendered toys is such a fraught and contentious one: what is at stake is not just the range of imaginative options available to particular children, but the way in which gendered toys institute models of behaviour, desire and aspiration that are decisive in producing our subjectivity – our understanding of who we are and what we want. Wider manifestations of gender identity (and related issues of sexual identity) are hereby fought over and negotiated in miniature form. While it would be too simplistic to suggest that toys straightforwardly produce adult subjectivities, it is certainly possible to look at toys and games as a site of cultural struggle where dominant ideas are reinforced and reproduced, tested and displaced.

This chapter will first consider 'cowboys and Indians' and the significant role of the 'red Indian'/'Native American' in shaping twentieth-century childhoods. It moves on to explore elements of multicultural programming on British preschool television, from references to Oriental culture to the interesting tendency in the representation of otherwise non-naturalistic characters to hold onto the visual markers of race. The chapter then considers the way in which racial difference figures as species difference in children's media, toys and games as race comes to be represented in animal form.

Cowboys and Indians

Just as with gender, toys and games can tell us an awful lot about the way that race works in our cultures, and the investments we have in it. Though the material culture of childhood tends to get broken and thrown away, collectors and museums provide ample evidence of the way in which racist attitudes and beliefs come to be expressed in the form of toys and games. The fact that people tend to want to protect their children from engaging with 'difficult' or controversial subjects underlines the unexceptional normality of racism when it has taken such a form. Take, for example, the toy rifle sold in the 1920s by US retailer Sears and Roebuck, which included for target practice, alongside game animals like elephants and bison, representations of Native Americans ('cardboard Indians') (see Barton and Somerville, 2012: 54). Shocking from a contemporary perspective, the 1920s toy rifle can be read as an index of dominant attitudes that survived further into the twentieth century than we might at first imagine. Commenting on the ubiquity of 'cowboys and Indians' in US popular culture until at least the 1970s, Michael Yellow Bird suggests that generations of American boys – among them presidents, politicians, judges and teachers – will have 'killed a lot of Indians during their boyhood war games believing it was the right thing to do' (Yellow Bird, 2004: 43). The evidence of such games provides a useful counterpoint to attempts to rewrite American history in more accommodating terms, and helps to demonstrate one of the ways in which colonial attitudes may survive and perpetuate themselves.[18]

It is not only in the context of American society that 'cowboys and Indians' has a cultural resonance. The global spread of US popular culture meant that such games had a transnational appeal. When my dad was growing up in an almost entirely white small town in Britain in the 1950s and 60s, he would regularly go to the cinema ('the pictures') on a Saturday morning, to watch the genre of film called the Western. This US cultural import, then already half a century old, told stories about the taming of the 'Wild West'. Depicting the romantic frontier struggle of heroic cowboys in a hostile landscape, Westerns crystallized an American mythology. They provided:

> an imaginative form which purveyed the experience, the thrill and exhilaration, of the exercise of enterprise. It is in the visceral qualities of the Western – surging through the land, galloping about on horseback, chases, the intensity and skill of fighting, exciting and jubilant music, stunning landscapes – that enterprise and imperialism have had their most undeliberated, powerful appeal.
>
> (Dyer, 1997: 33)

One of the fascinating things about the raw glamour of Westerns as they would have fed into my dad's games of cowboys and Indians is the social and geographical distance involved: the imaginative play of hundreds of thousands of prepubescent urban Britons was structured by historical stories set in rural nineteenth-century America, featuring encounters with racialized others for whom that audience would have had few, if any, points of comparison or association. A lack of reference points might be said, from one perspective, to consolidate the fantasy status of that play. Westerns share many features with the longstanding form of the quest narrative. As such their significance can be understood as an archetypal one: presenting an idealized fantasy model of white male domination and control over nature, law and foreign others.[19]

From another perspective still, the allure of 'cowboys and Indians' can be said to present a different set of pleasures that complicate the simpler readings of this game as straightforwardly involved in the re-enactment and reinforcement of imperial and colonial discourse. Though the cowboy may provide the primary locus of identification – even for non-white audiences (Yellow Bird, 2004: 39–42) – the figure of the 'red Indian' as represented in the genre of the Western is not always simply a cipher for 'the enemy'. While, as Sharon Wall notes in her study of white Canadian campers 'playing Indian' in the first half of the twentieth century, such engagements had little to do with 'honouring' or 'accurately portraying' Aboriginal tradition (Wall, 2005: 514), neither can they be understood only as a mode of cultural diminishment. Fascination with the mediated artefacts of 'Indian' culture –

peace pipes, totem poles, smoke signals, teepees, feathered headdresses and all the rest of it – alongside ideas about living in proximity to and in sympathy with 'nature', meant that representations of Native Americans have for a long time symbolized the appeal 'of alternative forms of community, belonging and pseudo-spiritual experience in an increasingly secular society' (ibid.: 518). The visceral qualities of the Western were not the sole property of the cowboy, and the game of 'cowboys and Indians' could provide a symbolic escape from whiteness, a contrastive experience and an alternative set of reference points to the cultural coordinates of post-war secular Western modernity (for more on this, see Bonnett, 2000, Chapter 4; 2006). It is no coincidence that many kids like my dad who grew up with Westerns embraced in adolescence a hippy culture where the exploration of alternative ways of living, thinking and experiencing the world would (through music, drugs, fashion, craft, environmentalist and peace politics and so on) draw heavily on the still-resonant childhood iconography of the 'red Indian'.

The figure of the 'red Indian', as experienced by children through Westerns and TV shows, toys and dressing-up clothes, and consolidated through imaginative play, thereby provided a considerable cultural resource that not only told stories about cultural difference but became a medium through which to think and act differently. Ideas about 'red Indians', developed and invested with meaning during a formative period of young lives, played a part in structuring the world-view of several generations of people in America, Europe and beyond. The racial politics of 'cowboys and Indians' are therefore not specific to the North American context that they reference, and neither are they contained within one particular time. 'Red Indians' can accordingly be read as a kind of barometer of changing attitudes to and investments in ideas about race and cultural difference. By the time we get to the end of the twentieth century, the 'red Indian' has been subject to a considerable degree of criticism and scrutiny, from the films known as 'revisionist Westerns' to a more general sensitivity or carefulness about representing difference: in the mid-1990s, for example, the UK ecosocialist youth organization the Woodcraft Folk dropped the Native American-inspired cry of 'how' from their ceremonies on the basis that it betrayed a lack of respect for other cultures (Nott, 2013). At the same time, the iconography of the 'red Indian', now renamed 'Native American', continues to be fed by the proliferation of ethnically branded commodities – the commodification of culture as intellectual property – that have become an important resource in the development of contemporary Native American culture (Comaroff and Comaroff, 2009: Chapter 4).

The figures represented on the cover of this book, made by German company Playmobil and sold to international consumers as 'Native American Warriors' as part of a 'Western' themed collection (other collections include 'Pirates', 'Knights', 'Dragons' and 'Future Planet'), accordingly bear a complicated legacy that prompts a range of questions that have no easy answers. Do figures like these present to contemporary children a primer in triumphant Western imperialism, or does their reproduction of an idea of Native American culture provide a platform for its contestation? Is it a problem that these figures were designed and manufactured in Germany, or does an insistence on the 'authenticity' of design and construction lead to an essentialization of Native American culture? Is it less a question of 'origin' and more a question of economics – is it a problem that people of Native American heritage do not share directly in the profits derived from this product, or does an economic frame provide a limited interpretation of cultural value? In the sense that the purchase of toys is a way for adults to recall or replay their own memories of childhood, is the purchase of such commodities by white parents or older relatives part of a nostalgia for their own twentieth-century childhood fantasies of white Western superiority, or do they symbolize their own continued investment, fascination and identification with a strong iconography of cultural difference? Does the reproduction of a profoundly historical version of Native American identity serve to consign it as belonging to another time and place, or does the rendering of the 'peace pipe' (calumet) in injection-moulded plastic draw that identity into the present? Do these toys offer contemporary Native Americans an opportunity to develop positive narratives of cultural history that resist the 'manifest destiny' of Euro-American colonization, does their containment within the genre of the Western preclude such resignification, or do contemporary Native Americans 'secretly wish we were more like the Indians in the movies' (Smith, 2009: 6)? Like the 'declared object of colonialism' discussed by Katrina Schlunke, the Native American figurine serves as the locus of a wide range of contesting meanings that 'confirm colonialism but also repudiate it, resist it and continue beyond it' (Schlunke, 2013: 18). The cultural productiveness that such objects channel overflows any particular meanings that might be imposed on them, and demonstrates that childhood games play a critical part in the cultural politics of race.

Though this complexity makes it impossible to decide and secure, once and for all, the racial meanings of 'cowboys and Indians', it is as I have already suggested certainly the case that there is today an increased carefulness or sensitivity towards representing cultural difference. While some of the first Playmobil figurines from 1974 were sold as 'Indians', their contemporary branding as 'Native Americans' indicates a changing language of racial reference. In other contexts, the Indian/Native American has slipped from popular-cultural view: though Woody the cowboy is the main protagonist of the Disney/Pixar *Toy Story* (1995), and is accompanied in its sequels by Jessie the Cowgirl, there are (as far as I can tell) no depictions of or references to Indians or Native Americans in any of the *Toy Story* movies. This is despite the fact that *Toy Story 2* features 'Woody's Roundup', a fictional 1950s TV show that provides Woody with a media back-story, and which is otherwise replete with a wide range of Western clichés. The centrality of Woody to *Toy Story* encourages us to read the absent Indians in terms of the franchise's nostalgia for a mid-twentieth-century version of American heroism that has since been displaced. According to evil gold prospector Stinky Pete in *Toy Story 2*, 'Woody's Roundup' was apparently cancelled when audiences turned from Westerns to Sci-Fi – '[o]nce the astronauts went up, children only wanted to play with space toys' (Animation Archive, 2013). This is a dislocation that echoes Andy's initial substitution of Buzz Lightyear for Woody as his favourite toy. *Toy Story* thus holds onto the model of the cowboy as the archetypal Western hero, but is a heroism that is symbolically located in America's past; it is both desired and explicitly recognized as old-fashioned and therefore in some sense unattainable.[20] Though 'Indians' are arguably an integral part of the Western genre that Woody embodies, their representation in the film would put into question Woody's unambiguous moral standing and thereby reveal the degree to which he symbolizes and is sustained by a nostalgic fantasy of white America. While Woody the Western hero shouldn't exist, he does, and because he exists, 'Indians' cannot. Though in some respects this rather neat solution to the otherwise disruptive nature of Native Americans means that the *Toy Story* franchise cannot therefore be charged with racial stereotype, it might be suggested that their symbolic erasure to avoid this charge is a troubling response to political struggles over representation.

Representing diversity on Cbeebies

While an increasing awareness of the politics of race in children's popular culture can lead, as with *Toy Story*, to its careful avoidance, this isn't of course the only creative strategy available. Besides a widespread moral argument, media institutions have not been slow to recognize the business case for representations of diversity. Sarah Banet-Weiser demonstrates how the animation show *Dora the Explorer*, on US 'diversity channel' Nickelodeon, draws on Latin-American themes in such a way that registers Dora's racial difference (she has dark skin, brown eyes and speaks Spanish), but which does not pin her down as belonging to any specific Latin American culture. This 'strategy of being racially specific but ethnically nonspecific', is used as a way 'to appeal to increasingly diverse and segmented audiences without alienating specific groups' (Banet-Weiser, 2007: 220, 214). The depiction of linguistic and racialized diversity fills a gap in a diverse global marketplace not only for parents of children with some kind of connection to Latin America, but also for wider audiences who derive value from that diversity. It is accordingly now not unusual to see non-white characters on children's television, particularly on channels run by public sector broadcasters, where they might be said to play a dual role – giving non-white children the opportunity to identify with representations of cultural difference (by diversifying representation), and by giving 'majority' audiences exposure to a culturally mixed mediascape (by representing diversity).

The recent output of Cbeebies, the preschool channel of British public sector broadcaster the British Broadcasting Corporation (BBC) provides a number of examples of this, and I want to focus for a while on the show *Waybuloo* (2009–present). According to one of its producers, the landscape of *Waybuloo* intentionally has 'a generic anywhere-world type of feel. It's a land that any kid could find just around the corner, in any country' (Rushton, 2009). Thus designed to appeal to global audiences with international sales and merchandising, each episode of *Waybuloo* features children from an intentionally 'diverse range of ethnic backgrounds' (ibid.). Despite this sense of using diversity as a way of maximizing audiences and revenue, *Waybuloo* makes some determinedly specific cultural references. It is set in a Japanese-style garden, and assembles a range of recognizably Oriental elements (bamboo buildings with pitched eaves, wind chimes, paper screens, Japanese Maples). Waybuloo's oriental influence is used as a resource as well as a context, for the show centres on the practice of 'yogo', a kind of children's yoga, which is practiced by the Piplings, its four central computer-generated characters. Within the narrative of Waybuloo, yogo has a strong emotional or spiritual dimension, an aspect of the show that is made clear in this programme information:

> When a Pipling is truly happy, does something good or makes another feel better, they achieve Buloo – a warm feeling of emotional harmony that is experienced as floating. A hug or a helping hand results in a small moment of Buloo. When children, Piplings and viewers co-operate, everyone achieves a shared moment of discovery or happiness, then Buloo is experienced as euphoric dancing, spinning and floating above the treetops and amongst the clouds.
>
> (BBC, 2009)

Oriental influences are a conduit in *Waybuloo* for this kind of eclectic, new-age style spirituality. Cultural difference serves as a resource that shapes the action within the show. Though *Waybuloo* derives its context and its themes from elements of Eastern culture, drawing on what might be thought of as a standardly clichéd repertoire of Oriental motifs, it would be over-simplistic to read this simply as the product of a monodirectional Western stereotyping, for its version of Oriental culture is a hybrid one. As cutsey wide-eyed creatures reminiscent of characters in the traditions of manga and anime, the Piplings certainly reference Japanese culture,[21] but as is widely recognized (though not without contestation) manga and anime are themselves strongly influenced by Western representational conventions. Thus *Waybuloo* is a Western (British-Canadian) cultural product that draws on ideas about the East influenced by Japanese visual culture which has in turn been influenced by Western comics and animation. There is a certain free-floatingness of referents here that helps us to recognize that cultural influence and appropriation is not a one-directional process: *Waybuloo* is in certain respects a transcultural production, where 'Eastern' qualities are not fixed by the social-geographical boundaries of the East, but are phenomena of global culture diversely called upon to signify certain ideas – in this case about the Zen-inspired relationship between the physical body and metaphysical contentment. There is no sense in trying to pin down exactly who might be 'borrowing' what from whom here because the diversity of influences do not lend themselves to the discovery of origins: a practice like yoga is a complexly hybrid cultural practice with transnational influences that links Indian antiquity to contemporary children's media culture picking up influences in places as diverse as China, Japan and Southern California. Like other examples of racial consumption though, yoga retains a symbolic attachment to south and east Asia, it doesn't 'belong' to anybody (despite the best efforts of the Indian government to assert a kind of 'ownership' (see Burke, 2010)). Certainly, *Waybuloo* might be involved in consolidating negative Western stereotypes of Eastern or Oriental culture, but it would be very unimaginative to think that this is the only thing it might do. To its Western audiences, it might stand as a model of otherness that could facilitate subsequent engagements with other non-Western cultural forms, or encourage forms of spiritual self-transformation that reject Judeo-Christian models (the show's unchristian spirituality is certainly the focus of many of its online critics).[22] The central point here is that manifestations of cultural difference in children's media are, as I have argued in relation to other examples, not necessarily fixed onto individual bodies but employed as a creative resource to tell particular stories and explore certain themes. Ideas about cultural authenticity – Japaneseness or Easternness – are important here, but they are always to a large extent fictional in the sense that they cannot be traced back to a point of cultural origin. It is the *perceived* rather than literal foreignness of cultural difference that provides it with a critical, reflective or transformative power.

Being black when you're green or blue

Over the following pages, I want to return to the question of how children's media self-consciously engage with the theme of representational diversity. While some productions employ codes of language, accent and gesture to express cultural identity (Disney movies are, for example, full of racialized crows, cats, dogs, monkeys and crabs (Byrne and McQuillan, 1999: Chapter 5)), TV shows for the youngest of preschool audiences, like *Waybuloo*, will often make lighter use of the anchoring power of language and mimetic cultural reference, adopting instead a less naturalistic aesthetic when it comes to characterization. This leads to some intriguing representational strategies, for as other human characteristics fall away, a number of shows concertedly hold on to phenotype – the visual markers of racial difference – as the only available signifiers of race. In the highly successful 1990s BBC show *Teletubbies* (1997–2001), the eponymous creatures are given subtly different coloured faces. Two of them, Tinky Winky and Po, share a pinky-cream skin tone; Laa Laa's is slightly darker, while the character called Dipsy has a brown face. Beyond its determined fantasy-play elements, *Teletubbies* accordingly encourages a kind of racial realism in its depiction of a miniature diverse 'society' where non-white characters live alongside a 'white' majority. This reading of racial realism is encouraged by the fact that the actor who wore the Dipsy costume, John Simmit, is of Cuban-Jamaican heritage. Is it simply coincidental that the 'black' teletubby is played by a black actor, or was Simmitt's casting deliberate? If deliberate, was this because it was thought inappropriate for a white actor to play a 'black' character (a distasteful echo of minstrelry), or because he would thereby bring particular characteristics to his performance, an interpretation perhaps encouraged by Dipsy's characterization on the programme's official website which arguably draws on some well-worn racial characterizations in its description of him as 'groovy' and 'super cool on the dancefloor' (*Teletubbies* website, 2013)?[23]

The trope of representational diversity is of continuing importance in children's TV, and a more recent Cbeebies show like *Nina and the Neurons* (2007–present) adheres to a set of similar conventions. While the five computer-generated characters are intended to represent sensory neurons – that is, nerve cells – with the properties of touch, hearing, sight, taste and smell, they are also anthropomorphized representations. Like the *Teletubbies'* Dipsy, one of their number, the sight neuron Luke, is racialized as black. While the neurons each have matching-coloured 'skin' and clothes, it is not coincidental that among green, pink, purple and blue neurons, Luke is given a racially mimetic light-brown colour. This reference to skin tone combines with eye colour in mimicry of a conventional phenotypal marker of race: while the other neurons have green, blue and purple eyes, Luke's are brown in colour. Though the neurons do not have hair but 'neuron dendrites' (the branches that transmit signals between neural cells), Luke's dendrites are 'designed to resemble dreadlocks' (BBC Scotland, 2013). This insistent racial referencing carries over, too, into Luke's characterization: again like Dipsy, Luke does not break with stereotype, and is described on a BBC webpage as 'laid back and relaxed' and 'very cool!' (BBC, 2013). The search for an actor to voice Luke was informed by the requirement to 'perform an Afro-Caribbean voice' (BBC Scotland, 2013), though the casting of the British Sierra-Leonean actor Patrice Naiambana in this role suggests that a degree of slippage has taken place between race (as describing Luke and Naiambana's shared blackness) and ethnicity (as the British-African actor mimics an African-Caribbean accent). Taken separately it is difficult not to read Luke and Dipsy – as surely is intended – as positive representations of racial difference. In combination, the relentless one-dimensionality of racial characterization, and the operation of an implicit representational code whereby African-Caribbean characters almost always invariably come to stand in for 'diversity', highlight some of the restrictions involved in the depiction of race in children's media culture.

Waybuloo also adheres to a kind of racial realism. The main characters in *Waybuloo*, the Piplings, are four anthropomorphized creatures: a rabbit, a bear, a monkey and a cat. In *Waybuloo*, eye colour and facial skin tone work together to designate race: while the lighter-skinned De Li, Yojojo and Lau Lau all have blue or green eyes, the darker-faced Nok Tok's eyes are brown in colour. The Piplings do not give us much else to go on in terms of accent or gesture, and we do not necessarily need to read them in terms of race, though these phenotypical factors clearly encourage us to do so. The marking of *Teletubbies*' Dipsy, *Nina and the Neurons*' Luke and *Waybuloo*'s Nok Tok as 'racial minorities' is as a result most probably an intentional strategy on the part of programme makers who are aware of the criticism that the absence of racial marking does not prevent media texts being read in racial terms: without the explicit figuration of difference, characters will be implicitly understood as white. To prevent this from happening, there is a determined insistence on the embodiment of racial realism in the face of an imaginative move away from other human elements.

Figure 6.1 Waybuloo. © The Foundation TV Productions Limited/Decode/Blue Entertainment 2014

In the case of *Nina and the Neurons*, Luke's ethnic/racial difference is part of an intentional strategy 'to represent our diverse audience' (BBC Scotland, 2013).

Race is not the only element that is insisted on in this fashion. As well as being phenotypically indexed to race, the characters in *Waybuloo* and *Nina and the Neurons* are also made to embody their gender identity. The female Piplings Lau Lau and De Li are rendered in the unambiguously feminized colours of lilac and pink, and the female neurons are likewise coloured pink and purple. The male Piplings Yoyojo and Nok Tok are coloured in a strong orange and blue, while the male Neurons are brown, green and blue. It appears that precisely because fantasy provides an abstraction from naturalistic convention there is an effort here to anchor aspects of human identity that otherwise risk being dissipated or dissolved. As I have just suggested, these shows' insistence on race may emerge from the perceived need to signify 'diversity' in an unambiguous way, but the resolute focus on gender norms through the conventions of colour-coding reminds us that such anchoring practices can be coercive too. Perhaps it is more generally the case that the move away from representational naturalism itself produces this insistence on certain identity markers, and it is precisely because of the central importance of race and gender to our understanding and interpretation of cultural texts that children's shows reference them both in such a strong fashion.

Bestial metonymy

There is certainly an argument to suggest that rather than think about a fantasy world like *Waybuloo* as a departure from social realities, it remains strongly tied up with them (the imagination does not, after all, operate outside of culture). Creative work in a less naturalistic realm, precisely because of its distance from 'reality', is, we might suggest, increasingly susceptible to being shaped by ways of thinking that would not be so readily admitted or embraced in a more naturalistic context (this is the basic psychoanalytic insight into the operation of fantasy). A media text like *Waybuloo* can accordingly make more apparent certain symbolic connections that would in more naturalistic contexts remain more carefully hidden. Take, for example, the relationship between gender and species in the show. While, from a zoological perspective, it is of course absurd to think of animal species as gendered, there nevertheless remains on a symbolic level a degree of meaning in the assignation of gender roles: Lau Lau and De Li, the female Piplings, are respectively a rabbit and a cat, while Yojojo and Nok Tok, the male Piplings, are a monkey and a bear. There is, clearly, an obvious association here that links femininity to domesticity via animals that we tend to think of as small, cuddly pets, and which links masculinity to animals that we conventionally regard as larger, wild and dangerous.

Gender identity is thus embodied in *Waybuloo* not just in terms of colour and dress, but is by the same associational logic mapped onto animal species too. Though all these associations are technically arbitrary (of course there isn't 'really' anything that connects bears and blue to maleness or pink and rabbits to femaleness), the Piplings' body colour and designated animal species both draw on longstanding and dominant cultural codes about gender that have shaped their representation. In turn, the show provides an educational modelling of those cultural codes, as a 'training programme' (Halberstam, 2011: 27) in gender normativity for *Waybuloo*'s preschool viewers.

The example of gender demonstrates how representational practice in *Waybuloo* is shaped by underlying cultural conventions that infer human meanings from animal sources. While gender is strictly speaking a property of humans rather than animals, it nevertheless saturates representations of animal life (see Mills, 2013). In other words, we can ostensibly be talking about animals when actually we're talking about people, because animals become a proxy for human characteristics (this is the basis for the critique of anthropomorphism: we do not treat animals like our pets as animals because we're forever trying to turn them into versions of ourselves). It is this same symbolic logic that consolidates the operation of race in *Waybuloo*'s characterization. Nok Tok's maleness, his blackness and his species identity as a bear are, in other words, interrelated, in just the same way that De Li's femaleness, whiteness and species identity as a rabbit are. Though the reasons are complex, it is not entirely coincidental that in the community of a rabbit, a cat, a bear and a monkey, the 'black' character turns out to be the bear, because the assignation of racial identity is shaped in part by the aforementioned relationship between femininity and domesticity, which in turn genders racial difference as masculine and 'wild'. Contemporary sensitivities towards explicitly racist historical representations mean that the non-white Pipling cannot possibly be a brown-faced, brown-eyed monkey, ergo Nok Tok is a bear.

Like the operation of gender in *Waybuloo*, what's significant here is the way in which the visual language of race can operate beyond its specific embodiment in racialized groups and individuals. The language of race, dispersed in culture, can come to be expressed or articulated through the representation of animal species just as readily as in human form. There is some crossover here between the practice of anthropomorphism (giving animals human characteristics) and that of zoomorphism (giving humans animal characteristics). Animal life comes to be understood in human terms, and human life comes to be understood in animal terms. If, as I have suggested, race is a key mechanism through which we understand, interpret and make sense of the world *and* is at the same time for various reasons disavowed, rejected and diminished as peripheral and insignificant, it is quite likely that race will have a particular tendency to irrupt in places where it is not explicitly marked or acknowledged. Even if we try to edit race out (on the basis, say, of the belief that it has no place in childhood), it will often find a way to creep back in.

The toy brand Sylvanian Families (manufactured since 1985 by the Japanese company Epoch, and sold as 'Calico Critters' in the US) is, like *Waybuloo*, a transcultural product, in this case a Japanese fantasy about an historically vague bucholic West, sold to international audiences. It also provides an example of the way in which ideas about race come to be expressed in terms not of difference within a single species but, as in *Waybuloo*, of difference across species. Sylvanian Families organizes its poseable flocked products into heterosexual 'families' of species-specific groupings, such as rabbits, hedgehogs, bears and mice. Parents, grandparents and children within families have the same features and colouration, and as a result Sylvanian Families places a stress on infra-species similarity. As such, it's possible to read Sylvanian Families as a model of a heteronormative multicultural social formation where difference – the species difference of particular families – reinforces the internal homogeneity of each family group. There is no evidence of hybridity and intermixture in Sylvanian families, and to read the brand in racial terms is to give credence to the logic of racial incommensurability. The self-evidence of species difference hereby informs and consolidates an idea of insurmountable human distinction: the ridiculousness of mixing together a dog and a cat (it doesn't happen in 'real life') makes this impossible for the Sylvanian Families too. And yet this tendency towards internal homogeneity on an animal model is contradicted by the inherent anthropomorphic sociality of the Sylvanian Families. The families share a human-like community and interact at grocers and cake shops, hospitals and markets, nurseries and hotels. The Sylvanian Families represent a shared community that is highly diverse and at the same time strongly and irretrievably striated, where difference is exhibited and yet contained within the simultaneous boundary of family/species. This is a multiculturalism without the possibility of miscegenation, where everybody is contained within their equivalent differences.[24]

This reading through a racial lens of the formal qualities of the Sylvanian Families product does not mean that the children who play with it will necessarily buy into its separate-but-equal model of multicultural community (for a discussion of a diversity of consuming practices in relation to Sylvanian Families, see for example Houlton and Short, 1995). Though what consumers do with any product can't be determined by its designers and manufacturers, it cannot be denied that Sylvanian Families provide a model of practice, and insofar as the brand encourages us to read the animals as human (they live in society, drive cars and go to school), it is not altogether improbable to think that their ostensibly animal characteristics (species difference) might signify, in human terms, as racial difference. As such, it's worth thinking critically about what toys like this tell us about the kind of relationships we should have with one another within and across the apparent boundaries of race.

Africans and monkeys

An example like the Sylvanian Families suggests that the stuff of children's culture is necessarily involved in the production and reproduction of race. Given the extent to which racial meanings are denied or unacknowledged in this location, it can be particularly interesting to think about how an otherwise universally rejected racism might be given some succour at the ambiguous interface of zoomorphism and anthropomorphism. Take the familiar racist trope that associates monkeys with people of African heritage. This should most obviously be read in terms of the legacy of scientific racism – the evolutionary association of non-whites with 'lesser' species. But it could also be argued that the way in which children's cultural forms invariably anthropomorphize monkeys as children (messing about, monkeying around) draws too on a developmental logic, for while the monkey – and in scientific racism, the African – figure as an earlier stage in the human species, the child is conceived as an earlier stage in the development of a single human organism. It is arguable that the widespread association in the culture of childhood between monkeys and children draws implicitly on both of these associations, simultaneously developing ideas about cognitive, physical and developmental capacities from the conceptual vocabularies of race, infancy and animal life. A perspective like this gives us wider opportunities to think about how race might be involved in our understanding of the different states or stages of what it is to be a human being.

But perhaps one of the reasons for the resilience of racist monkey jokes is not the residual irruption of scientific racism per se, but rather the persistent way in which we map together ideas about racial 'origin' and the 'natural' location of animal species like monkeys. A strong association is already there, in other words, between African people and monkeys because of the 'common sense' that reads them as inhabiting the same geographical space. The near-ubiquitous presence of the banana in children's monkey literature, for example, serves to cement this link between identity and geography, so that even when a monkey loses some of the other signifiers of place, the banana continues to make that connection back to a point of origin. This same tendency can be seen, for example, in the Sylvanian Families 'Around the World' series, where animals are chosen and dressed to represent particular nationalities (a Brazilian Rabbit wears a carnival costume; a British dog wears a busby; a Spanish cat wears a flamenco dress). Or consider the iPad app Dr Panda's Restaurant, which simulates cooking processes for preschool children. Though Dr Panda teaches an Americanized version of international cuisine, her/his restaurant has an upstairs room done up with Chinese lanterns where chopsticks are laid out and where 'oriental' music

Figure 6.2 'African Village' at Manor House Wildlife Park

plays. These are perhaps trivial and rather unexceptional examples, but they clearly demonstrate a continual slippage in children's toys and media between animals and humans that are thought to occupy the same geographical space. In doing so, the criteria used to understand and interpret animals come to be applied to ideas about human culture, and vice versa.

This is a tendency that is perhaps reinforced by contemporary zoos, those places where we take children to experience animals at first hand.[25] I'm thinking here particularly of the way in which contemporary zoos place increasing emphasis on communicating ideas about 'natural' habitats. Although zoos are necessarily involved in quite a radical decontextualization of animals from their 'nature', the welfare of 'wild' animals remains associated with the mimicry of that nature. Zoos therefore call on a theatrical repertoire of place to reinforce these symbolic associations. The 'African Village' at the Manor House Wildlife Park, near Tenby in south Wales, is typical of the way in which the simulation of natural habitat is shored up through the intimation of human life: the village's straw-roofed 'African' huts thereby provide anthropological references that help to geographically position its inhabitants (in this case including lemurs, meerkats and tortoises), against the more immediate evidence of Pembrokeshire's northern maritime climate. The creation of 'enriched environments' for animals is accompanied by a discourse of cultural enrichment, as in this text from the Manor House website: 'African culture is rich and diverse – the beauty of African Villages, set in strikingly colourful landscapes, and the traditional lifestyle of their inhabitants is often the envy of us in the Western World' (Manor House Wildlife Park, 2013).

While zoos are ostensibly 'about' animals, they facilitate imaginative journeys like the one suggested here in human culture. They show us how those ideas about cultural difference are always produced through associations with non-human elements like landscape, flora and fauna. The human and the non-human bring one another into being, giving meaning to one another and in doing so making each other mutually intelligible. Rather than base our anti-racism on the humanist separation of human and animal, and in doing so implicitly maintain 'the pejorative metaphorics that animal alterity provides', it is well worth considering what we might gain from breaking down this binary in an affirmation of human animality (Pearson, 2013: 8). When all humans are animals too, it becomes harder for racism to hive off some humans as less-than-human.

In this chapter I have suggested that the evidence of children's toys, games and media can provide us with some critical insights into the ways in which our ideas about race can be informed by practices that do not at first glance have anything to do with it. Rather than being a race-free zone, the objects, images and representations of childhood constitute an arena where racial knowledge is developed and performed. As such, attention to the stuff of childhood can provide us with some interesting ways of thinking about where ideas about race come from, and how they get reproduced. Race is, again, not the product of some kind of unmediated encounter between ostensibly different groups of people, but is rather a way of understanding the world we live in and our own place within it. In the next chapter I want to explore in some more detail the relationship touched on here between race and nature, focusing on the domestic garden as a space of intersection between ideas about the environment and human belonging.

Chapter 7

Animals and plants

Natural gardening and non-native species

What has race got to do with plants and animals? At first glance, the very idea of understanding these in terms of race might seem odd – even a bit silly. Race is a category we use to understand human life, so surely plants and animals, by definition, have nothing to do with it? A Yorkshire Terrier might chase an Afghan Hound, but it's not being racist is it?

The answer to this question is that, no, of course it's not. And yet while it is true that, as a social category, it is theoretically invalid to project human ideas about race directly onto plants and animals, this does not mean that plants and animals do not get caught up in raced practices of human meaning-making. As I have suggested throughout this book, it is very limiting to think that the ideas we have about race are simply restricted to groups and individuals we regard as explicitly 'raced'. The meanings of race are distributed far more widely than that, and it is only by understanding the extent of these meanings that we can begin to get to grips with the profound ways in which race shapes our everyday lives, in ways that we do not always expect or anticipate.

This basic recognition prompts us to start looking for race in some unusual spaces and places – locations that haven't necessarily been recognized as having anything to do with race at all. This chapter's focus on animals and plants asks us to do just this. This chapter will begin by considering how environmental discussions of native and non-native species in Britain draw on and in turn inform discourses of human identity and belonging. Exploring the way in which the definition of native species is based on an idea of extra- or pre-human nature, I go on to consider the relationship between humans and the environment in discourses of 'natural gardening', demonstrating a close interrelationship here between ideas about nature, nativity and national belonging, and in particular the way in which the defence and encouragement of nature roots the natural gardener in a specifically national context. I then turn to the red squirrel as an 'iconic' native species, and show how nature serves as a particularly rich site for the expression of ideas about race and national identity. It is the ultimate fantasy of nationalism to become coextensive with nature, and – unexpectedly perhaps –

contemporary environmentalist-inspired discourses are one place in which this claim is underpinned. I conclude this chapter by outlining some of the ways in which a rethinking of the relationship between nature and culture might provide some useful resources for challenging still-dominant discourses of race and nation. If, as Kate Soper suggests, ' "nature" is a concept through which humanity thinks its difference and specificity' (in Moore *et al.*, 2003: 1), then reworkings of nature indicate some possibilities for challenging racially exclusive territorial claims, though as I will suggest a cosmopolitan ecology does not necessarily mitigate continuing nationalist exclusions.

Non-native species

The GB Non-Native Species Secretariat is a governmental organization set up in 2006 and funded mainly by DEFRA, the Department for Environment, Food and Rural Affairs. The development of the Non-Native Species Secretariat demonstrates the British state's increasing involvement in thinking about, surveying, reporting and managing what are called 'non-native species'. As the term suggests, non-native species are plants and animals that are understood to be living outside of their 'natural' distribution (I will explore what this means in more detail below), and are equivalent to what are in other contexts known as 'alien', 'introduced' or 'exotic' species. Most non-native species are considered to have a benign effect on native ecosystems, or to be welcome on the basis of their contribution to 'economic and social wellbeing' and 'Britain's natural heritage' (DEFRA, 2008: 2). Some, however, are categorized as 'invasive', and it is with these that the GB Non-Native Species Secretariat is primarily concerned. Invasive non-native species are defined for an audience of stakeholders and the general public as having the 'ability to spread causing damage to the environment, our health, and the way we live' (NNSS, 2010: 7).

While most invasive non-native species are not widely recognized by the public (ibid.: 16), a few species have attained a degree of notoriety. The grey squirrel, for example, is the most well-known non-native species, crowding out and supplanting the weaker, native, red squirrel, which is now largely confined to Scotland, Anglesea and parts of northern England. Another well-known non-native species is the Japanese knotweed, a herbaceous perennial native to eastern Asia, which can overtake other herbaceous species and whose root system is capable of damaging human-made structures, breaking through concrete and undermining foundations. Japanese knotweed presents a very dramatic example of the rhetoric that can circulate around invasive non-native species: take, for example, the website of the private company Japanese Knotweed Solutions (jksl.com), which includes on its front page a timelapse-like animation of the plant erupting through paving slabs, accompanied by these sentences, which follow one another in quick succession:

THIS COUNTRY HAS BEEN INVADED BY A HOSTILE ENEMY
AN ALIEN CONQUERING NEW TERRITORY EVERYDAY
AN ALIEN LEAVING DAMAGE AND DESTRUCTION IN ITS WAKE
AN ALIEN WHICH IT IS ALMOST IMPOSSIBLE TO DESTROY
THE ALIEN IS JAPANESE KNOTWEED AND WE ARE THE SOLUTION

Clearly, one doesn't have to be an expert in the subtleties of discourse analysis to make a connection between this rhetoric of enemy invasion and a popular anti-immigrant language of race. The website's repetitive layering of capitalized hyperbole references the conventions of a cinema trailer, drawing us into the genres of horror or sci-fi, themselves so often used to treat the subject of race in symbolic form (Nama, 2008; Sardar and Cubitt, 2002). The national designation 'Japanese' also facilitates the transference or sharing of meaning from one realm to another, so that the frame of race makes the horticultural legible (and dramatic). As Figure 7.1 shows, this kind of strategy is not confined to the commercial sector. The GB Non-Native Species Secretariat themselves draw on the theatrics of invasion in the production of what their website describes as a 'wanted poster' for this eastern European 'killer shrimp'. The shrimp itself, in reality only a few millimetres across, is blown up to the size of a small dog, and depicted as if on the verge of some kind of martial arts-style attack.

I use these examples of the cross-fertilization of meanings not to support some cheap point about 'racism against plants and crustaceans' (although actually there is as I will show more mileage in this than one might first expect), but rather to demonstrate the discursive fluidity between flora, fauna and human life. Japanese knotweed and killer shrimps are not alone in inspiring this kind of rhetoric, and the frequent recourse to the description of alien immigrant invasions, weak native hosts bedevilled by larger, more aggressive, rapidly reproducing foreign parasites, stable sustainable environments upset and jeopardized by Malthusian overpopulations, and so on, suggests that there is something more significant at work here than simply a glib analogy between otherwise incommensurable objects. While we may try to keep them apart, discourses of race, plant and animal life have a sometimes unnerving habit of getting mixed up with one another. When the GB Non Native Species Secretariat's strategic communications plan includes in its risk assessment the possibility of 'accusations of "racism"' (NNSS, 2010: 27), this fact is on some level acknowledged. It should be noted that I'm not so much interested here in questioning the veracity of the claims made about the damaging potential of invasive non-native species (though I am aware that such a critique is not entirely inappropriate either). My interest here resides in the racial language of nativity and non-nativity, and in particular the ways in which ideas about the non-human shape and inform conceptions of human culture.

KILLER SHRIMP
Dikerogammarus villosus

What is it?

A highly invasive non-native species that has spread from the Ponto-Caspian Region of Eastern Europe. As a voracious predator it kills a range of native species, including young fish, and significantly alters ecosystems.

© Michel Grabowski

How do you identify it?

➤ Usually found among hard surfaces in water bodies where Zebra Mussels are present.

➤ Key distinguishing feature is the cone shaped protrusions on the tail.

➤ Can be large (up to 30mm) but often 10-20mm.

➤ May have a striped pattern (but sometimes not).

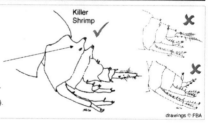

Killer Shrimp ✓ ✗ ✗

drawings © FBA

STOP THE SPREAD
INVASIVE AQUATIC SPECIES
CHECK·CLEAN·DRY

Help stop the spread of this species by:

➤ Inspecting and cleaning boats and kit before and after use.
➤ Inspecting and cleaning launching trailers.
➤ Draining all bilge water from boats before leaving the site.
➤ Disinfecting angling kit before and after use.
➤ Making sure no lake water is taken away with your kit.
➤ Not transferring bait between water bodies.

If you find this species, please send a photo and details of the sighting to:

alert_nonnative@ceh.ac.uk

www.nonnativespecies.org/alerts/killershrimp

Figure 7.1 Killer shrimp 'wanted' poster. © The GB Non-native Species Secretariat

Interestingly, the slippage between human and non-human categories occurs too in the language of those who seek to question the xenophobic bent of some environmentalist discourses. Take Judy Ling Wong, Honorary President of the Black Environmental Network, who notes how the practices of Rhododendron control ('Rhodo-bashing') 'resonate too closely to Paki bashing' (Ling Wong, 2001: 2). It is hard not to read Ling Wong's defence of the idea that 'all plants have a place in the right setting' and that 'In many settings indigenous plants and animals, garden plants, introduced plants and animals all support each other, provide shelter and feed on each other' (ibid.: 4) as inflected by anthropocentric (that is, human-centred) concerns. Likewise, when Mark Cocker in the *Guardian* suggests that 'we should avoid a blanket condemnation of "aliens" and take each case – each non-native species – on its individual merits' (Cocker, 2013), it is difficult not to read this argument through the frame of an ethics of human migration. Similarly, when Syd Singer, writing in the *Hawaii Reporter*, argues that '[f]ear of species from other ecosystems' represents a 'bio-xenophobia' that goes 'against the Aloha spirit' (Singer, 2013), his words are clearly shaped by recognition of a correspondence between the human and the non-human. Whatever the merits of their arguments, I would suggest that the connections being made here by Ling Wong, Cocker and Singer are not entirely inappropriate ones. Rather than assert some kind of scientific distinction between categories, I want to explore in what follows the profound interrelationship between human and non-human, nature and culture, and its implications for the politics of race.

To do this, I first want to return to the distinction that gets made between native and non-native species. The website of the Non-Native Species Secretariat provides a useful working definition for the British context:

> When the Ice Age ended over 10,000 years ago the ice that covered most of Britain retreated northwards. Following behind this retreating ice were waves of plants and animals that slowly colonised Britain as conditions warmed up. These plants and animals got to Britain under their own steam as there was still a connection (the land bridge) attaching us to the European mainland.
>
> However as the ice melted so sea levels rose and the connection was flooded. This effectively stopped any more colonisation by species that couldn't cross the water. All these plants and animals – the ones that established themselves in Britain naturally – are called native species.
>
> Some species (like elk and lemmings) died out naturally as the climate continued to warm up. Other species such as wolves and beavers were eradicated by man only relatively recently – in the last few hundred years.

Man first arrived in Britain about 8,000 years ago and virtually all new land animals and plants that have become established since this date have been brought here by man. These are all non-native species.

(NNSS, 2013)

The difference, in short, between native and non-native is set roughly eight millennia in the past, when the melting of the last ice age finally submerged the landmass known as Doggerland to create what is now the southern part of the North sea, cutting off the landmass we now call the British Isles from the landmass we now call Europe. The difference between native and non-native is, in other words, measured in geological time, the end of the last ice age serving as a kind of foundational ecological moment, a moment that is interestingly coincidental with the creation of what will, thousands of years later, be thought of as the territorial integrity of the political entity we call Great Britain. There are all sorts of anomalies and incongruities when we sort out the plant and animal world in these terms: we find that species that we often think of as native – like beech or sycamore trees, or rabbits, or crocuses – become lined up among the Japanese knotweeds and killer shrimps as, technically, non-native or alien species. As the Non-Native Species Secretariat website makes clear, the distinction between native and non-native is, of course, an anthropogenic one: it centres on the role that humans have played, whether intentionally or inadvertently, in shaping the environment of the British Isles.

Though definitions like this seem at face value quite reasonable – we're used to thinking about 'nature' as something outside of or distinct from human influence, it is worth thinking critically about the implications of this. What does it mean to think about the environment without people? Why are we invested, with the concept of native species, in giving a particular status to plants and animals 'as if' the enormous impact of human beings over millennia was undone or put to one side? From this perspective, nativity seems a rather abstract or technical concept. Certainly, it potentially has a legitimate place in the science of ecology, where it is meaningful to think about ecosystems in terms of very long temporal scales, but outside of this you might not think it would be considered particularly relevant or meaningful. A niche interest perhaps, equivalent to something like the hypothetical elaborations of counterfactual history, where we might as a thought experiment imagine what the world would be like without human beings. Though it can be argued that the concept of native species remains of use in the sense that it helps us to make a distinction between species and so tackle some of the genuine problems presented by those that get labelled as invasive (I'm not denying the possibility that in some circumstances these exist), there is a lot more that gets caught up with this idea of nature without people that's worth exploring in more detail. While in one sense this notion seems invested in keeping apart the codefining categories of (human) culture and (non-human) nature, in other respects and perhaps unexpectedly it underlines their inseparability. To explore this problematic, I would like to think about the ways in which, in a very everyday sense, approaches to animal and plant life are shaped by this same idea of an extra- or pre-human nature.

Natural gardening

Popular ideas about 'the environment' and behaving in 'environmentally friendly' ways will often draw on conceptions of an 'original' or 'unspoiled' nature. As such, they tend to be invested in an idea of ecosystems that are untouched, or at least uncorrupted, by human influence. Negative human influences like industrial pollution can be tackled and, according to narratives of ecological restitution, be 'returned' or 'given back' to nature. The conflict that tends to be assumed here between natural and human life, inflected as it is by the idea that human beings are temporary interlopers in otherwise non-human environments, is clearly informed by the idea of nature without people. The fact that this peopleless conception of nature is so central to dominant ways in which we conceptualize the environment makes it very interesting to think about the hold it has on consuming practices that are intended to have some kind of 'environmentally friendly' outcome.

Take, for example, a recent trend towards what sometimes gets called 'natural gardening', a term used to organize a variety of ideas about gardening in a more environmentally-friendly fashion. The British-based web company The Natural Gardener is typical of this trend, selling a range of garden products – including handmade 'traditional' wooden tools – with a crudely hand-drawn logo that reads 'natures natural cycle' and the strapline 'Putting something back – Organic, Sustainable, Biodegradable – Just growing Natures way' [sic] (The Natural Gardener, 2013). Text on the website of 'Sustainable Living Supplies' web company Wiggly Wigglers asserts that 'native British species are best', enjoining its customers to '[r]emember, when you plant native British species, you are working with nature, everything goes together and the result suddenly becomes much more than just the sum of its parts' (Wiggly Wigglers, 2013). The website of the garden designer Alice Bowe states that she 'firmly believes in working with nature, not against it' (Bowe, 2012), while gardening broadcaster and writer Bob Flowerdew entreaties his readers to 'go further – not just co-operating with nature but enticing her' (Flowerdew, 2003: 7).

The ethos of natural gardening brings to mind a memorable passage in Zygmunt Bauman's *Modernity and the Holocaust*, where Bauman employs a gardening analogy to suggest how the holocaust can be understood as an expression of 'the spirit of modernity' (Bauman, 1989: 93). In Bauman's reading, the gardener's attention to design and the rationality of distinguishing between plants and weeds has its social correlative in the orderly rationalization of genocidal extermination (ibid.: 91). Bauman's analogy depends for its success on our unquestioned acceptance of this simple logic of selection, distinction and spatial management. To Bauman's gardener, nature and culture are codefining opposites, and artificial order is maintained only on the basis of the destruction of and defence against the natural world.

The contemporary trend towards natural gardening appears to depart from Bauman's model. Natural gardening deliberately refuses to police the binary distinction between plant and weed, and indeed seeks to redefine the meaning of both. The fascistic exterminationist logic of Bauman's modernist horticulture has apparently given way to the inclusive tolerance of the natural garden. And yet things are not quite as harmonious as they may at first seem. While Bauman is concerned with gardening as a metaphor for the social, I'm interested here in thinking about the social as a metaphor for gardening, or, more properly, about what kinds of social relationships are implicated in or worked up through practices of natural gardening, and how these might go on to inform wider cultural orientations in twenty-first century Britain. In the sense that gardening exemplifies a conception of human-ecosystem relations, I want to consider how the way people think about their gardens may predispose them to certain ideas about the character of human populations, and in particular those that come to be organized by the idea of race.

Coffee table gardening books provide a useful resource to show some of the ways that the advocates of natural gardening establish a relationship between people and the 'natural' environment. Though actually quite nuanced in his treatment of nature's 'natural' credentials, Noël Kingsbury picks up the common theme of ecological desire in *Natural Garden Style*:

> The widespread and very popular desire to be 'natural' in the garden is part and parcel of a much greater sense of unease about the way the human race has been managing (or mismanaging) the world; it is also about optimism and hope: that as private individuals we can do something in our own personal spaces to create a more harmonious relationship with the natural world.
>
> (Kingsbury, 2009: 8)

In *Home Grown*, Hugh Fearnley-Whittingstall similarly entreat us 'to remember that we are all part of the same natural system as the animals, insects, plants and land that surrounds us' (Soil Association, 2009: 8), while Alys Fowler suggests in *The Edible Garden* that 'in order to know your place, and where you belong, you need to understand you are part of an ecosystem far bigger than your needs, and that you are responsible for its health and must be a good caretaker' (Fowler, 2010: 12).

In these and similar accounts of natural gardening, a strong relationship is set up between gardener and environment. The natural gardener, according to these writers, facilitates a return to nature, reinstating a harmony put out of joint by the activities of humans (remember: the definition of native plants and animals is a definition of nature without people in it). The natural gardener plays an important role in this refounding or rediscovery of nature, albeit 'a refined and tidied-up version' (Kingsbury, 2009: 8). While the natural gardener refuses Bauman's modernist distinction between plants and weeds, she or he is still the gardener, still the agent of change and bearer of horticultural law. In the case of natural gardening, the gardener is the arbiter of nativeness and non-nativeness, desirous of a nature outside of or 'before' human influence, on the basis that it is somehow more right, more appropriate, more fitting, more 'natural'. There is a strong parallel here with my discussion of 'ethnically appropriate' consumption in Chapter 3. Though strictly speaking the subject position of the natural gardener is an oxymoronic impossibility (for the very definition of the thing that is desired excludes the gardener's presence), an ecological imperative to mitigate the damaging effects of humans on the environment provides the natural gardener with an important role as the custodian or steward of nature: nature cannot survive without her or his personal intervention.

There is therefore a sense in which, by serving as the conduit or medium of nature, some of nature's 'naturalness' rubs off on the natural gardener. To make some sense of this relationship between the native garden and the gardener, it is helpful to introduce the nation as a third term that serves to articulate them together. On account of it being both a social term to describe a human population *and* a geographical or territorial term to describe a space or landscape, the idea of the nation helps to organize the relationship between human and non-human populations that exist within it. In the British case, I want to suggest that there is a specific affinity between native plant and animal species and the group of people for whom the possession or ownership of the nation has, in the popular imagination, invariably defaulted: that is, white British people. Now of course there is no sense in which white people really are the 'natural' inhabitants of Britain – that idea is simply a myth of racial nationalism built on a selective and simplifying reading of human history. It does, however, remain the case that dominant discourses of national belonging repeatedly and unfailingly position white people in this custodial or proprietorial role over the nation (see Hage, 1998). There is, in other words, a structural homology between the positioning of white people and native species as originary and rightful occupants of the national space. Both natural gardening discourse and dominant forms of race discourse symbolically position the non-white and non-native as outsiders, immigrant interlopers interrupting the (for all intents and purposes) ahistorical stasis of natural and native population. With nature under threat from outside forces, natural gardening, as a practice for managing the national space and deciding what does and does not belong within it, cements the 'native' status of the gardener. Native plants serve as a compass of belonging, providing, according to natural gardener Caroline Foley 'a sense of place in an increasingly homogenized world' (Foley, 2009: 10). It is not particularly surprising to learn that the genocidal project of the Nazis was accompanied by a horticultural attempt 'to give the German people its characteristic garden and to help guard it from unwholesome alien influences' by establishing with native plants the 'blood-and-soil-rooted' garden (Pollan, 1994). While it would be unhelpfully reductive to suggest that all forms of natural gardening are motivated by the explicit racism of the Nazi model, there nevertheless remains a relationship between nationalism and the championing of native species. It's not that opposition to non-native species is necessarily motivated by racism – a question that Daniel Simbeloff (2003) ties himself in knots about – but rather that there exists a degree of conceptual interplay between 'nature', 'nation' and 'native', assisted in part by the derivation of all three terms from the same Latin root (Peretti, 2010: 29).

Restoring Squirrel Nutkin

To explore in some more detail the close relationship between these terms, it is useful to return to the red squirrel, described by the Non-Native Species Secretariat as an 'iconic native species' (NNSS, 2010). The iconicity of the red squirrel relates of course to its status in the national cultural imaginary, where, as I suggested in Chapter 6, childhood features as a particularly important site of cultural reproduction. From Beatrix Potter's Squirrel Nutkin to Axel Scheffler's contemporary northern European woodscapes, the red squirrel – and its reputed threat from the non-native grey squirrel, is an instance of where a native species has come to symbolize and stand in for a range of issues and ideas related to British national identity, and is a particularly clear example of a more general shift or slippage between 'native' and 'British', a slippage that links together ahistorical ideas of nature with racialized narratives of political community and rightful ownership. When Prince Charles writes for the Red Squirrel Survival Trust that he 'cannot bear the thought that one day they might disappear for ever, driven out by the relentless Northern march of the greys' (RSST, 2012), the language of a military campaign clearly signals that his rhetoric is operating within a national, rather than ecological framework. Charles's defence of the red's 'rightful place in this country' likewise helps to collapse together nature and nation. When Eric Robson of BBC Radio 4's Gardener's Question Time writes that '[t]ogether we'll get Squirrel Nutkin back where he belongs!' (RSST, 2013), he draws on the same rhetorical resources of natural gardening discourse by positing a necessary relationship between the agents of change, in this case the supporters of the Trust, and the rightful restitution of the red rodent. The act of 'getting back' produces not only a return to nature, but confers a special connection between that nature and those who have restored it. Elsewhere on the imaginative fringes of a far right discussion forum, the fate of the red squirrel is linked to 'the extinction of the indigenous White race in Britain' (Stormfront, 2011), while the 'red squirrel' blog compares 'non indigenous grays [sic]' to 'fast breeding hostile Islamists whose barbaric practices will one day sweep our heritage and culture away' (quoted in Engage, 2009). Peter Coates catalogues a long history of British nationalism informing debate around the red and grey squirrel, from the ways in which the red squirrel, a 'charming, feisty little chap', has been associated with a 'truly British' character to the widespread rumour, circulating in the early twentieth century, that the grey male 'castrated its red counterpart by biting off its testicles' (Coates, 2011: 44, 43). These kind of fantasies circulating around the red squirrel reveal the gendered psychodynamics of national identification, and provide an illustration of the ways in which cultural feelings of sexual inadequacy, themselves produced through a nature-culture binary that associates the triumphs of British civilization with a declining generative capacity, are then in turn projected onto poor old 'British' nature. The red squirrel suffers from the malaise of a cultural identity preoccupied with the worry that it might be firing blanks.

We might suggest that the red squirrel serves as a particularly rich symbol for nationalist identification precisely because, like other native species, it functions as a stolidly material referent of nationalism. It gives shape and substance to what is otherwise a profoundly abstract category of social identity. This is, as discussed throughout this book, another example of racial metonymy, where in this case 'nature' and the qualities of nature are substituted for the culture or society that makes a claim of possession over it. Nature is hereby territorialized as land or landscape. The projection of 'culture' onto 'nature' provides a highly comprehensible way of imagining a territory to be defended, as in times of war (vide Prince Charles above). Territory then becomes, as Kevin Grove suggests, 'a strategy bound up in securing identity and subjectivity' (Grove, 2009: 212). But as the red squirrel clearly demonstrates, this is not a transferral that takes place in only one direction, because it facilitates a kind of feedback where 'nature' in turn works on and gives shape to 'culture'. A changing environment, by its intimate association with the human, simultaneously indicates a change in the character of the nation. Threats to British native species trigger an associative threat to the integrity of the British nation, an integrity produced through the articulation of nature, nation and a native, proprietorial whiteness. When Divya Toila-Kelly suggests, after Raymond Williams, that 'racialized taxonomies of "native" and "non-native" [. . .] are deeply embedded in cultural geographies of Britain and the structures of feeling around national identity' (Toila-Kelly, 2008: 286), she correctly highlights the sense in which the two-way flow of meaning between nation and nature occurs through an aesthetic and affective (emotional) register. The otherwise dry and abstract husk of nationalist ideology is given importance (and arguably attains its significance) through an experiential 'filling up' with the stuff of a nationalized nature, helping to form the 'instinctive responses' of national identification (James, 1963: 152). The way in which an idea of 'original' nature becomes coextensive with an idea of the 'original' nation should come as no surprise to any student of nationalism, who will know that the nationalism is so often about concealing the arbitrariness of its claim in the smoke and mirrors of eternity; the idea that 'things have always been this way'.

Because of the sense in which nations 'are imagined not only as social categories [but also] entities possessing a geographic and historical "reality" that somehow exceeds their human membership' (Wallwork and Dixon, 2004: 22), nature and the defence of nature provide particularly potent sites for the expression of racialized ideas around national identity and belonging. Because these expressions work through racial metonymy, they are far less prone to the charge of racism, and it might be suggested that some of the more complex, ambivalent, denied or disavowed feelings around race and national identity find their expression not in statements about racial difference per se but in the language of nature, place and landscape.[26] The expressive material of 'postcolonial melancholia' (Gilroy, 2004) may just as readily be formed from woods, fields, meadows and pasture as the more familiar substance of national sports teams, political speeches and newspaper columns. Indeed, attempts to account for the resilience of dominant discourses of race might benefit from turning our critical gaze away from the usual suspects to explore instead some of these less examined regions of the cultural life of nations. It is, perhaps, the subterranean elemental stuff of nature that, like nutrient-rich compost, particularly enriches and gives succour to nationalist imaginaries.[27] Could it be, then, that our parks and gardens are under-recognized barricades in the struggle for racial equality? Could the garden centre equip us with some of the tools by which we might start to consume race differently?

Doing nature differently

Is the desire that motivates the planting of a 'native' hedge necessarily a xenophobic one? Does the uprooting of 'foreign' species betray an unacknowledged taste for 'ethnic cleansing'? Not necessarily. You don't have to be white to engage in practices of nature conservation and natural gardening and neither do you have to sign up to the idea that white people have some kind of priority membership of the British nation. And yet, insofar as a phenomenon like natural gardening expresses a desire to maintain geographically demarcated distinctions in so-called 'original' biological populations, it retains a symbolic affinity with ideas of racial purity and socio-geographies of separate development. If we add to this the ways in which ideas about British nature have drawn on a stock of symbols that – like the red squirrel – are evocative elements of nationalist imaginaries, it is hard to contest that there is a close relationship between discourses of race and nature. In exploring something of 'the busy traffic of nature and culture that articulates racial formations' (Moore *et al.*, 2003: 1; Haraway, 1989), this chapter has been invested less in making the charge of racism and more with exploring the ways in which race, nation, nature and nativity work on and in doing so help to constitute one another. As such, it has suggested that we should remain alert to the possibilities and tendencies operating in their complex interrelationship, rather than think of these terms as discrete and incommensurable.

One reason to maintain critical attention in this area is a marked tendency in some environmentalist discourses to deploy a nostalgic or otherwise backward-looking vision of nature. The association of ecological sustainability with some kind of 'return' feeds off and is sustained by fictive ideas about the ideal or appropriate character of and relationship between human and non-human populations, as explored in this chapter.[28] Visions of pristine or untouched nature are fed by an 'ecological nostalgia for an imagined past' (Gandy in Grove, 2009: 214). While the 'environmental crisis often provokes a feeling of hopelessness and a longing to "turn back the clock"' (Peretti, 2010: 34), it is important that such an idea of nature gets disentangled from racialized mythologies of 'native' or 'original' human populations. Simply because nationalism tends to define itself in an ahistorical language, falsely making its territorial claims on nationalized natures as if for all time, it does not mean we should take such claims at face value. These ideas can be challenged not just by foregrounding the overextending contingency of the nationalist claim, but also through the recognition that it is simply inaccurate to think about nature as static and immobile, 'inactive and at home' (Clark, 2002: 107). By recognizing that nature may be as 'cosmopolitan' as humans are, ecologists have developed an understanding of environmental dynamism that does not recognize a qualitative difference between 'native' and 'non-native' species (ibid.: 113). The idea of nature and the distinction between native and non-native hereby become social phenomena, such that the 'problem' of invasive species is best understood not as a concern of biology but 'as an expression of human culture' (McNeely, 2011: 19).

One interesting element of this denaturalization of nature and the recognition of the inseparable interconnections between human and non-human life – neatly summed up in Donna Haraway's coinage of 'naturecultures' (Haraway, 2003) – is the way in which it requires us to reconsider the way in which the boundaries between nature and culture have been informed by colonial thinking. Built on the opposition of a 'civilized' West to a 'primitive' outside, Western colonialism is predicated on a nature/culture binary. Challenging work on contemporary postcolonies refuses the temptation to advance a critique of Western colonialism by assigning to 'Western' plant and animal species a non-native (or 'alien') status, partly because to do so would reinforce the supposed 'natural' status of the non-West and so consolidate that binary. Instead, scholars recognize that precolonial landcapes were just as shaped by human influence as postcolonial or Western contexts (Clark, 2002: 114; Ross, 1994: 32). As Franklin Ginn suggests, the 'idea of a pre-colonial baseline' empties nature 'of any politics or history' and 'substitutes an origin myth for learning to live with historically layered relations – relations that have made "us" who we are today' (Ginn, 2008: 348). Such insights can be usefully brought to bear on the contemporary British context: if all 'nature' everywhere is anthropogenic then we are always in truth dealing with naturecultures. There is no original nature, just versions of nature. While the idea of a 'return' to nature is not an option, there *is* always a possibility of other, alternative relationships between human beings and nature. While naturecultures can, as Ginn suggests, be 'eco-nationalist', they do not have to be. This recognition of the possibility of understanding the relationship between human and non-human species in such a way that refuses an idea of purity or a point of origin 'could help us understand and manage the damaged, cosmopolitan nature that our global, cosmopolitan society has helped produce' (Peretti, 2010: 34). New versions of nature that depart from dominant articulations of race, nation and nativity then have the potential to feed back and produce new understandings of human culture (see, for example, Mortiner-Sandilands and Erickson, 2010).

Jean and John Comaroff strike a cautionary note here in their exploration of the role of 'alien' species in the consolidation of national identity in post-apartheid South Africa. While citizens within contemporary nation-states are able to imagine nationhood in pluralist terms – 'in such a way as to embrace the ineluctability of internal difference' – the limits of that difference are still definitively marked by autochthony, that is, the nation-state as a place of birth or origin (Comaroff and Comaroff, 2001: 635). In other words, the fact that contemporary forms of national identity are culturally diverse does not prevent a policing of who does and does not belong on the grounds of origin. While in the Comaroffs' argument non-native species are, unlike South Africa's cosmopolitan human population, considered to be alien even if they have settled and reproduce themselves within the nation-state (their eradication becoming a focus for contemporary practices of nation-building), it is surely possible for non-native species to be assimilated into the national fold. Indeed, this seems precisely to have been what has happened in the British context where non-natives like chestnut trees and most rose varieties persist on the basis that they do not appear to trouble – and in certain cases actively contribute to – national ecological imaginaries. The large populations of rose-ringed parakeets that live in the parks and gardens of south London have likewise been 'adopted' by admiring Londoners who arguably see in them some animal reflection of the capital's cultural pluralism (aided by the racial flavour of the urban myths that attribute their presence to an act of avian psychedelia by Jimi Hendrix, or an open door on the set of *The African Queen* (Coward, 2010)). The Chief Executive of the London Wildlife Trust advances a cosmopolitan ecology when he characterizes that the bird is 'as British as curry' (Gray, 2009). Yet in a similar way to which multiculturalism can become a resource for the rejuvination of nationalist exclusions (Pitcher, 2009), it is surely the case that the explicit diversity of London's ecology does not prevent its parakeets from the possibility of simultaneously symbolizing the limits of 'native' hospitality, as is the implicit logic of all discourses of tolerance: this far, but no more.

While, in other words, it is clearly possible to imagine nature beyond the binary of native and non-native, this does not mean that cosmopolitan versions of nature will not on some level still reproduce the terms of national belonging, on the basis of a reworked idea of autochthony. Anxieties over climate change are fed by the sense in which it is impossible to tell whether the presence of new species has an anthropogenic cause, even if these species appear to have arrived under their own steam. Under these conditions, recourse to an idea of nature is tempting, whether in the form of natural gardening or a more augmented form of cosmopolitan ecology. The implicit horizon of the nation here as the container of nature means that such visions of nature are always capable of informing – and being informed by – an exclusionary politics of race. A rethinking of nature in the context of climate change offers a potential solution here, because it allows us to conceive of the entire planet as anthropogenic; it allows us to recognize that there is no nature without culture – that naturecultures are all we have, and that nobody and nothing, human and inhuman, has a claim to territorial belonging that trumps that of anyone or anything else. In the context of tightening immigration regimes, this rethinking can prevent nature being lined up as a resource to bolster still-dominant discourses of race and nation, and help to produce new ways of thinking about the complex interrelationships between human and non-human life.

Chapter 8

Stories about race
Knowledge and form

Stories and form

One reason race is such a significant part of our cultures is that we're continually telling stories about it. Race fascinates; it grabs the attention. It provides a content that seems perpetually novel and is a subject of which audiences never seem to tire. The objective of this chapter is to look at a range of stories about race, paying some attention to the different forms or genres in which these stories get told. It begins with the 'controversies' about racism produced through the interaction of old and new media, where news stories get worked up through microblogging sites like Twitter. It moves on to explore stories about race in popular fiction, before considering, with reference to the reception and discussion of the Islamophobic 'film trailer' *Innocence of Muslims*, how stories about race can work to express ideas about cultural conflict. Finally, this chapter considers the stories about race that get produced in the US HBO television show *The Wire*, and in particular the way that the show fulfils a demand for 'progressive' representation that produces a racial politics that is far more ambiguous than may at first appear.

The point about all these different forms – new and old media, popular literature, YouTube videos and TV – is that they all generate different stories about race, and collectively contribute a diverse and complex texture to race in contemporary culture. They each facilitate different engagements with the subject, while at the same time informing, crossing over, and interacting with one another. As this book has repeatedly suggested, cultural artefacts, objects and practices simultaneously reproduce existing ideas about race and are necessarily involved in the transformation and reshaping of those ideas. Take, for example, the phenomenon of race online. Counter to predictions that race (along with other forms of identity such as gender and sexuality) might be transcended or left behind in online contexts, the actual experience of race in our fledgling internet culture suggests something altogether different. As even early theorists of the internet recognized, the 'meat world' of race necessarily intrudes online, as our identity performances occur through 'sign systems [we] already inhabit'

(Gonzáles, 2000: 43–4); at the same time, the characteristics of online culture feed back into and give new shape to experiences and practices of race. In this sense, there is nothing special about the experience of race online: online contexts do the same thing as other cultural forms in hosting, expressing, and shaping the meanings of race, contributing their own particular characteristics and giving their own 'flavour'. Different forms organize racial meanings in different ways, presenting alternative ways of experiencing time, space, proximity, affinity, emotions, identity and so on, telling different stories about race in the context of our protean cultures.

This chapter's brief overview of some stories about race and the cultural forms in which they are produced also sets out to consider these stories as the locus or repository of racial knowledge. Stories get produced and consumed, in other words, as part of the processes by which we develop our understanding of and orientation to questions of race. They give us the opportunity to figure stuff out, and to make issues and problems legible. It is in relation to stories about race that we develop aspects of our self-image, our moral framework in respect of race and racism, and our relationship to racialized others. Stories about race help us to sort, filter and assign meaning to differences; defining the extent of our hospitality, excitement or fear. Stories about race express our want for racial distance, proximity or familiarity, they help us find a place we are happy to occupy in our complex multicultural social formations. Stories provide meaningful opportunities for us to live and work through race, forms of engagement that are as real and significant to the formation of our beliefs and understanding as the space of face-to-face relationships and encounters. Of course these stories all have a political dimension, and they can just as easily be deceptive and self-serving as liberating and enlightening. Racial knowledge does not have to be 'true' to give us a means of navigating through culture. And so it is by attending to the grammar of racial desire – the things we want race to 'do' and 'be' in the stories we tell about it – that we can learn quite a lot about the characteristics of the racial present.[29]

Online stories: new media anti-racism

Discussing the significance of mediation in shaping dominant discourses of race, Lentin and Titley usefully borrow from Michel De Certeau the idea of a 'recited society' as defined by media stories and their continuous citation and recitation (in Lentin and Titley, 2011: 21). De Certeau's description captures something of the specific temporality of mediated race discourse, which has of course been subject to a considerable acceleration in the twenty-first century where 24-hour rolling news feeds off and into new media. One particularly visible kind of recited race discourse in contemporary Britain circulates around unguarded racist speech acts caught on camera: public figures say the wrong thing; reality TV stars let their guard down; 'civilians' riding public transport under the influence of drink, drugs or medication get papped by phone wielding citizen journalists and posted to YouTube. Interactive social media feeds into and feeds off these transmitted nuggets of racist excess, drawing in a diverse range of actors – from celebrities to politicians to internet activists – to the latest race spectacular. The particular forms these stories take, the mechanisms of their recitation, and the broader context of their reception all play a part in shaping what is meant by racism in British popular culture, which, as Paul Gilroy has suggested, has become narrowly focused on individual conduct and its subsequent legal prosecution (Gilroy, 2012: 381).

Consider, from among the hundreds of possible examples, the characteristics of the minor media controversy in 2012 where a British footballer retweeted a message which referred to another British footballer as a 'choc ice' (see Ogden, 2012). Twitter's 140 character limit provides a marvellously decontextualizing format that delivers forms of super-haiku hate speech with the clarity and economy required of TweetDeck journalism. The microblogging site provided a space where a story could be stoked, and where football clubs and professional bodies – sensitive to the very real legacies of football racism – were drawn in to a now-familiar narrative of prohibitive fines and public apologies. Such new mediated recitations tame race discourse, wrestling its complexity into a set of verboten words and phrases. One of the most important elements of this chef-like process of reduction and concentration is the stripping away of all ambiguity: because it's the words themselves that come to matter rather than the contexts in which they are used, what might under other circumstances be interpreted as part of a debate involving two footballers (both of British Caribbean heritage) regarding different ways of exhibiting black identity at the top of British football becomes a matter of revealing and policing bad words, a disinfecting of race discourse. As I have already implied, this process is one that is repeated again and again in contemporary culture, and while the particular culprits are usually new each time (these kind of stories comprise a litany of first offences), their recursivity bears some thinking about. Why do we keep telling them? What does it tell us about the cultures we live in that we are drawn to such repetitions?

There is more at work here than the triumph of clarity, bureaucracy and legal judgment in the politics of race. These elements facilitate a convenient packaging of racism in quickly and easily accessible examples, but the reason this packaging happens in the first place is, I want to suggest, because it fulfils a cultural demand for the popular expression of anti-racism. What is of central importance here is the way that new media have become host to the public performance of anti-racism, the procedural activity of identifying and admonishing bad words and, by association, the 'bad' people who intentionally or involuntarily let them slip their lips. A sense of new media producers and consumers as involved in some kind of collective practice is key here, the idea that there is a community of people who collectively go through the stages of outrage, condemnation and reproval (depending on the details of the story, this might figure as a national community, an international one, or a more specialized demographic within the blogosphere). This is not to say that the pursuit of racism in such contexts is pointless, or that it is not often motivated by admirable sentiments. Rather, that what is primarily important about this kind of new media anti-racism is that it fulfils the important social need to 'be' anti-racist, to express anti-racism, to be seen to be anti-racist. A theatre of mass disapproval is fed by anti-racist desire, and in some cases we might say that racism only exists in such fora to be rejected and condemned (see Pitcher, 2007). Like the policing of other practices that have come to stand as markers of the betrayal of contemporary moral standards (sexual violence, paedophilia), what's going on here is arguably often more to do with shoring up the moral probity of the shocked and outraged than a serious engagement with the culture that produces those practices in the first place. And so, while endemic and established racisms continue to adversely shape the life chances of racialized minorities in Britain across the realms of education, employment, law, criminal justice and so on, these excited recitations of hate speech retain a monopoly on dominant understandings of what racism means today.

It is useful, therefore, to point to the limitations of this kind of new media anti-racism: its inability to get to grips with the subtleties and complexities of race, and to deal with forms of racism that cannot be rendered in 140 characters or interpreted within the given parameters of moral expression. As Zoe Williams puts it '[n]obody ever made the world fair by hitting "like" on YouTube' (Williams, 2011). A focus on the 'correct' use of language, for example, takes us into a territory whereby definitions of linguistic facility may be inflected by the hidden scapegoating codes of class or cultural specificity (consider, in relation to this, the demotic discourse of racism as produced by a distinction between the educated and uneducated: 'she's ignorant'). In spite of such obvious criticisms, the policing of race discourse can nevertheless tell us a lot about some of the things that race has come to mean in the twenty-first century. It helps us to understand the spatial and temporal characteristics of contemporary race thinking, about 'where' race takes place, and how it happens. In particular, it is informative about popular orientations to the question of racism: while posited solutions to racism may often be weak, there is nevertheless an acknowledgement that racism exists, and that it's a problem. While the theatrics of racism's pursuit and prosecution are often overhasty, premature and self-serving, they paint a picture of a culture that is invested on some level in the idea of trying to deal with it. New media anti-racism expresses a social consensus that is dissatisfied with aspects of contemporary race culture, and though the tools used are so often woefully inadequate to the job, the desires they express are nevertheless very real.[30]

Stories in books: popular pedagogy

Popular literature is another interesting site where stories about race get told in contemporary culture. The pace is less frenetic than that of new media controversies, and while by no means free from contention, popular literature opens up a space where a very different set of concerns come to be aired and worked through. Here, I want to briefly discuss the twenty-first-century phenomenon of what might be called the popular race novel. In the British context, this might include books such as Zadie Smith's *White Teeth* (2000), Monica Ali's *Brick Lane* (2003) and Angela Levy's *Small Island* (2004), all bestselling, shortlisted or prize-winning novels by non-white female authors that centre their realist stories on the experiences of British minority cultures in the second half of the twentieth century. While I do not have the space here for a detailed engagement with the specificity of these texts and their readerships (for this, see the 'Devolving Diasporas' project (2011) which studied the engagement of reading groups with these and other 'diasporic' texts), I want to provide a basic reading of the role that books like these might play in contemporary culture. Noting the 'immensely positive' reception of *Brick Lane* by critics and reviewers, Rehana Ahmed records the tone of discovery and revelation that characterizes much of this material: to one reviewer, the novel revealed 'a rich, fresh and hidden world', taking another 'into a life and culture I knew so little about'; to another still it 'opened up a world whose contours I could recognize, but which I needed Monica Ali to make me understand' (Ahmed, 2010: 35). It seems reasonable to suggest that this orientation in the reviews of *Brick Lane* to the novel as a mechanism of knowledge and understanding describes something of the book's appeal to its wider readership. If we move away from a narrow understanding of literature as to do with the hermeneutics of great writing and consider the wider cultural contexts of their production and consumption, which includes the materials of promotion and publicity, media reports, discussion and review (Benwell *et al.*, 2011), then we are in a position to begin to think about some of the things that popular race literature might 'do' within a wider cultural formation.

Without reducing such books to the job of fulfilling a crude social function, it is worth noting both the status of the novel form itself as a tool of popular education (Barney, 1999), and that books taking race as their subject have long played a legitimate, albeit contested, role as mechanisms of compassion and understanding (Gilroy, 2010: 65). It might in this light be argued that the cross-cultural consumption of popular race literature (for by definition all bestselling books exceed the niche of a specific minority audience) represents a longstanding interest in learning about, discovering and making connections across the boundaries of race (see also Gunning, 2010: 9). I suspect that this desire to know is, in the contemporary British context, formed out of the experience of living in a multicultural society but being ill-equipped to understand in any detail the terms under which it came about.

These are not, after all, stories in which race figures as foreignness; *White Teeth*, *Brick Lane* and *Small Island* are all immigrant stories, focusing on the conflicts and accommodations that have beset first and second generation Bangladeshi and Jamaican heritage citizens in postcolonial Britain. They are, in other words, novels about race in Britain, and as such might be said to serve a purpose in 'filling in the gaps' for a readership whose formal educational experience dealt inadequately with the history of empire, decolonization and postcolonial immigration. The skill in their writing resides in the way these books build on a limited skeleton of existing race-historical reference (*Small Island*, for example, features the iconic Empire Windrush; *Brick Lane* is named after the street that is a well-known symbol of Bengali Britain; *White Teeth* features the infamous 'Rushdie affair'). Serving as a common ground of intelligibility, these elements of a recognizable history provide the novels' readers with the opportunity to teach themselves aspects of an unknown history that they feel they should know more about. Novels provide a form of pedagogy for readers in search of greater knowledge and understanding, but cater at the same time to the psychological requirement not to reveal to others an ignorance they might be embarrassed or ashamed of. It is precisely because novels present themselves as fictional that they enable this kind of concealed learning: the popular race novel is not explicitly 'about' the multicultural education on which its popularity is arguably founded.

In so doing, the novel form, just like that of the mediated microblog, gives a particular kind of shape to the knowledge it produces. With parallels to the individualization of racism in new media race discourse, novels are well equipped to communicate qualities of individual experience, and popular race fiction typically cultivates gendered sympathies and empathies with the experiences and struggles of strong female characters in adverse social conditions. As Kimberly Davis suggests of the majority white and majority female audience of Oprah Winfrey's US TV book club (where over twenty per cent of the books selected were written by African American authors), 'black' texts may facilitate forms of personal identification with fictional characters, and in doing so 'foster identification with the emotional pain and joyful triumphs of black women' (Davis, 2004: 401, 400). Against 'the predominant critical view that cross-racial sympathy is inevitably imperialistic' (ibid.: 399), Davis remains open to 'the complexity of the sympathetic emotions' in fostering 'micropolitical, intersubjective change' (ibid.: 406, 402).

As Davis recognizes, cross-racial emotional and sympathetic responses can also work in a less positive direction, reinforcing racial hierarchies of power and privilege: they can be egocentrically invested in self-satisfied benevolence, or prematurely minimize racial differences in a desire to connect with black characters 'as women' (ibid.: 407). Vron Ware's informal survey of non-fiction 'Eastern studies' flags up a further problem with the relationship between race and gender in popular writing. Books 'by women from east of Istanbul writing autobiographically' (Ware, 2006: 541), may offer educational insights into cultural difference, but their structural reliance on narrating the personal experiences of non-Western women means that such books have a tendency to reinforce Orientalist stories about Eastern patriarchy. Identification with the struggles of 'Eastern' women is accordingly at cost of a certain pathologization of non-Western cultures. As Ware suggests, such books – and even the genre of 'Eastern studies' itself – are the product of a broader cultural formation implicated in the Islamophobic geopolitics of what came to be known as the War on Terror. The knowledge that gets produced in such books about 'Eastern' women is in part dependent on (and in its turn helps to consolidate) dominant readings of repressive and sexist Islamic culture, such that women's writing becomes 'an indispensable instrument of foreign policy and international relations' (Ware, 2011: 55). The popularity of fictional and non-fictional narratives about Afghan culture post-2001 suggests not only that books are a way of understanding or processing world events, but that at the same time they also play a part in shaping wider cultural orientations to them.

Ware reminds us that the content of a particular cultural text is only part of what it 'means': we also need to be able to take into account the diverse contexts of its production and consumption. It is often the case that there is a dialogue or movement between content and context, between text and paratext, for interpretive frameworks 'internal' to a particular narrative may be repeated or mirrored 'outside' of it. As Rehana Ahmed remarks in her interpretation of *Brick Lane*, 'the binary of individual freedom versus communal/religious repression' that is present in the novel was repeated in the protests against the book and subsequent film by some groups who objected to *Brick Lane*'s portrayal of British Bangladeshis (Ahmed, 2010: 29). In a reading like this, what *Brick Lane* comes to be 'about' has rather less to do with the content of the book and more to do with the way in which the novel becomes a point of focus around which a polarized 'debate' is organized that pits the pursuit of 'artistic freedom' against those who hold to 'the commitments of social identity' (Benwell *et al.*, 2011: 99). This is, it hardly needs saying, a debate whose outcome has been decided in advance, for the refusal to give priority to artistic freedom – indeed, protestors' refusals to read the book and in doing so engage with it on literary terms – will tend to be interpreted as an expression of 'Muslim intransigence, irrationality, extremism' (ibid.: 95).

Stories about images: 'Muslims can't read media texts'

This same interpretive binary of artistic freedom versus cultural conservatism is characteristic, too, of many of the flashpoints that give life to stories about clashing civilizations and the supposed incommensurability of 'Islamic' and

'Western' values. I want to turn here to thinking about a recent example of a Muslim-baiting provocation, the YouTube-released US-produced short video (posing as the trailer for a movie that appears not to have been made) that came to be known as *Innocence of Muslims*. First uploaded in mid-2012, the video subsequently led to international protests, some of which were violent, in which people got killed (for an overview, see Al Jazeera, 2012). There is a story here that is largely shared not only by the Islamophobic producers of the video and those who protested most virulently against it, but also and most interestingly by the mainstream audiences who would otherwise seek to distance themselves from identification with either of these groups. As such, it bears some critical scrutiny. It is a story that centres on the place of images in Islamic culture, and in particular on the assumption that images are somehow understood differently by Muslims and non-Muslims.

This common assumption is rooted in an idea about representation and god, and the practice in the tradition of the Abrahamic religions – with reference to the first commandment – of the theological ban on idolatry, the worshipping of what are sometimes referred to as 'graven images' or false idols. Writing about the power of images in postmodern culture, Jean Baudrillard references the clash in Christian theology between the Iconolaters, those who used images and idols as part of their religious practice, and the Iconoclasts, who sought to destroy those idols (Baudrillard, 2001: 172). The usual way of reading the position of the Iconoclasts is that they were interested in protecting the special status of god as exceeding the capacity for human understanding. According to this interpretation, god cannot be represented because god is simply not fully comprehensible to human beings. Any representation of god falls short of god's truth, and is therefore a betrayal of god. This idea (an idea that is there too in Platonism) is certainly central to the Iconoclasts' self-image. But in Baudrillard's reading, this idea gets turned on its head. Rather than despise and deny images because of their insufficiency, Baudrillard argues that the Iconoclasts are those who accord images their actual worth, their true value, because they are able to recognize (if not fully admit) that the power of god resides in the image. The representation of god exists, in other words, to distract us from the fact that god does not exist beyond god's representation. It is not that the true existence of god is concealed by the false representation, because the idea of god itself resides in the simulation of god. According to this reading, representations do not actually conceal anything. Quite the reverse: they conjure that thing into existence.

How does this insight help us to understand *Innocence of Muslims* and its destructive legacies? First, I want to suggest we should steer clear of straightforwardly assigning the roles of Iconoclasts and Iconolaters to Muslims and non-Muslims: as it played itself out, the row over *Innocence of Muslims* was not an internal theological dispute between co-believers, but typically between representatives of a religion – Islam – and what (rather euphemistically) gets called 'secular society'. Instead, what Baudrillard's discussion helps us with is an acknowledgement of the key role of representations – of images – in the contemporary world. This is a fact that the producer of the video, playing the classic role of the *agent provocateur*, knew only too well. With very few resources (material or creative), he was able to construct a global media spectacle that inspired some tremendous political mobilizations, protests and violence. As is widely recognized, the video was released and promoted with the calculated intention to push buttons, to inflame 'the Muslim world', and lo and behold this is precisely what happened. The video was taken in certain quarters as US-Zionist propaganda, providing confirmation of Muslim victimhood and a premise for revenge, with the destructive and murderous consequences I have already noted.

While this is clearly what *Innocence of Muslims* set out to do, I'd suggest that this kind of reading is likely to fall prey to an unthinking assumption about Islamic culture that gets smuggled in through the back door, and which is all the more invidious and damaging because of it. What I'm referring to here is the way that dominant responses to the video and its aftermath, even those that charge it with a divisive Islamophobia, invest in the very same story that the video itself promotes: the idea that there is a fundamental attitudinal or conceptual distinction between 'ourselves' and the protestors, which comes to be generalized as a fundamental attitudinal or conceptual distinction between Muslims and non-Muslims.

In other words, what is ultimately the most serious and damaging outcome of the *Innocence of Muslims* affair are not the immediate and short-term protests (destructive and deadly though they undoubtedly were), but rather the way that the video rather cleverly encourages the idea among secular, liberal audiences that, because of some kind of doctrinal adherence to the first commandment, Muslims are somehow incapable of reading media texts 'properly'. Audiences who generally find the video abhorrent on account of its Islamophobia are hereby drawn into an agreement with its central Islamophobic premiss. This story about Islam and the politics of representation is one that comes up again and again – from the aforementioned excitement around the *Brick Lane* movie in 2006, the protests against the publication in the Danish newspaper *Jyllands-Posten* of cartoons of Mohammed in 2005, or further back in time to the Rushdie affair of the late 1980s. It is a story that reproduces the idea that 'we' (liberal, secular, Western) are somehow better equipped at dealing with representations, that we can recognize irony, that we can tolerate commentary and controversy, that we can quite literally take a joke. (This is, incidentally, a position that *Innocence of Muslims* actively produces if you sit down to watch it through its shoddy acting, its amateur use of bluescreen, and its farcical dubbing of calculated insult). What *Innocence of Muslims* and the discussion around it were most successful in doing was reproducing a broad cultural consensus invested in the idea that there is a fundamental, civilizational divide between Muslims and non-Muslims. Here, as usual, the actions of a violent minority of protestors are read as the expression of an essential truth about the Islamic faith. The widespread interpretation of the video and its protests feeds off and feeds into other widespread civilizational distinctions – of Western tolerance and liberty versus Eastern intolerance and suppression, of freedom of speech versus doctrinal adherence to religious diktat. The seductive idea of our own tolerance creates in its mirror image a notion of intolerant others, who are on some level patronized and pitied for the inappropriateness and excessiveness of their reaction (for more on the modalities of tolerance, see Brown, 2006).

This story about Muslims and representation should be resisted, I would argue, because it is simply and self-evidently not the case. It seems a ridiculous point to have to make, but Muslims are just as capable of reading images and interpreting texts as anybody else. Sure, depictions of Mohammed don't hang in the mosque, but Muslims are just as much a part of our image-saturated societies as non-Muslims. Muslims watch TV, go to the movies and surf the web. Muslims are just as likely as non-Muslims to have a sense of humour, to appreciate irony, to be capable of distinguishing fact from fiction, because Muslims inhabit the same cultures as the rest of us. The lives the vast majority of Muslims lead in the twenty-first century are just as image-laden, are just as in thrall to the spectacular, as everyone else's, religious or non-religious. Baudrillard's insight about the significance of images in the contemporary world does not apply differentially; despite the widespread propaganda of which *Innocence of Muslims* is a part, Muslims do not exist in a different century from the rest of us. The fact that a minority of protesting Muslims would eagerly self-identify as Iconoclasts does not demonstrate a 'truth' about Islamic culture, but rather the interdependency of Muslim-baiting Islamophobes and groups and individuals with specific political agendas of their own. For an example of the Islamic exploitation of stereotype in the production of counter-stereotype, see Tarlo (2005).

By refusing the easy and divisive distinction about Islam and representation that is deeply embedded in our contemporary culture, we are in a position to read the realm of representation as an intrinsic part of a culture that is shared by Muslims and non-Muslims alike. We can begin to recognize the power that images hold over us all, whether secular or religious, and that we are not somehow divided by fundamental ontological or cognitive differences in how we relate to or understand them. We might, to use Baudrillard's terms, say we are all alternately Iconoclasts and Iconolaters as we attempt to develop a sense of who we are and what's important to us in the context of a culture of images. We then begin to occupy a position that can think about the ethics of representation, an ethics that attributes to cultural producers a degree of responsibility for recognizing the contexts in which representations are produced and disseminated. These contexts can be anticipated, and deserve to be understood. Such a position shifts the focus of blame away from the invariably poor and under-educated individuals who were in the case of *Innocence of Muslims* typically the foot-soldiers of Iconoclastic protest, and towards those, Islamist and Islamo-phobe alike, who are invested in talking up stories about essential human difference.[31]

'Good' stories about race: 'progressive' representation and white desire

The last part of this chapter gives a reading of representation that, rather than providing a stage for racialized divide and distinction, seems on the surface to do just the opposite. Like Kimberly Davis's argument above about popular fiction's capacity for cross-racial intersubjective identification, I want to explore the sense in which stories about race appear to facilitate a kind of knowledge about racialized others that challenges and dispels prejudice. The particular media text I want to consider here is the acclaimed US HBO drama series *The Wire* (2002–8), a show that, in the estimation of the *Observer* newpaper, 'started as a cop show about drug gangs in Baltimore, and grew into an epic, shifting portrait of a city in the grip of poverty and crisis' (*Observer*, 2008). In the discussion that follows, I first want to focus on the widespread idea that the show expresses a socially informative take on the politics of race, and suggest that in fact the 'good' stories it tells might be more accurately thought of as the production of its audience's desire for 'progressive' forms of racial representation. I will then move on to consider in broader terms the idea that *The Wire* provides audiences with a 'sociological' insight into contemporary US culture, and suggest that this, too, needs to be understood in terms of a desire for knowledge of the social.[32]

As many of the show's fans agree (see, for example, Reed, 2006), what sets *The Wire* apart from the usual run of US TV cop shows is the sense in which it appears to avoid some of the genre's lazier clichés. *The Wire* seems to challenge a dominant regime of representation, particularly in respect of its depiction of race and sexuality. Resisting an unthinking recapitulation of the formulaic and caricatured, the show presents to its audience a number of ostensibly stereotype-challenging characters, and makes a concerted break with the model of compulsory heterosexuality and casual homophobia that continues to define the standard US TV repertoire of urban blackness. Characters like Omar Little, the homosexual stick-up man, can accordingly be read as a corrective to the common-sense discourse of TV racism. Omar can be thought of as a 'good' (unstereotypical) representation countering 'bad' (stereotypical) representations (see, for example, Hill Collins, 2004: 175). Omar's sexuality tells a truth about social diversity – the fact of black homosexuality – that otherwise goes suppressed and unacknowledged. In this sense Omar is pedagogic: he is an agent of truer knowledge of social reality.

Implicit in these notions of 'good' and 'truer' representation are ideas about how representations work on TV audiences. While it would be wrong to dismiss these ideas out of hand, it is important to be sceptical of imputing a function to representational practice in *The Wire* that reads 'good' cultural politics as the straightforward and unambiguous outcome of 'good' representation. Indeed, the reading I want to make of *The Wire*'s politics of representation casts doubt not only on the show's 'progressive' character but also on the notion that it is, at a minimal level, even socially informative. In order to do this, it is useful to consider the circuit of audience desire and gratification that is at work in *The Wire*.

To think about the desires of *The Wire*'s audience is to think reflexively about where a character like Omar Little comes from. As 'good' representation, as the refutation of a stereotype, I want to suggest that his origins lie not in the social reality that he is taken to embody, but rather in the yearning of *The Wire*'s audience for 'good' representation. It is not simply that Omar's transgressiveness makes him attractive to *The Wire*'s audience, but moreover that this transgressiveness is itself willed and thus effectively determined by that audience. As such, Omar can be thought of as little more than the projection of the desire of *The Wire*'s socially liberal, predominantly middle-class and predominantly white audiences troubled by 'bad' media representation (for a discussion of the show's demographics, see Bramall and Pitcher, 2013: n.3). To *The Wire*'s pay TV/DVD-box-set fanbase, Omar can be said to have a dual function as both the refutation of negative stereotype and the supposed agent of 'truer' knowledge of the social. Omar is able to assuage both the audience's guilt in respect of the politically regressive nature of 'bad' representation and, as a direct result of this, appear to manifest a better, truer, more sociologically accurate representation of contemporary black urban life.[33] Despite the naturalistic allure of *The Wire*'s 'progressive realism' (Shohat and Stam, 1994: 180), we might suggest that Omar is a bourgeois fantasy of urban blackness: his strict ethical code and his refutation of certain dominant modes of black identity make him in many respects an ideal middle-class dinner party guest. As the projection of *The Wire*'s audience's greatest desires into the text, Omar provides a mechanism for the white middle classes to feel at home in poor black Baltimore. Audiences are not easily positioned to admit the determining status of their desire for 'good' representation precisely on account of the show's supposed 'realism'. As is often the case, the realist mode brings with it a pretence of objectivity and a pose of moral neutrality that can admit to only 'true' or 'false' representations. Omar is thus read by audiences as 'true' rather than as a reflection of the desire for truth.

This naturalistic fantasy of racial truth actually reproduces some deep-rooted racial prejudices, for Omar's 'good representation' implicitly stands as a critique not only of 'bad representation' but also of 'black homophobia', that is, the 'bad black people' that are present in *The Wire*. Progressive stereotypes of 'good representation' thus beguile and distract socially liberal audiences from the extent to which *The Wire* confirms what is actually an unremittingly negative and racially problematic representation of poor black America (of sadistic, ultra-violent, homophobic heterosexuality, of animalistic anti-sociality and so on). If this reading of the fantastical figure of Omar as a kind of 'liberal white person's black person' is right, then Omar's physiognomical blackness provides the culturally necessary alibi for a racially regressive critique of unruly blacks. The murderous violence of Omar's revenge for the murder of his own boyfriend Brandon can in this light be read as a figuration of a repressed but disturbing white liberal desire to punish illiberal black homophobia.

It is not only in the realm of characterization that a show like *The Wire* can be said to convey, echo and reflect its audience's desires. One particularly interesting area to think about is how dominant readings of *The Wire* consider the show to provide a means of understanding or developing knowledge of the social. Helena Sheehan and Sheamus Sweeney (2009) make a common assessment when they argue that *The Wire*'s plots 'open into an analysis of the social-political-economic system shaping the whole. The series has demonstrated the potential of television narrative to dramatize the nature of the social order.' Such understandings of the show are reinforced by the expressed intentions of *The Wire*'s creator and head writer, David Simon. In '*The Wire* bible', a document widely available online that apparently served as the show's pitch to HBO, Simon writes that the show is not 'an exercise in realism for its own sake', but rather exists 'to serve something larger' (Simon, 2000: 3). Referencing Euripides and Eugene O'Neill, Simon makes a case for *The Wire* as the expression of 'a national existentialism'. It should, he argues, 'be judged not merely as a descendent of *Homicide* or *NYPD Blue*, but as a vehicle for making statements about the American city and even the American experiment' (ibid.: 2). Based on the claim that the show makes contemporary social life more comprehensible, these readings of *The Wire* position the show as a tool of knowledge production. As such they have much in common with a Lukácsian reading of the nineteenth-century novel as a form uniquely capable of grasping and representing the social totality (Lukács, 1978). *The Wire*'s systematic approach to its depiction of educational, media and policing institutions certainly appears to be 'an attempt to portray a whole social structure', and gives credence to an idea of Simon, as one blogger puts it, as 'the Balzac of Baltimore' (Beggs, 2008).

It is important not to take these 'sociological' claims at face value. Indeed, it can be suggested, as before, that they reveal as much about the desires of *The Wire*'s audience as any nascent social truth. *The Wire* can thus be read as a 'realist' fantasy: it doesn't describe an ideal world – its portrayal of racism and racialized inequality means that its vision is certainly not an escapist or utopian one – but rather it depicts an ideal knowledge of, or orientation to, the world. *The Wire*'s institutional approach to social conflict and its apparent engagement with the complexities of post-industrial global capitalism offers a seductively intelligible vision of social and cultural complexity, and this intelligibility is again the product of audience desire. By appearing to set out a cognitive map of contemporary social life, *The Wire* seems to confer legibility on the social, yet in truth only really reflects back its audience's yearning for social legibility. In this reading, the show is a machine for the production of epistemological gratifications, a means of conjuring a fantasy of total knowledge in the face of the postmodern disruption of its very possibility.[34] As with *The Wire*'s ultimately narcissistic politics of representation, just because something reads like, looks like (and from its creator's admission actually purports to be) a conduit for knowledge and understanding of contemporary social life, this doesn't mean it necessarily provides anything more than the simulation of that knowledge, structured and shaped by the fashions, prejudices and moralities of its audience.

One reason why this simulation of knowledge of the social might be considered problematic is that it is in many respects a backward-looking one. The social legibility that *The Wire* appears to confer is channelled through and enabled by a prelapsarian vision of US society, culture and institutions that surfaces, for example, in the residual ethics of the newsroom in series five. *The Wire*'s pessimism for the present is counterbalanced by this romanticization of an American past. This structure of redemption has in particular quite negative implications for *The Wire*'s racial politics, for while recourse to the past might figure as a solution to some of the problems of the present, it is also implicitly a return to a world beset by racial segregation and routine discrimination. Kent Ono remarks on a similar issue with the racial politics of *Mad Men* (2007–14), the AMC series set in 1960s adland. While, like *The Wire*, the show 'contains a thoughtful and thought-provoking representation of racial politics', its 'realist' maintenance of 'historical demographic segregation' and a related failure to develop non-white characters means that *Mad Men* 'reports the past from the perspective of white people' (Ono, 2013: 304–5, 315). Though *The Wire* is set in the present, its moral investments in mid-twentieth-century America suggest that it, too, is at least in part the product of a white world view.

Stories about race

This chapter has surveyed a broad and eclectic range of stories about race. The thread that ties all these stories together is the sense in which they all develop and produce varieties of racial knowledge, and in doing so provide ways by which we navigate and negotiate our contemporary cultures of race. As such, these diverse stories can all be said to express, in their own specific ways, some of the particular racial demands or needs of those cultures: the desire to exhibit anti-racism; the desire to know more about racialized others; the desire to understand racialized conflict; the desire to challenge racial stereotypes. As such, these stories provide examples of racial tropes that surface again and again. Collectively, they might be said to describe desires to register a distance from racial pasts characterized by discrimination, ignorance and prejudice. Yet they all elaborate a cultural politics of race that remains in some sense conflicted: recited condemnations of microblogged racism, like *The Wire*'s 'good' stories about race, can wind up being self-serving; feminist empathy can tip over into the generation of civilizational stories about patriarchal oppression, and the desire to defend Muslims from Islamophobia can lead to an exaggeration of differences that refuses the fact of a common cultural experience. These contradictions reveal some of the complexity of our contemporary racial formations. They show how the cultural politics of race is not a simple question of deciding whose side you're on, and that we are frequently tripped up or undone by the very thing we are trying hard to surmount or get beyond. This is of course not a reason to give up trying: while 'good intentions' in the cultural politics of race don't always produce the intended results, consideration of these 'failures' can nevertheless contribute to a greater understanding of how race works. Take, to return to the last example, a problem like Omar Little. As a 'good' representation he certainly has his problems. But the stereotype he challenges is arguably even more divisive. There is no 'answer' here because the problem isn't one that can be solved by uncovering the 'perfect' representation. There is no way of breaking the representational cycle whereby stereotype gets replaced by counter-stereotype, which in time inevitably becomes the very thing it sets out to critique. The project of telling stories about race is not one that ever ends, but thinking critically about the stories we tell can give us some clues about the other kind of stories that we might want to try telling.

Chapter 9

Conclusion

This book has explored some of the ways in which we are all of us involved in the production and reproduction of racial meanings in acts of everyday consumption. It has suggested that race is very much a part of the ordinary business of being a human being in the contemporary world. An engagement with race on the terms set out in this book undermines racial essentialisms, working against investments in race as the property of particular groups and individuals. As I have shown, racial meanings can – as everybody already knows – be divisive and destructive by elaborating harmful distinctions between groups and individuals: racial meanings can produce racisms, practices of discrimination and inequality. Yet as I have also shown, the meanings of race exceed racism. As a mechanism of desire, understanding, exploration and transformation, race is also a creative resource that we use to navigate our way through our contemporary cultures. To engage with race does not make you a racist, any more than engaging with gender makes you a sexist.

The analogy with gender is a useful one, and not only because, like race, it has historically tended to be indexed to and guaranteed by ideas about biological essence. Certainly, we can (and should) use gender to talk about inequality, but we also can (and should) use gender to talk in broader terms about the production of human differences, differences that it makes absolutely no sense to think about in terms of 'right' or 'wrong' or 'good' or 'bad'. As poststructuralist feminist theory so adeptly shows, we can (and should) also use gender to talk about challenging, redefining and reworking those differences, in the name of freer, fairer, alternative or more interesting futures. The 'end' of gender is hypothetically possible, but we only get there by 'doing' gender in gendered cultures, not through fantasy mechanisms of transcendence and overcoming. I would make precisely the same points about race: we can (and should) talk about race in critical, descriptive and transformative terms; there is no reason why we should confine ourselves only to the first of these, because in fact these terms are all implicated in and require one another.

One way that it might be useful to think about this is in relation to what is often conceived of in discussions of racism as the determining force of racial histories. Because of the resilient way in which race continues to be a part of our cultures, it is common to think about race in terms of a kind of stubborn 'weight' of history. Histories of race can be afforded a real force and agency that is used to explain race's persistence in the contemporary world. In such analyses, it is as if racial histories quantify race, turning it into a heavy object inexorably bearing down upon and patterning human culture. Race as a determining force is often present, too, in the language of 'structure' and 'institutions' that anti-racists often deploy to describe race's apparent 'depth' of cultural embeddedness, the way in which racist cultures cannot simply be changed like an individual might change their mind. These metaphors of weight and structural depth can all provide some useful ways of thinking about the cultural politics of race, but it is nevertheless important that we hold on to the fact that they *are* metaphors, and be careful that they do encourage us to think about race as an entity or phenomenon beyond human intervention.

Whether intentionally or otherwise, there is often a curious tendency to evasion in anti-racist pronouncements that, intent on stressing the seriousness and profundity of race, seem to close the subject off to thinking in any detail about how it actually gets made and remade (how, in other words, that historical weight and depth is manifested). We get a portentous sense of the importance of race, but not much of a grasp of how and why it has this status, potentially leaving us with the feeling that we probably can't do very much about it. This book has tried to make an argument that helps to fill in some of those conceptual gaps, and refuse the fatalism that can accompany such a strong sense of racial determination. I have tried in this book's examples to show some of the ways in which we are all enmeshed and invested in the production of racial meanings. Race is implicated in multiple aspects of our social and cultural lives. The metaphor of 'depth' might be better conceived as 'breadth', for as I have been arguing, race is not a 'narrow' thing (to do with just racism), but is dispersed right across the realm of human experience.

The advantage of this recognition – which is an acknowledgement that we are necessarily involved in race, but that this does not necessarily make us racists – is that it gives us an idea of how we might productively engage with the subject. From this perspective, race is no longer an inaccessible and unfathomable thing, reaching up from the depths of history to be treated with a fearful reverence. Race is something that touches and entangles us all. The cultural politics of race become an active and ongoing question of and for the present, of living relationships not dead relationships. This does not mean we can vanish racism in a utopian gesture of wishing it away, but it does mean we can examine in a more clear-sighted way the terrain of racial practice.[35] This terrain, as I have been arguing, is a complex and complicated one. It does not have the false clarity derived from counterposing racism and anti-racism as a description of race. Every single cultural reference and preference – from a choice of clothing to a taste in literature to a taste in men to the act of typing a search term into a web browser – is potentially an act of consuming race, and can be scrutinized as such. Every single cultural move potentially positions us within and contributes to the activity of racial formation. To see what race is, and what it does, we need to open our eyes to it and start looking everywhere about us, the space of our desire and pleasure as well as our responsibility. We may have arrived, at the end of this book, with a renewed orientation towards the injustices and inequalities of race, but this has only been made possible by what I would suggest is a necessary detour through a series of themes in which injustice and inequality are not necessarily the first, most obvious, or indeed most significant elements. It is a detour that helps us to understand that anti-racism is not only to do with taking a stance on some setpiece act of racism (important as this may be), but a complicated process that we all of us live through, day by day, as we go about the practice of being human beings. At a historical moment when anti-racist hegemony prompts for many the suggestion that we might have got 'beyond' race, it is useful to be reminded how racial meanings are, in truth, absolutely everywhere we look.

Notes

1 Introduction

1 The ways in which Bob Marley has lent a certain mobility to Rastafarian culture does not necessarily gain the approval of the self-appointed guardians of that culture – as made evident in the Ethio-Africa Diaspora Union Millennium Council's insistence to the US rapper Snoop Dogg that 'smoking weed and loving Bob Marley and reggae music is not what defines the Rastafari Indigenous Culture!' (TMZ, 2013).

2 The meaning in this particular image is not clarified by the ambiguity of the accompanying hand gesture, which might reference the American Sign Language for 'I love you', but could also reference infidelity, the devil, heavy metal or (rather less probably) George Clinton's P-Funk, among other things.

3 The difference that is figured in sexual encounters with racialized others can allow subjects to mark a distance from their own norms of social identity and behaviour, and in doing so facilitate processes of exploration and self-transformation. For example, when (as was recently described to me) an otherwise heterosexual male tourist spends his holiday in Thailand snogging 'ladyboys', a kind of sexual experimentation is occurring that would not necessarily have been entertained at 'home'.

2 Theorizing racial consumption

4 This is a point that might also be made in the opposite historical direction, for it's clear that people have for thousands of years been using images, objects and texts to describe and understand cultural difference, and for the purposes of interaction and exchange. This recognition goes against some of the dominant ideas we hold in our cultures about race. As Gilbert Rodman suggests, the 'phenomenon of cultural exchange between "different" racial populations [. . .] has a long and tangled history, but such exchanges are often treated as if they were a dangerous new phenomenon' (Rodman, 2009: 97). There is a very hard-to-shake investment in 'common-sense' ideas about race that different groups spent most of human history living separately and autonomously from one another. While mixture – both biological and cultural – is a product of human movement, an activity 'as old as homo sapiens' (Goldberg, 2009: 251), many people continue to think and act as if the fact of living and interacting with difference is limited just to the more recent past.

5 For another example of the disruption of a naturalized conception of race, consider the common experience of migrants or the decendents of migrants who

retain a symbolic hold on 'back home' as a key element of their cultural identity. So often, people in this position experience a profound sense of estrangement when they actually go 'home', because they will tend to be treated like tourists: their voice, hair style, clothing or some other subtle element of their racial performances will have set them out as strangers to the culture they had hitherto regarded as their 'own'.

6   In her reading of the symbolic as 'the sedimentation of social practices', Judith Butler suggests that 'radical alterations in kinship demand a rearticulation of the structuralist presuppositions of psychoanalysis and, hence, of contemporary gender and sexual theory' (Butler, 2000: 19). While I would reject the idea that it is possible to build a general theory of race on a psychoanalytic reading of racial meaning, I would suggest that, insofar as dominant theoretical approaches to race posit a fundamental structuring role to processes of othering (inclusion and exclusion; us and them), the logic of Butler's argument is that these too might be (subtly) redefined, challenged, undermined and reworked by new trans-national configurations of race and culture. As she later suggests of reworkings of the family form, we might 'accept that the ideality of the norm is undone precisely through the complexity of its instantiation' (ibid.: 79).

3   Ethnic appropriateness: white nostalgia and Nordic noir

7   This observation should be read as an apology of sorts to Matt Wray for what I now note was an unfairly hard review of his book *Not Quite White* (2006).

8   The example here of the articulation of gender and race as co-constitutive categories of identity is axiomatic of my approach to race throughout this book. Racial meanings are always produced alongside and in relation to ideas about gender, class, sexuality and so on. For a more developed discussion, see for example Barnard (1999).

9   Thanks to Sarah Elsie Baker for suggesting I take a look at this text.

10 This relationship between the Nordic countries and an aesthetic/climatic white-ness in the British cultural imagination is underwritten, as Jakob Stougaard Nielsen has suggested to me, by the tendency of English translations of Nordic crime fiction to feature snowy landscapes on their covers, while their Nordic language editions do not. A work of Nordic crime fiction in English can have a snowy cover even when there is no mention of snow in the book itself. I explore the taste for 'Nordic noir' towards the end of this chapter.

11 This is, incidentally, a regular and apologetic observation that white students make of themselves in culturally diverse seminar groups in discussion of culture and identity. They genuinely feel they have nothing of interest to say on the matter.

4   Engaging whiteness: black nerds

12 In Ron Eglash's black nerds article, Afrofuturism is conceived of as an alternative to the technocultural imaginary of the black nerd (Eglash, 2002: 59–60). Though Afrofuturism certainly provides some interesting ways of configuring the past in the present, the figure of the retro nerd here provides us with an alternative temporality and a different set of cultural resources.

13 This doesn't mean that non-white people haven't made an appearance as antiques experts: Lennox Cato was recruited as an expert on the BBC show *Antiques Roadshow* in 2005, while Philip Merrill featured on the PBS version from 1996 (albeit as an appraiser of 'Black Memorabilia').

14 These practices, tellingly, take place in the context of a critique of *contemporary* black cultural forms. This trope of contemporary critique and historical appropriation is a longstanding feature of white relationships to black musical culture, from jazz and blues through to hip hop, dubstep and beyond. The markers of a music's unacceptability have included a predictable litany of moral objections (unlawfulness, violence, sexual explicitness, and more recently sexism and homophobia) and aesthetic considerations (commercialism, insincerity, inauthenticity). But somehow the passing of time takes the edge off these and transforms 'dangerous' musics into cultural forms that are assimilable into a mainstream culture structured by whiteness (it is no accident, for example, that it is an early 1980s reggae style that features on the preschool BBC TV show Rastamouse).

5   The taste of race: authenticity and food cultures

15 An interesting phenomenon in these technologies of display is the separation in contemporary retail between what the Tesco supermarket website calls 'cooking sauces and meal kits' (arranged into the categories 'Indian', 'Italian', 'Mexican' and 'Oriental') and what it calls 'foods of the world' (categorised in terms of 'African Groceries', 'American Groceries', 'Asian Groceries', 'Caribbean Groceries' and so on). While the former are oriented towards any consumer intent on culinary tourism, the latter – with obscurer brands and bulk packets of commodities like rice and pulses – are clearly pitched at those with a specific 'ethnic' claim of their own, also enabling those with sufficient cultural confidence to engage in a more adventurous form of ethnic food tourism (see tesco.com/groceries). The geopolitical regionalization of ethnic food will likely seem very strange to future generations, at once an expression of contemporary global interconnectedness and a symbolic struggle against that recognition. For more on this problematic, see Brown (2010).

16 Another great example of improbable culinary eclecticism is the UK-based Red Planet Pizza/Jasmine Garden Oriental Cuisine franchise, whose takeaway menus promise an intriguing combination of Chinese, Thai, Malaysian, Italian, American, Caribbean, Belgian, Mexican and Japanese cuisines, united in their dissimilarity by the offer of 'criss cuts' chips (free with every order over £35).

6   Race and children: from anthropomorphism to zoomorphism

17 This is not the 'earliest' point at which we might think about the cultural politics of race. As Khiara Bridges suggests, racial formation is a process that takes place in utero (Bridges, 2011). A chapter of this book that didn't get written, but which is a theme I want to return to in the future, is a consideration of pregnancy and early childcare as a particularly important site for engagements with ideas about racial difference, from the philosophies of 'natural', 'attachment' or 'continuum concept' parenting to anti-consumerist approaches to the material cultures of infancy.

18 To give another example of race in the material culture of childhood: I have a photograph of myself as a toddler in the late 1970s wearing a pair of dungarees onto which has been stitched the image of a 'gollywog', then used in Britain as the emblem of Robertson's Jam. To look at this image now is to be reminded of the rapidly changing norms of racial representation. Though we rightly read this image today as an unequivocally racist caricature, its meaning will have been somewhat different in late 1970s Britain. This is not to excuse that context

of its racism, but to recognize that it was unlikely that whoever put me into those dungarees had a malevolent racist intent. Indeed, it is to recognize that this image was perfectly acceptable – even appealing – according to the prevailing norms of the culture in which it was displayed. Though we fix on objects and images as the bearers of racist meanings, our indictment of them is not an indictment of the object or image itself, or of its producers or consumers as if they were producing or consuming it today (which most probably would be considered more straightforwardly racist practices). To judge an image from the past and find it wanting is to register a rupture with that past and our distance from and dissimilarity to the culture in which such images were enjoyed. (For a discussion of 'contemptible collectables', see Dant 1999: 149–50.)

19   The model of the Western has a certain interchangeability with other mid-twentieth-century gendered narratives that secure masculine identity through conflict and violence. In this sense the Western has much in common with 'cops and robbers' or games of war where 'the Germans' can be substituted for 'the Indians' while leaving the hero's identity largely unmodified and intact.

20   One marker of this ambivalence in the movie is Woody's shifting cultural value in the US. While in *Toy Story 2* he is left, broken on a shelf, by his owner Andy, Woody is pursued by a toy collector seeking to make a fortune by selling him to Mr Konishi of the Konishi Toy Museum, Japan (Pixar Wiki, 2013).

21   This association is reinforced by *Waybuloo's* name for its live-action children – cheebies – which appears to refer to the *chibi* (or 'super deformed') style of Japanese drawing that the big-eyed, large-headed piplings closely resemble (TV Tropes, 2013a). For a discussion of the Japanese origins of a globalized culture of cuteness, see Granot *et al.* (2013).

22   The sense in which childhood provides a model of a different way of thinking to adult life (as simpler, perhaps, less cynical or less alienated) probably explains why 'non-Western' religious themes are often explored in or in relation to childhood culture: consider, for example, the Taoist influence on the books and animations in the *Bod* series, or the Taoist reading of A. A. Milne's Winnie the Pooh (see Cole, 2002; Hoff, 1983).

23   The idea that *Teletubbies* have racial phenotypes that seamlessly match that of their actors is perhaps troubled a little by Po, an ostensibly 'white' teletubby, who was played by the British Chinese actor Pui Fan Lee, and who augmented her character's baby talk with some Cantonese. In other respects, a biographical reading of characterization consolidates some racial interpretations of the programme. When the *Teletubbies* actors toured America on the occasion of the show's tenth anniversary in 2007, the *Today Show* 'Behind the scenes' feature rather improbably claimed that Simmitt 'adds reggae to his tellytubby speak' (*Today Show*, 2007).

24   Though there does not in the main appear to be any social stratification of the different animal families, the one rather Orwellian exception are horses, which remain on four legs and are ridden or given carts to pull around Sylvania.

25   For a comprehensive discussion of the relationship between zoos and the colonial display of human groups for education and entertainment, see Blanchard *et al.* (2008).

7   Animals and plants: natural gardening and non-native species

26   For discussions of the way in which ideas of whiteness inform understandings of rural landscape and park spaces, see Neal (2002) and Byrne (2011) respectively.

27   In doing so, flora and fauna does not necessarily need to work in the service of dominant articulations of race and nation. Refugee communities, for example,

frequently mediate their memories of a lost home and 'engender the feeling of being "at home" in exile' by growing plants and tending gardens (Taylor, 2009: 172–214). For further discussions of gardening among migrant cultures, see Rishbeth (2005) and Horst (2008).

28 It should be noted that this is not the only possible figuration of environmentalism and cultural difference. As Elspeth Probyn notes of the history of organic farming in the West 'many of our ideas about organic or sustainable farming came first from the South and moved to the North' (Probyn, 2011: 110).

8 Stories about race: knowledge and form

29 While the following examples do circulate around significant issues in the cultural politics of race, it should be noted that stories about race can also serve to make legible and explicable problems and issues that in truth many actually have very little to do with race: race can be called upon as a handy 'answer' to what can appear to be otherwise impossible questions (see Butler, 1997: 23; Valluvan et al., 2013; Pitcher 2009: 105–8).

30 Another mediated site of antiracist desire is the 'wishful multiculturalism' of soap opera, which typically depicts racism as an 'interpersonal encounter between the voices of bigotry and reason' amidst an otherwise 'effortless process of negotiating difference' (Cohen, 1997: 34). Or consider the ways in which cross-racial empathies and friendships are played out among 'ordinary' people who would otherwise be strangers to one another on TV quiz shows like Deal or No Deal. The social levelling staged by such formats in their representations of contestant/audience diversity is clearly a proxy and substitute for the practice of offscreen multicultural community.

31 For another example of this kind of interpretive framing in the contemporary politics of race, consider the widespread critique of materialistic hip hop culture that was drawn upon in the interpretation of the riots in England in 2011: 'It is precisely the presence of a public already literate in the representational cues of a degenerate materialism tied to alarmist evocations of black hip hop which renders instantly recognizable a general (across race) ascription to the rioters of a morally aimless cultural drive' (Valluvan et al., 2013: 9).

32 This section is a version of a longer argument about The Wire and cultural studies published as Bramall and Pitcher (2013).

33 In so doing, the representation of Omar signals a reflexive acknowledgement of the history of racial representation. New stories about race are necessarily in dialogue with older stories about race. Because in older narratives racialized figures so often occupied the position of the 'bad guy', it has become a contemporary representational convention to provide some novelty by subverting this idea and introducing as objects of suspicion racialized characters (particularly, of course, shady Muslims) that are in the course of the narrative revealed to be nothing more than law-abiding citizens going about their ordinary business. This has, in turn, become such a convention – particularly of the contemporary whodunit – that it is almost a structural impossibility that racialized characters are ever guilty of anything more than behaving in studiedly unstereotypical ways. Consider, for an example of this, the cycle in the first series of the Danish television show The Killing (2007) whereby suspicion is focused on and then removed from the innocent Iranian schoolteacher Rahman Al Kamel and Nanna Birk Larsen's Muslim-heritage boyfriend Amir El' Namen.

34 The suggestions made by John Kraniauskas (2009) and Jeff Kinkle and Alberto Toscano (2009) that The Wire confers not social legibility but rather dramatizes the impossibility of representing postmodern capitalism confirm in fact that they

too remain in thrall to this fantasy, for to argue that *The Wire* provides knowledge of the limits of knowledge is to fall short of interrogating the centrality of epistemological desire in the production of knowledge of those limits.

9   Conclusion

35 I do get a sense that the time has probably come for this kind of openness to thinking about race. From the debates in the US around 'post-black' African-American culture (see Chapter 4), to the emergence of a global 'Afropolitan' demographic (Selasi, 2005), to the recognition of 'super-diversity' in policy debate (Vertovec, 2007), there are plenty of indications that those engaged in thinking about race are recognizing the need for a greater conceptual complexity and the limitations of reducing the horizons of race to the question of racism.

Bibliography

95percentshop (2013) '95% Danish – the home to Danish design', available at: www.95percentshop.co.uk/acatalog/danish.html [27.03.13].

Ahmed, R. (2010) 'Brick Lane: a materialist reading of the novel and its reception', *Race & Class*, 52(2): 25–42.

Al Jazeera (2012) 'Anti-Islam Video Protests Live Blog', available at: http://blogs.aljazeera.com/liveblog/topic/anti-islam-video-protests-10701 [27.06.13].

Ali, M. (2003) *Brick Lane*, London: Doubleday.

Amin, A. (2012) *Land of Strangers*, Cambridge: Polity Press.

Animation Archive (2013) 'Toy Story 2 Script', available at: http://animationarchive.net/Pixar%20Studios/Films/Toy%20Story%202/Script/ [23.04.13].

Appadurai, A. (ed.) (1986) *The Social Life of Things: commodities in cultural perspective*, Cambridge: Cambridge University Press.

Baker, S. (2013) *Retro Style: class, gender and design in the home*, London: Bloomsbury.

Banchs, E. (2013) 'Desert Sounds – Kalahari metalheads pursue a dream', 10 February, available at: www.guardian.co.uk/world/2013/feb/10/kalahari-metalheads [10.06.13].

Banet-Weiser, S. (2007) 'What's Your Flava? Race and postfeminism in media culture', in Y. Tasker and D. Negra (eds) *Interrogating Postfeminism: gender and the politics of popular culture*, Durham, NC: Duke University Press.

Bannister, M. (2006) *White Boys, White Noise: masculinities and 1980s indie guitar rock*, Aldershot: Ashgate.

Barnard, I. (1999) 'Queer Race', *Social Semiotics*, 9(2): 199–212.

Barney, R. A. (1999) *Plots of Enlightenment: education and the novel in eighteenth-century England*, Stanford: Stanford University Press.

Barton, C. P. and Somerville, K. (2012) 'Playthings: children's racialized mechanical banks and toys, 1880–1930', *International Journal of Historical Archaeology*, 16: 47–85.

Baudrillard, J. (1996) *The System of Objects*, trans. James Benedict, London: Verso.

Baudrillard, J. (2001) 'Simulacra and Simulations', in *Selected Writings*, Cambridge: Polity Press.

Bauman, Z. (1989) *Modernity and the Holocaust*, Cambridge: Polity Press.

Bauman, Z. (2007) *Consuming Life*, Cambridge: Polity Press.

Bauman, Z. (2011) *Collateral Damage*, Cambridge: Polity Press.

BBC [British Broadcasting Corporation] (2009) 'Network TV BBC Week 20 Feature', available at: www.bbc.co.uk/pressoffice/proginfo/tv/2009/wk20/feature_waybuloo.shtml [14.03.12].

BBC [British Broadcasting Corporation] (2013) 'Nina and the Neurons', available at: www.bbc.co.uk/cbeebies/grownups/shows/nina-and-the-neurons [18.04.13].

BBC Scotland (2013) 'Questions about Luke Neuron', e-mail from *Nina and the Neurons* Series Producer [12.04.13].

Beggs, M. (2008) 'Balzac of Baltimore', available at: http://scandalum.wordpress.com/2008/01/13/balzac-of-baltimore/ [30.12.2009].

Benwell, B., Proctor, J. and Robinson, G. (2011) 'Not Reading *Brick Lane*', *New Formations*, 73: 90–116.

Best, A. (2012) 'Post-Racial Ironies and Counterfactual Histories: a commentary on hipsters', *Darkmatter*, 9(2), available at: www.darkmatter101.org/site/2012/11/29/post-racial-ironies-and-counterfactual-histories-a-commentary-on-hipsters [10.06.13].

Bestor, T. C. (2005) 'How Sushi Went Global', in J. L. Watson and M. L. Caldwell (eds) *The Cultural Politics of Food and Eating: a reader*, Oxford: Blackwell.

Binkley, S. and Littler, J. (2008) 'Introduction: cultural studies and anti-consumerism: a critical encounter', *Cultural Studies*, 22(5): 519–30.

Black Nerds Network (2006) Press Pack, available at: www.blacknerdsnetwork.com/BNN_PressPack.pdf [31.05.13].

Blanchard, P., Bancel, N., Boëtsch, G., Deroo, É., Lemaire, S. and Forsdick, C. (eds) (2008) *Human Zoos: science and spectacle in the age of colonial empires*, Liverpool: Liverpool University Press.

Bonnett, A. (2000) *White Identites: historical and international perspectives*, Harlow: Pearson Education.

Bonnett, A. (2006) 'Pale Face, Red Mask: racial ambiguity and the imitation of "American Indian" facial expressions', *Cultural Politics*, 2(3): 319–38.

Booth, H. (2013) 'What Could an Umlaut Do for You?', *Guardian* Shortcuts Blog, 27 May, available at: www.guardian.co.uk/science/shortcuts/2013/may/27/what-could-umlaut-do-for-you [29.05.13].

Bowe, A. (2012) 'Alice Bowe', available at: www.alicebowe.co.uk [29.07.12].

Bowman, P. (2010) *Theorizing Bruce Lee: film-fantasy-fighting-philosophy*, Amsterdam: Editions Rodopi.

Bradotti, R., Hanafin, P. and Blaagaard, B. (eds) (2013) *After Cosmopolitanism*, London: Routledge.

Bramall, R. (2013) *The Cultural Politics of Austerity: past and present in austere times*, Basingstoke: Palgrave Macmillan.

Bramall, R. and Pitcher, B. (2013) 'Policing the Crisis, or, Why We Love *The Wire*', *International Journal of Cultural Studies*, 16(1): 85–98.

Bridges, K. M. (2011) *Reproducing Race: an ethnography of pregnancy as a site of racialization*, Berkeley, CA: University of California Press.

Britain's Finest (2013) 'The Bilash', available at: www.britainsfinest.co.uk/restaurants/restaurants.cfm/searchazref/920011015337 [23.04.13].

Brown, W. (2006) *Regulating Aversion: tolerance in the age of identity and empire*, Princeton: Princeton University Press.

Brown, W. (2010) *Walled States, Waning Sovereignty*, New York: Zone Books.

Browning, C. (2007) 'Branding Nordicity: models, identity and the decline of exceptionalism', *Cooperation and Conflict*, 42(1): 27–51.

Bryce, D. (2013) 'The Absence of Ottoman, Islamic Europe in Edward W. Said's *Orientalism*', *Theory, Culture & Society*, 30(1): 99–121.

Buettner, E. (2008) ' "Going for an Indian": South Asian restaurants and the limits of multiculturalism in Britain', *The Journal of Modern History*, 80: 865–901.

Burke, J. (2010) 'Yoga Heritage: don't even think about stealing it, says Indian government', *Guardian*, 8 June, available at: www.guardian.co.uk/world/2010/jun/08/yoga-heritage-india-filming-asanas [25.07.13].

Butler, J. (1990) *Gender Trouble: feminism and the subversion of identity*, London: Routledge.

Butler, J. (1997) *Excitable Speech: a politics of the performative*, London: Routledge.

Butler, J. (2000) *Antigone's Claim: kinship between life and death*, New York: Columbia University Press.

Butler, J. (2006) 'Imitation and Gender Insubordination', in J. Storey (ed.) *Cultural Theory and Popular Culture: a reader*, third edition, Harlow: Pearson Education.

Byrne, B. (2006) *White Lives: the interplay of 'race', class and gender in everyday life*, London: Routledge.

Byrne, E. and McQuillan, M. (1999) *Deconstructing Disney*, London: Pluto Press.

Byrne, J. (2011) ' "When Green is White": the cultural politics of race, nature and social exclusion in a Los Angeles urban national park', *Geoforum*, 43: 595–611.

Cahill, S. (2009) 'Battleground: war rugs from Afghanistan', *The Journal of Modern Craft*, 2(2): 229–32.

Chandler, M. (2012) ' "Don't Jerk Us Around": museum's plans to extend alcohol licence anger people who remember "pandemonium" at chicken festival', *News Shopper*, 25 April.

Chouliaraki, L. (2010) 'Post-Humanitarianism: humanitarian communication beyond a politics of pity', *International Journal of Cultural Studies*, 13(2): 107–26.

Chow, R. (2002) *The Protestant Ethnic and the Spirit of Capitalism*, New York: Columbia University Press.

Clark, N. (2002) 'The Demon-Seed: bioinvasion as the unsettling of environmental cosmopolitanism', *Theory, Culture & Society*, 19(1–2): 101–25.

Clarke, J. (2004) *Changing Welfare, Changing States: new directions in social policy*, London: Sage.

Coates, P. (2011) 'Over Here: American animals in Britain', in I. D. Rotherham and R. A. Lambert (eds) *Invasive and Introduced Plants and Animals: human perceptions, attitudes and approaches to management*, London: Earthscan.

Cocker, M. (2013) 'In the British Countryside, Alien Species are not Always Undesirables', *Guardian*, 23 February.

Cohen, P. (1997) 'Beyond the Community Romance', *Soundings*, 5: 29–51.

Cole, A. (2002) *Bod's Way: the meaning of life*, London: Contender.

Comaroff, J. and Comaroff, J. L. (2001) 'Narrating the Nation: aliens, apocalypse and the postcolonial state', *Journal of Southern African Studies*, 27(3): 627–51.

Comaroff, J. L. and Comaroff, J. (2009) *Ethnicity, Inc.*, Chicago: University of Chicago Press.

Condry, I. (2007) 'Yellow B-Boys, Black Culture, and Hip Hop in Japan: towards a transnational cultural politics of race', *Positions: East Asia Cultures Critique*, 15(3): 637–71.

Cook, I. and Crang, P. (2003) 'The World on a Plate: culinary culture, displacement and geographical knowledges', in D. B. Clarke, M. A. Doel and K. M. L. Housiaux (eds) *The Consumption Reader*, London: Routledge.

Coward, M. (2010) 'The Parakeets of London', *Fortean Times*, available at: www.forteantimes.com/strangedays/mythbusters/2725/the_parakeets_of_london.html [17.04.13].

DailyCandy (2011) 'Viet-Van Banh Mi Sandwiches Are Pho Real', available at: www.dailycandy.com/london/article/113107/Viet-Van-Banh-Mi-Vietnamese-Sandwiches [24.04.13].

The Daily City (2013) 'Publix Banh Mi Debuts as Asian BBQ Sub', available at: www.thedailycity.com/2013/04/publix-banh-mi-debuts-as-asian-bbq-sub.html [23.04.13].

Dalal, F. (2002) *Race, Colour and the Process of Racialization: new perspectives from group analysis, psychoanalysis and sociology*, Hove: Brunner-Routledge.

Dant, T. (1999) *Material Culture in the Social World: values, activities, lifestyles*, Buckingham: Open University Press.

Davis, J. C. (2007) *Commerce in Color: race, consumer culture and American literature 1893–1933*, Ann Arbor, MI: University of Michigan Press.

Davis, K. C. (2004) 'Oprah's Book Club and the Politics of Cross-Racial Empathy', *International Journal of Cultural Studies*, 7(4): 399–419.

DEFRA [Department for Environment, Food and Rural Affairs] (2008) *The Invasive Non-Native Species Framework Strategy for Great Britain*, London: DEFRA.

Deleon, J. (2013) 'The 15 Stages of Kanye West's Style', *Complex Style*, 23 April, available at: www.complex.com/style/2013/04/the-15-stages-of-kanye-wests-style/ [07.06.13].

Derbyshire, J. (2008) 'Performing Blackness', *Prospect*, 20 December, available at: www.prospectmagazine.co.uk/magazine/performingblackness/#.UbHhX4X9nbk [07.06.13].

Devolving Diasporas (2011) 'Publications and Papers', available at: www.devolvingdiasporas.com/papers.htm [25.06.13].

Digital Spy (2013) 'Indian Restaurants and Flock Wallpaper?', available at: http://forums.digitalspy.co.uk/showthread.php?p=65322436 [23.04.13].

Duruz, J. (2011) 'Quesadillas with Chinese Black Bean Puree: eating together in "ethnic" neighbourhoods', *New Formations*, 74: 46–64.

Dyer, R. (1997) *White*, London: Routledge.

Dyer, R. (2002) *The Matter of Images: essays on representations*, second edition, London: Routledge.

Eat Ban Mi (2013) 'Menu', available at: www.eatbanmi.com/#!menu/cccq [23.04.13].

Economist (2013) 'Creativity: cultural revolution', 2 February, available at: www.economist.com/news/special-report/21570839-one-worlds-blandest-regions-has-become-one-its-most-creative-cultural-revolution [26.03.13].

Eglash, R. (2002) 'Race, Sex and Nerds: from black geeks to Asian American hipsters', *Social Text*, 20(2): 49–64.

Engage (2009) 'ChSC BNP Report Underplays Anti-Muslim Prejudice', available at: www.iengage.org.uk/news/449-cfsc-bnp-report-underplays-anti-muslim-prejudice [15.04.13].

Fanon, F. (1967) *Toward the African Revolution*, New York: Grove Press.

Fanon, F. (1986) *Black Skin, White Masks*, London: Pluto Press.

Featherstone, M. (2007) *Consumer Culture and Postmodernism*, London: Sage.

ferm LIVING (2013) 'About', available at: www.ferm-living.com/pages/webpage. aspx?articleid=58127 [26.03.13].

Fiell, C. and Fiell, P. (2008) *Decorative Art 50s*, Köln: Taschen.

Flowerdew, B. (2003) *Bob Flowerdew's Organic Bible: successful gardening the natural way*, revised edition, London: Kyle Cathie.

Foley, C. (2009) *The Natural Garden Handbook*, London: New Holland Publishers.

Fowler, A. (2010) *The Edible Garden: how to have your garden and eat it*, London: BBC Books.

Freeman, H. (2009) 'Kanye West: design guru?', *Guardian*, 29 January, available at: www.guardian.co.uk/artanddesign/2009/jan/29/kanye-west-design-guru [07.06.13].

Freidman, J. (1997) 'Global Crises, the Struggle for Cultural Identity and Intellectual Porkbarrelling: cosmopolitans versus locals, ethnics and nationals in an era of de-hegemonisation', in P. Werbner and T. Modood (eds) *Debating Cultural Hybridity: multi-cultural identities and the politics of anti-racism*, London: Zed Books.

Frostrup, M. (2010) 'Scandinavian Special', *Observer Food Monthly*, 18 April: 34–7.

Fryer, P. (1984) *Staying Power: the history of black people in Britain*, London: Pluto Press.

Gilbert, J. (2008) *Anticapitalism and Culture: radical theory and popular politics*, Oxford: Berg.

Gilroy, P. (1990) 'The End of Anti-Racism', in Wendy Ball and John Solomos (eds) *Race and Local Politics*, Basingstoke: Macmillan.

Gilroy, P. (1993) *The Black Atlantic: modernity and double consciousness*, London: Verso.

Gilroy, P. (2004) *After Empire: melancholia or convivial culture?*, Abingdon: Routledge.

Gilroy, P. (2010) *Darker than Blue: on the moral economies of black Atlantic Culture*, Cambridge, MA: Harvard University Press.

Gilroy, P. (2012) '"My Britain is Fuck All": zombie multiculturalism and the race politics of citizenship', *Identities: Global Studies in Culture and Power*, 19(4): 380–97.

Ginn, F. (2008) 'Extension, Subversion, Containment: eco-nationalism and (post)colonial nature in Aetearoa New Zealand', *Transactions of the Institute of British Geographers*, 33: 335–53.

Giroux, H. A. (1994) 'Consuming Social Change: the "United Colors of Benetton"', *Cultural Critique*, 26: 5–32.

Goldberg, D. (2009) *The Threat of Race: reflections on racial neoliberalism*, Oxford: Wiley Blackwell.

Gonzáles, J. (2000) 'The Appended Subject: race and identity as digital assemblage', in B. E. Kolko, L. Nakamura and G. B. Rodman (eds) *Race in Cyberspace*, London: Routledge.

Goodman, M. K. (2004) 'Reading Fair Trade: political ecological imaginary and the moral economy of fair trade foods', *Political Geography*, 23: 891–915.

Goodman, M. K. and Barnes, C. (2011) 'Star/Poverty Space: the making of the "development celebrity"', *Celebrity Studies*, 2(1): 69–85.

Granot, E. Alejandro, T. B. and Russell, L. T. M. (2013) 'A Socio-Marketing Analysis of the Concept of Cute and its Consumer Culture Implications', *Journal of Consumer Culture*, published online 7 May, DOI: 10.1177/1469540513485274.

Gray, H. (2013) 'Race, Media and the Cultivation of Concern', *Communication and Critical/Cultural Studies*, published online 18 July, DOI: 10.1080/14791420. 2013.821641.

Gray, L. (2009) 'Parakeets Cull is Racist, Say Researchers', *Telegraph*, 2 October, available at: www.telegraph.co.uk/earth/earthnews/6254939/Parakeets-cull-is-racist-say-wildlife-experts.html [17.04.13].

Grillo, I. (2008) 'Mexico's Emo-Bashing Problem', *Time*, 27 March, available at: www.time.com/time/arts/article/0,8599,1725839,00.html [10.06.13].

Grosrichard, A. (1998) *The Sultan's Court: European fantasies of the East*, London: Verso.

Grove, K. (2009) 'Rethinking the Nature of Urban Environmental Politics: security, subjectivity and the non-human', *Geoforum*, 40: 207–16.

Guardian (2011) Travel Section, Saturday 3 September.

Gunkel, H. and Pitcher, B. (2008) 'Editorial: racism in the closet: interrogating postcolonial sexuality', *Darkmatter*, 2, available at www.darkmatter101.org/site/2008/05/02/racism-in-the-closet-interrogating-postcolonial-sexuality/ [28.03.13].

Gunning, D. (2010) *Race and Antiracism in Black British and British Asian Literature*, Liverpool: Liverpool University Press.

Hage, G. (1998) *White Nation: fantasies of white supremacy in a multicultural society*, Annandale NSW: Pluto Press Australia.

Hage, G. (2003) *Against Paranoid Nationalism: searching for hope in a shrinking society*, Annandale NSW: Pluto Press Australia.

Halberstam, J. (2005) *In a Queer Time and Place: transgender bodies, subcultural lives*, New York: New York University Press.

Halberstam, J. (2011) *The Queer Art of Failure*, Durham, NC: Duke University Press.

Hall, S. (1981) 'Notes on Deconstructing "The Popular"', in R. Samuel (ed.) *People's History and Socialist Theory*, London: Routledge and Kegan Paul.

Hall, S. (1992) 'The West and the Rest: discourse and power', in S. Hall and B. Gieben (eds) *Formations of Modernity*, Oxford: Polity Press.

Hall, S. (1996) 'New Ethnicities', in Morley, D. and Chen K.-H. (eds) *Stuart Hall: critical dialogues in cultural studies*, London: Routledge.

Halle, D. (1993) 'The Audience for "Primitive" Art in Houses in the New York Region', *The Art Bulletin*, 75(3): 397–414.

Halter, M. (2000) *Shopping for Identity: the marketing of authenticity*, New York: Schocken Books.

Hansen, B. (1991) 'Translations: everything you need for Vietnamese cooking', 14 March, available at: http://articles.latimes.com/1991–03–14/food/fo-11_1_vietnamese-restaurants [23.04.13].

Haraway, D. (1989) *Primate Visions: gender, race and nature in the world of modern science*, London: Routledge.

Haraway, D. (2003) *The Companion Species Manifesto: dogs, people and significant otherness*, Chicago, IL: Prickly Paradigm Press.

Harman, N. (2012) 'Hop and Spice', *Foodepedia*, available at: www.foodepedia.co.uk/restaurant-reviews/2012/mar/hop_and_spice_balham.htm [24.04.13].

Haus (2013) 'Haus – about us', available at: http://hauslondon.com/pages/about-us [27.03.13].

Hemma Magazine (2011) 'Kånken: from nerd to trend', available at: http://hemma magazine.co.uk/fashion/kanken-from-nerd-to-trend [26.03.12].

Hesse, B. (2011) 'Self-Fulfilling Prophecy: the postracial horizon', *The South Atlantic Quarterly*, 110(1): 155–78.

Highmore, B. (2008) 'Alimentary Agents: food, cultural theory and multiculturalism', *Journal of Intercultural Studies*, 29(4): 381–98.

Hill Collins, P. (2004) *Black Sexual Politics: African Americans, gender, and the new racism*, London: Routledge.

Hoff, B. (1983) *The Tao of Pooh*, London: Penguin.

Hollows, J. (2006) 'Can I Go Home Yet? Feminism, post-feminism and domesticity', in J. Hollows and R. Moseley (eds) *Feminism in Popular Culture*, Oxford: Berg.

hooks, b. (1992) *Black Looks: race and representation*, Boston, MA: South End Press.

Horst, H. (2008) 'Landscaping Englishness: respectability and returnees in Mandeville, Jamaica', *Caribbean Review of Gender Studies*, 2(22): 1–18.

Houlton, D. and Short, B. (1995) 'Sylvanian Families: the production and consumption of a rural community', *Journal of Rural Studies*, 11(4): 367–85.

Howes, D. (ed.) (1996) *Cross-Cultural Consumption: global markets, local realities*, London: Routledge.

Huffington Post (2013) 'Post-Racial America', available at: www.huffingtonpost. com/tag/post-racial-america [10.07.13].

Jaffe, R. (2010) 'Ital Chic: Rastafari, resistance and the politics of consumption in Jamaica', *Small Axe*, 14(1): 30–45.

James, C. L. R. (1963) *Beyond a Boundary*, London: Stanley Paul.

Jameson, F. (1991) *Postmodernism, or, the Cultural Logic of Late Capitalism*, London: Verso.

Jameson, F. (1993) 'On "Cultural Studies"', *Social Text*, 34: 17–52.

Jamie's Great Britain – the East End and Essex (2011) TV Programme, Fresh One for Channel 4, 25 October, 9pm.

Jones, J. and Seamons, H. (2012) 'Women's White: key fashion trends of the season', *Guardian* 19 December, available at: www.guardian.co.uk/fashion/gallery/2012/dec/19/womens-white-fashion#/?picture=400899471&index=1 [17.05.13].

Jones, R. L. (2008) *What's Wrong With Obamamania? Black America, black leadership and the death of political imagination*, Albany: State University of New York Press.

Joseph, J. (2012) 'The Practice of Capoeira: diasporic black culture in Canada', *Ethnic and Racial Studies*, 35(6): 1078–95.

The Killing [*Forbrydelsen*] (2007–12) TV series, Danish Broadcasting Corporation.

Kingsbury, N. (2009) *Natural Garden Style: gardening inspired by nature*, London: Merrell.

Kingston, S. (1999) 'The Essential Attitude: authenticity in primitive art, ethnographic performances and museums', *Journal of Material Culture*, 4(3): 338–51.

Kinkle, J. and Toscano, A. (2009) 'Baltimore as World and Representation: cognitive mapping and capitalism in *The Wire*', *Dossier*, 8 April, available at: http://dossier journal.com/read/theory/baltimore-as-world-and-representation-cognitive-mapping-and-capitalism-in-the-wire/ [28.03.10].

Kitwana, B. (2005) *Why White Kids Love Hip Hop: wankstas, wiggas, wannabes, and the new reality of race in America*, New York: Basic Civitas.

Kraniauskas, J. (2009) 'Elasticity of Demand: reflections on *The Wire*', *Radical Philosophy*, 154: 25–34.

La Ganga, M. L. (1988) 'Business is Rising: French bakeries of Little Saigon keep cross-cultural tradition alive', *Los Angeles Times*, 1 March, available at: http://articles.latimes.com/1988–03–01/business/fi-220_1_vietnamese-business-directory [23.04.13].

Lægaard, S. (2009) 'Normative Interpretations of Diversity: the Muhammad cartoons controversy and the importance of context', *Ethnicities*, 9: 314–33.

Laclau, E. (1990) *New Reflections on the Revolution of Our Time*, London: Verso.

Lazzarato, M. (2013) 'Immaterial Labour', available at: www.generation-online.org/c/fcimmateriallabour3.htm [20.07.13].

Lentin, A. and Titley, G. (2011) *The Crises of Multiculturalism: racism in a neoliberal age*, London: Zed Books.

Levy, A. (2004) *Small Island*, London: Review.

Lewis, G. (2007) 'Racializing Culture is Ordinary', *Cultural Studies*, 21(6): 866–86.

Ling Wong, J. (2001) *The 'Native and Alien' Issue: a discussion paper*, available at: www.ben-network.org.uk/resources/publs.asp [20.07.13].

Littler, J. and Naidoo, R. (eds) (2005) *The Problem of Heritage: the legacies of 'race'*, London: Routledge.

Lott, E. (1999) 'Racial Cross-Dressing and the Construction of American Whiteness', in S. During (ed.) *The Cultural Studies Reader*, second edition, London: Routledge.

Lucas, C., Deeks, M. and Spracklen, K. (2011) 'Grim Up North: Northern England, Northern Europe and black metal', *Journal for Cultural Research*, 15(3): 279–95.

Lukács, G. (1978) *The Theory of the Novel*, London: Merlin Press.

Lury, C. (2011) *Consumer Culture*, second edition, Cambridge: Polity Press.

Lyotard, J. F. (1984) *The Postmodern Condition: a report on knowledge*, Manchester: Manchester University Press.

McClintock, A. (1995) *Imperial Leather: race, gender and sexuality in the colonial context*, London: Routledge.

McNeely, J. A. (2011) 'Xenophobia or Conservation: some human dimensions of invasive alien species', in I. D. Rotherham and R. A. Lambert (eds) *Invasive and Introduced Plants and Animals: human perceptions, attitudes and approaches to management*, London: Earthscan.

McRobbie, A. (2009) *The Aftermath of Feminism: gender, culture and social change*, London: Sage.

Mad Men (2007–14) TV series, Lionsgate Television for AMC.

Mankikar, P. (2005) ' "Indian Shopping": Indian grocery stores and transnational configurations of belonging', in J. L. Watson and M. L. Caldwell (eds) *The Cultural Politics of Food and Eating: a reader*, Oxford: Blackwell.

Manor House Wildlife Park (2013) 'African Village News', available at: www.manorhousewildlifepark.co.uk/African-Village-news [28.02.13].

Marable, M. (2009) 'Racializing Obama: the enigma of post-black politics and leadership', *Souls*, 11(1): 1–15.

Marx, K. and Engels, F. (1992) *The Communist Manifesto*, Oxford: Oxford University Press.

Mercer, K. (1994) *Welcome to the Jungle: new positions in black cultural studies*, London: Routledge.

Micheletti, M. (2003) *Political Virtue and Shopping*, second edition, Basingstoke: Palgrave Macmillan.

Miller, D. (2010) *Stuff*, Cambridge: Polity Press.

Mills, B. (2013) 'The Animals Went in Two by Two: heteronormativity in television wildlife documentaries', *European Journal of Cultural Studies*, 16(1): 100–14.

Mills, G. (2013) 'My Dream Wintery Bedroom – The White Company', 10 January, available at: http://mymillsbaby.co.uk/2013/01/my-dream-wintery-bedroom-the-white-company/ [19.03.13].

Möhring, M. (2008) 'Transnational Food Migration and the Internationalization of Food Consumption: ethnic cuisine in West Germany', in A. Nützenadel and F. Trentmann (2008) *Food and Globalization: markets and politics in the modern world*, Oxford: Berg.

Moore, D. S., Kosek, J. and Pandian, A. (eds) (2003) *Race, Nature and the Politics of Difference*, Durham, NC: Duke University Press.

Mortiner-Sandilands, C. and Erickson, B. (eds) (2010) *Queer Ecologies: sex, nature, politics, desire*, Bloomington, IN: Indiana University Press.

Mukherjee, R. (2011) 'Bling Fling: commodity consumption and the politics of the "post-racial"', in M. G. Lacy and K. A. Ono (eds) *Critical Rhetorics of Race*, New York: New York University Press.

Murji, K. and Solomos, J. (eds) (2005) *Racialization: studies in theory and practice*, Oxford: Oxford University Press.

Muuto (2013) 'Muuto Designer Profile – the leading scandinavian designers', available at: www.muuto.com/showdesigner.aspx [26.03.13].

Naidoo, R. (2005) 'Never Mind the Buzzwords: "race", heritage and the liberal agenda', in J. Littler and R. Naidoo (eds) *The Politics of Heritage: the legacies of 'race'*, London: Routledge.

Nakamura, L. (2008) *Digitizing Race: visual cultures of the internet*, Minnesota: University of Minnesota Press.

Nama, A. (2008) *Black Space: imagining race in science fiction film*, Austin, TX: University of Texas Press.

The Natural Gardener (2013) 'The Natural Gardener', available at: www.thenatural gardener.co.uk/ [04.04.13].

Nava, M. (2007) *Visceral Cosmopolitanism: gender, culture and the normalisation of difference*, Oxford: Berg.

Neal, S. (2002) 'Rural Landscapes, Representations and Racism: examining multicultural citizenship and policymaking in the English countryside', *Ethnic and Racial Studies*, 25(3): 442–61.

Newman, F. and Gibson, M. (2005) 'Monoculture Versus Multiculinarism: trouble in the Aussie kitchen', in D. Bell and J. Hollows (eds) *Ordinary Lifestyles: popular media, consumption and taste*, Maidenhead: Open University Press.

Nicholls, W. (2008) 'The Banh Mi of My Dreams', *Washington Post*, 6 February, available at: www.washingtonpost.com/wp-dyn/content/article/2008/02/05/AR2 008020500888.html [23.04.13].

Nigel Slater's Simple Cooking – sweet and sour (2011) TV Programme, BBC Bristol for BBC One, 23 September, 7.30pm.

Nina and the Neurons (2007–) TV series, BBC Scotland for BBC.

NNSS [GB Non-Native Species Secretariat] (2010) *The Invasive Non-Native Species Strategic Communications Plan for Great Britain*, available at: https://secure.fera. defra.gov.uk/nonnativespecies/index.cfm?sectionid=14 [20.12.11].

NNSS [GB Non-Native Species Secretariat] (2013) 'What are Invasive Non-Native Species?', available at: https://secure.fera.defra.gov.uk/nonnativespecies/index.cfm?sectionid=15 [04.04.13].

Nordicana (2013) Flyer, Picked up at Scandinavian Kitchen, 61 Great Titchfield Street, London.

Nott, J. (2013) 'Woodcraft Folk Creed', e-mail [11.03.13].

Obama, B. (2007) *Dreams From My Father: a story of race and inheritance*, Edinburgh: Canongate Books.

Observer (2008) 'Is This the Best TV Series Ever Made?', *Observer*, 20 July, available at: www.guardian.co.uk/media/2008/jul/20/television.irvinewelsh [28.06.13].

Ogden, M. (2012) 'Sir Alex Ferguson Condemns Twitter after Rio Ferdinand is Fined £45,000 for "Choc Ice" Tweet', *Telegraph*, 17 August, available at: www.telegraph.co.uk/sport/football/teams/manchester-united/9483803/Sir-Alex-Ferguson-condemns-Twitter-after-Rio-Ferdinand-is-fined-45000-for-choc-ice-tweet.html [24.06.13].

Olesen, B. B. (2010) 'Ethnic Objects in Domestic Interiors: space, atmosphere and the making of home', *Home Cultures*, 7(1): 25–42.

Omi, M. and Winant, H. (1994) *Racial Formation in the United States: from the 1960s to the 1990s*, second edition, London: Routledge.

Ono, K. (2013) '*Mad Men's* Postracial Figuration of a Racial Past', in L. M. E. Goodlad, L. Kaganovsky and R. Rushing (eds) *Mad Men, Mad World: sex politics, style & the 1960s*, Durham, NC: Duke University Press.

Oswalt, P. (2010) 'Wake Up, Geek Culture: time to die', *Wired*, December 27, available at: www.wired.com/magazine/2010/12/ff_angrynerd_geekculture/ [07.06.13].

Pearson, C. (2013) *Bestial Traces: race, sexuality, animality*, New York: Fordham University Press.

Peretti, J. (2010) 'Nativism and Nature: rethinking biological invasion', in S. Johnson (ed.) *Bioinvaders*, Cambridge: Cambridge University Press.

Peterson, C. (2013) 'Sorry, Nerds, but Obama was Right about the Jedi Meld (and Metaphysics)', MIT Center for Civic Media, 1 March, available at: http://civic.mit.edu/blog/petey/sorry-nerds-but-obama-was-right-about-the-jedi-meld-and-metaphysics [07.06.13].

Pham, M.-H. T. (2010) 'More Native Appropriations, Heritage Capitalism, and Fashion on Antiques Roadshow', *Threadbared* blog, available at: http://iheart threadbared.wordpress.com/2010/05/24/more-native-appropriations-heritage-capitalism-and-fashion-on-antiques-roadshow/ [3.06.13].

Pitcher, B. (2007) 'Racism for Anti-Racism', *Darkmatter*, 1, available at: www.darkmatter101.org/site/2007/05/07/racism-for-anti-racism-2/ [24.06.13].

Pitcher, B. (2009) *The Politics of Multiculturalism*, Basingstoke: Palgrave Macmillan.

Pitcher, B. (2010) 'Obama and the Politics of Blackness: antiracism in the "post-black" conjuncture', *Souls*, 12(4): 313–22.

Pitcher, B. (2011) 'Radical Subjects after Hegemony', *Subjectivity*, 4(1): 87–102.

Pitcher, B. (2012) 'Race and Capitalism Redux', *Patterns of Prejudice*, 46(1): 1–15.

Pixar Wiki (2013) 'Konishi Toy Museum', available at: http://pixar.wikia.com/Konishi_Toy_Museum [09.07.13].

Pollan, M. (1994) 'Against Nativism', available at: www.nytimes.com/1994/05/15/magazine/against-nativism.html [15.04.13].

Povinelli, E. (1998) 'The State of Shame: Australian multiculturalism and the crisis of indigenous citizenship', *Critical Enquiry*, 24(2): 575–610.

Prashad, V. (2001) *Everybody Was Kung Fu Fighting: Afro-Asian connections and the myth of cultural purity*, Boston, MA: Beacon Press.

Probyn, E. (2011) 'Feeding the World: towards a messy ethics of eating', in T. Lewis and E. Potter (eds) *Ethical Consumption: a critical introduction*, London: Routledge.

Quinn, B. (2003) *Scandinavian Style*, London: Conran Octopus.

Reed, J. (2006) 'Watch The Wire', *PopMatters*, available at: www.popmatters.com/pm/feature/watch-the-wire [30.12.09].

Rishbeth, C. (2005) 'Gardens of Ethnicity', in N. Kingsbury and T. Richardson (eds) *Vista: the culture and politics of gardens*, London: Frances Lincoln.

Rodman, G. B. (2009) 'Race . . . and other Four Letter Words: Eminem and the cultural politics of authenticity', *Popular Communication*, 4(2): 95–121.

Rogers, S. (2012) 'Census 2011: religion, race and qualifications – see how England and Wales have changed', *Guardian* datablog, 11 December, available at: www.guardian.co.uk/news/datablog/2012/dec/11/census-2011-religion-race-education [14.05.13].

Rollock, N., Vincent, C., Gillborn, D. and Ball, S. (2013) '"Middle Class by Profession": class status and identification amongst the Black middle classes', *Ethnicities*, 13(3): 253–75.

Root, D. (1996) *Cannibal Culture: art, appropriation and the commodification of difference*, Boulder, CA: Westview Press.

Ross, A. (1994) *The Chicago Gangster Theory of Life: nature's debt to society*, London: Verso.

RSST [Red Squirrel Survival Trust] (2012) 'HRH The Prince of Wales', available at: http://rsst.org.uk/about-us/hrh-the-prince-of-wales/ [16.04.13].

RSST [Red Squirrel Survival Trust] (2013) 'Ambassadors', available at: http://rsst.org.uk/about-us/ambassadors/ [16.04.13].

Rushton, K. (2009) 'Waybuloo', *Broadcast*, 6 May.

Said, E. (1995) *Orientalism: Western conceptions of the Orient*, London: Penguin Books.

Saldanha, A. (2007) *Psychedelic White: Goa trance and the viscosity of race*, Minneapolis, MN: University of Minnesota Press.

Samuel, R. (1994) *Theatres of Memory*, volume 1, London: Verso.

Sardar, Z. and Cubitt, S. (eds) (2002) *Aliens R Us: the other in science fiction cinema*, London: Pluto Press.

Sawyer, M. (2010) 'How Nando's Conquered Britain', *Observer*, 16 May, available at: www.guardian.co.uk/lifeandstyle/2010/may/16/nandos-fast-food-chipmunk-tinchy [17.05.13].

Scandinavia Show (2012) 'Welcome to the Scandinavia Show', available at: www.scandinaviashow.co.uk/index.html [26.03.13].

Schlunke, K. (2013) 'One Strange Colonial Thing: material remembering and the Bark Shield of Botany Bay', *Continuum: Journal of Media & Cultural Studies*, 27(1): 18–29.

Schwarz, B. (2011) *Memories of Empire, Volume 1: the white man's world*, Oxford: Oxford University Press.

Seal, R. (2010) 'How to Cook the Scandinavian Way', *Observer Food Monthly*, 18 April, pp. 39–43.

Selasi, T. (2005) 'Bye-Bye Barbar', *The Lip Magazine*, available at: thelip.robertsharp. co.uk/?p=76 [29.07.13].

Sheehan, H. and Sweeney, S. (2009) 'The Wire and the World: narrative and meta-narrative', *Jump Cut*, 51, available at: www.ejumpcut.org/currentissue/Wire/4.html [30.12.09].

Sheller, M. (2003) *Consuming the Caribbean: from Arawaks to zombies*, London: Routledge.

Sherman, J. (2009) 'The Colour of Muscle: multiculturalism at a Brooklyn body-building gym', in A. Wise and S. Velayutham (eds) *Everyday Multiculturalism*, Basingstoke: Palgrave Macmillan.

Shire, G. (2008) 'Introduction: race and racialization in neoliberal times', in S. Davison and J. Rutherford (eds) *Race, Identity and Belonging: a soundings collection*, London: Lawrence and Wishart.

Shohat, E. and Stam, R. (1994) *Unthinking Eurocentrism: multiculturalism and the media*, London: Routledge.

Simbeloff, D. (2003) 'Confronting Introduced Species: a form of xenophobia?', *Biological Invasions*, 5: 1759–92.

Simon, D. (2000) *The Wire Bible*, available at: http://kottke.org/09/04/the-wire-bible [30.12.09].

Singer, Syd (2013) 'Invasive Species Agenda Promotes Racism', *Hawaii Reporter*, 7 March, available at: www.hawaiireporter.com/invasive-species-agenda-promotes-racism/123 [03.04.13].

Skeggs, B. (2004) *Class, Self, Culture*, London: Routledge.

Smith, H. (2010) 'Greek Man Wins €160,000 for Turkish Yoghurt "Slur"', *Guardian*, 15 July, available at: www.guardian.co.uk/world/2010/jul/15/greek-pensioner-sues-over-turkish-yoghurt [08.07.13].

Smith, P. C. (2009) *Everything You Know about Indians is Wrong*, Minneapolis, MN: Minnesota University Press.

Smith, Z. (2000) *White Teeth*, London: Hamish Hamilton.

Soil Association (2009) *Home Grown: a practical guide to self-sufficiency and living the good life*, London: Gaia.

Sommar, I. (2003) *Scandinavian Style: classic and modern Scandinavian design*, London: Carlton Books.

Stormfront (2011) Discussion forum thread 'Caring about Red Squirrels Extinction is "Racist" Eco-Xenophobia', available at: www.stormfront.org/forum/t641617/ [15.04.13].

Stuff White People Like (2008) '#116 Black Music that Black People Don't Listen to Anymore', November 18, available at: http://stuffwhitepeoplelike.com/2008/11/18/116-black-music-that-black-people-dont-listen-to-anymore/ [07.06.13].

Szeman, I. (2006) 'Cultural Studies and the Transnational', in G. Hall and C. Birchall (eds) *New Cultural Studies: adventures in theory*, Edinburgh: Edinburgh University Press.

Tarlo, E. (2005) 'Reconsidering Stereotypes: anthropological reflections on the jilbab controversy', *Anthropology Today*, 21(6): 13–17.

Taylor, H. (2009) *Narratives of Loss, Longing and Daily Life: the meaning of home for Cypriot refugees in London*, unpublished PhD thesis, University of East London, UK.

Teletubbies (1997–2001) TV series, Ragdoll Productions for BBC.

Teletubbies website (2013) 'Dipsy', available at: www.teletubbies.com/en/eh-oh-dipsy.asp [12.03.13].

Thompson, H. (2011) 'Handy Scandi', *Guardian* Weekend Magazine, 17 September, pp. 82–3.

Thomson, C. (2012) 'Help Please! Nordic culture and the British zeitgeist', *Nordic Noir Book Club* [blog], 20 August, available at: http://scancrime.wordpress.com/2012/08/20/help-please-nordic-culture-and-the-british-zeitgeist/ [28.03.13].

Time Out (1999) 'Banzi', available at: www.timeout.com/london/restaurants/banzi [23.04.13].

TMZ (2013) 'Snoop Lion REJECTED by Bunny Wailer and Rastas', available at: www.tmz.com/2013/01/23/snoop-lion-snoop-dogg-rejected-bunny-wailer-rastarians-reincarnated/ [25.07.13].

Today Show (2007) 'Behind the Scenes: how does it work? The Teletubbies', 29 March, available at: www.youtube.com/watch?v=SlaRHYni17A [12.03.13].

Toila Kelly, D. P. (2008) 'Investigations into Diasporic "Cosmopolitanism": beyond mythologies of the "non-native"', in C. Dwyer and C. Bressey (eds) *New Geographies of Race and Racism*, Farnham: Ashgate.

Touré (2011) *Who's Afraid of Post-Blackness? What it means to be black now*, New York: Free Press.

Toy Story (1995, 1999, 2010) Film and Sequels, J. Lasseter *et al.*, USA: Disney/Pixar.

Tripadvisor (2013) 'Little India: restaurant reviews', available at: www.tripadvisor.co.uk/ShowUserReviews-g187045-d3377704-r151320408-Little_India-Peterborough_Cambridgeshire_England.html [23.04.13].

TV Tropes (2013a) 'Super Deformed', available at: http://tvtropes.org/pmwiki/pmwiki.php/Main/SuperDeformed [31.05.13].

TV Tropes (2013b) 'Rule 34', available at: http://tvtropes.org/pmwiki/pmwiki.php/Main/RuleThirtyFour [31.05.13].

Urry, J. (2002) *The Tourist Gaze*, second edition, London: Sage.

Valluvan, S., Kapoor, N. and Kalra, V. S. (2013) 'Critical Consumers Run Riot in Manchester', *Journal for Cultural Research*, 17(2): 164–82.

Varul, M. Z. (2008) 'Consuming the Campesino: fair trade marketing between recognition and romantic commodification', *Cultural Studies*, 22(5): 654–79.

Varul, M. Z. (2013) 'Towards a Consumerist Critique of Capitalism: a socialist defence of consumer culture', *Ephemera: Theory & Politics in Organization*, 13(2): 293–315.

Vertovec, S. (2007) 'Super-Diversity and its Implications', *Ethnic and Racial Studies*, 30(6): 1024–54.

Wall, S. (2005) 'Totem Poles, Teepees, and Token Traditions: "playing Indian" at Ontario summer camps, 1920–1955', *The Canadian Historical Review*, 86(3): 513–44.

Wallwork, J. and Dixon, J. A. (2004) 'Foxes, Green Fields and Britishness: on the rhetorical construction of place and national identity', *British Journal of Social Psychology*, 43: 21–39.

Ware, V. (2006) 'Info-War and the Politics of Feminist Curiosity: exploring new frameworks for feminist intercultural studies', *Cultural Studies*, 20(6): 526–51.

Ware, V. (2011) 'The New Literary Front: public diplomacy and the cultural politics of reading Arabic fiction in translation', *New Formations*, 73: 56–77.

Watts, E. K. and Orbe, M. (2002) 'The Spectacular Consumption of "true" African American Culture: "whassup" with the Budweiser guys?', *Critical Studies in Media Communication*, 19(1): 1–20.

Waybuloo (2009–) TV series, Decode Entertainment/The Foundation for BBC.

Webster, J. (2012) 'Banh Mi, the Vietnamese Sandwich that Took New York by Storm, arrives in Ann Arbor', 26 July, available at: www.annarbor.com/ entertainment/food-drink/ann-arbor-banh-mi-lunch-room-bona-sera-vietnamese-sandwich/ [23.04.13].

Werbner, P. (2002) 'The Place which is Diaspora: citizenship, religion and gender in the making of chaordic transnationalism', *Journal of Ethnic and Migration Studies*, 28(1): 119–33.

White, F. R. (2013) ' "We're Kind of Devolving": visual tropes of evolution in obesity discourse', *Critical Public Health*, published online 18 March, DOI: 10.1080/ 09581596.2013.777693 [05.04.13].

The White Company (2012a) Autumn 2012 Catalogue.

The White Company (2012b) Winter 2012 Catalogue.

The White Company (2012c) Christmas 2012 Catalogue.

The White Company (2013a) Spring 2013 Home Collection Catalogue.

The White Company (2013b) 'Our Story', available at: www.thewhitecompany.com/ help/our-story/ [21.03.13].

The White Company Careers (2013a) 'Diversity', available at: www.thewhite companycareers.co.uk/index.php?path=white-life/diversity/ [19.03.13].

The White Company Careers (2013b) 'Our Story', available at: www.thewhite companycareers.co.uk/index.php?path=the-story-so-far/ [22.03.13].

Wiggly Wigglers (2013) 'Wildflowers – plants', available at: www.wigglywigglers. co.uk/native-plants/wildflowers.html# [04.04.13].

Williams, Z. (2011) 'Truth and Fairness are the First Casualties of Video Vigilantes' war', *Guardian*, 16 December, available at: www.guardian.co.uk/theguardian/ 2011/dec/16/truth-fairness-casualties-video-vigilantes [25.07.13].

Willis, S. (1990) 'I Want the Black One: is there a place for Afro-American culture in commodity culture?', *New Formations*, 10: 77–97.

Wilson, B. (2010) 'The Kitchen Thinker: Vietnamese filled baguettes', *Telegraph*, 16 April, available at: www.telegraph.co.uk/foodanddrink/7593718/The-kitchen-thinker-Vietnamese-filled-baguettes.html [24.04.13].

Wilson, R. and Pickett, K. (2010) *The Spirit Level*, London: Penguin Books.

Wintour, P. (2011) 'David Cameron Tells Muslim Britain: stop tolerating extremists', *Guardian*, 5 February, available at: www.guardian.co.uk/politics/2011/feb/05/ david-cameron-muslim-extremism [28.03.13].

The Wire (2002–8) TV series, Blown Deadline Productions for HBO.

Wise, A. and Velayutham, S. (2009) 'Introduction: multiculturalism and everyday life', in A. Wise and S. Velayutham (eds) *Everyday Multiculturalism*, Basingstoke: Palgrave Macmillan.

Wood, N. T. and Muñoz, C. L. (2007) ' "No Rules, Just Right" or is it? The role of themed restaurants as cultural ambassadors', *Tourism and Hospitality Research*, 7: 242–55.

Woods, J. (2012) 'Why Do We Love Scandinavian culture?', *Telegraph*, 23 April, available at: www.telegraph.co.uk/lifestyle/9221267/Why-do-we-love-Scandanavian-culture.html [27.03.13].

Wray, M. (2006) *Not Quite White: white trash and the boundaries of whiteness*, Durham, NC: Duke University Press.

Wray, M. and Newitz, A. (1997) *White Trash: race and class in America*, London: Routledge.

Yellow Bird, M (2004) 'Cowboys and Indians: toys of genocide, icons of colonialism', *Wicazo Sa Review*, 19(2): 33–48.

Yelp (2012) 'Bánhmì11', available at: www.yelp.co.uk/biz/b%C3%A1nhm%C3%AC11-london-5 [23.04.13].

Yilmaz, F. (forthcoming) *The New Politics of Immigration: how politics in Europe moved to the right through the question of immigration*, Ann Arbor, MI: Michigan University Press.

Young, R. J. C. (1995) *Colonial Desire: hybridity in theory, culture and race*, London: Routledge.

Index

CPSIA information can be obtained at www.ICGtesting.com
Printed in the USA
BVOW03s0838160714

359338BV00003B/50/P